ASIA IN THE MODERN WORLD

Prepared by specialists in the field of Asian studies, this comprehensive introduction to the peoples, countries, and history of Asia offers a complete and objective view of the continent's past heritage . . . and political future.

The text is divided into three sections. The first introduces the reader to Asia by way of her literature, art, music, and living religions—by way of her rich contribution to civilization. The second section presents a study of the individual countries; included are China, India, Japan, Korea, Pakistan, and Southeast Asia. The third section deals with Asia since World War II—the internal problems of modern Asia and the relationship of the Asian countries to each other and to the world.

Maps of Asia and of the individual countries are used extensively to illustrate the text. Also included are a bibliography and a résumé of resources.

HELEN G. MATTHEW, editor of this Mentor volume, received her B.A. from Hunter College and her M.A. from Columbia University. A Ford Foundation grant to The Asia Society enabled Mrs. Matthew to make a survey of the teaching materials used in Asian studies by American schools and colleges.

MENTOR Books of Related Interest

ASIA
In the Modern World

EDITED BY
HELEN G. MATTHEW

MENTOR ▶ *A MENTOR BOOK*
Published by The New American Library

To R. J. M.

MENTOR BOOKS are published *in the United States* by
The New American Library of World Literature, Inc.,
501 Madison Avenue, New York, New York, 10022,
in Canada by The New American Library of Canada Limited,
156 Front Street West, Toronto 1, Ontario,
in the United Kingdom by The New English Library Limited,
Barnard's Inn, Holborn, London, E.C. 1, England

Printed in the United States of America

... general American understanding of the problems of Asia forms one of the most important frontiers of knowledge, or at least of education, in the whole world today. In this sense, the greatest foreign-policy frontier this country faces does not lie in Europe or even in Asia but right here, on the campuses of our colleges, in primary and secondary-school rooms, and in the forums of public debate.

... It is our Asian frontiers of knowledge which today offer the greatest challenge both as a field of basic research about human society and as a field of general education that requires urgent development.

Edwin O. Reischauer
U. S. Ambassador to Japan

Acknowledgments

I AM so deeply indebted to others in the preparation of this book that to list them all would be impossible.

First and foremost I am indebted to those who assumed the responsibility for the major sections of this book and whose names appear elsewhere.

I relied heavily upon the works of others throughout preparation of the book. Among those who should be mentioned are Derk Bodde, E. A. Burtt, Donald Keene, Jacques Fradier, Wilfred Cantwell Smith, Chitoshi Yanaga, Joseph Needham, Alan Watts, and Joseph Gaer.

I am especially grateful to Richard C. Rowland for his assistance on the literature section of "The Treasure House of Asian Arts."

I should like to express my profound appreciation and indebtedness to Phillips Talbot, to whom I owe more than can ever be said, without whom the concluding section, "Asia in the Modern World," would not have been possible.

Robert I. Crane and Ward Morehouse were particularly helpful in the planning and organization of this book.

I owe much indeed to Barbara Keyser, with whom this book was first envisaged, and whose critical comments and advice throughout preparation of the entire book were invaluable, and upon whom I relied heavily as consultant.

I am grateful to all those who gave time and thought to the reading of particular sections: Derk Bodde, W. Norman Brown, E. A. Burtt, John K. Fairbank, Edward Feurwecker, Teg Grondhal, John Hall, Donald Keene, Ward Morehouse, Douglas Overton, Edwin O. Reischauer, Donald Cole, William Skinner, Quincy and Louise Wright, and August Maffry.

This book is the culmination of a search for materials on Asia that resulted from the keen interest of my students at Hunter College High School. A grant from the Ford Foundation to The Asia Society made it possible for me to continue the search through consultation with many of the experts at the Asian centers in universities throughout the country as well as with teachers, curriculum directors, and administrators in secondary schools.

I am indebted to UNESCO House in Paris, Merrill F. Hartshorn, Alvin Ulrich, Paul Shebert, and Ward Morehouse in the field of teaching materials.

Although this list of acknowledgments may seem long, I cannot conclude it without expressing thanks to Victor Weybright for his appreciation of the need for this book.

Preface

COMPETENT AND outstanding scholars in the field of Asian studies have united together in the difficult and almost overwhelming task of compressing within a relatively few pages a portrayal of Asia and its people. This book grew out of the conviction that there is an urgent need for one book covering the whole of Asia that could serve as a basic text in secondary-school and introductory college courses. Its purpose is to provide a greater understanding of Asian countries, their past history and culture, the revolutionary changes that are transforming them into modern states, and why each country is so different in its development.

It is so designed that it can be used as a whole or as separate units within a wide variety of courses in the social studies and humanities. Considerable variety of presentation and emphasis reflect the differences in approach by the various contributors.

There are three distinct divisions. The first is intended as an introduction to Asia as a whole, to its vast treasure house of riches in literature, art, music, and living traditions. The emphasis on geography, lands, and people stresses the changing political and economic geography in order to provide a more basic understanding of the processes that are transforming Asia. The second is concerned with the presentation of individual countries, the nature and significance of their traditional cultures and history, the continuity of their civilizations, the changes that have occurred over the centuries, the challenges now facing those civilizations and the responses being made to them. India, China, and Japan are considered in greater depth than the countries of Southeast Asia because of their long history, the rich civilizations they developed, and their importance and influence throughout the centuries. Lack of space prohibited the inclusion of all countries and in the case of Korea and Pakistan only brief accounts were possible, but it should also be noted that the past of Pakistan is also that of India and that the history of Korea is intervened with that of China and Japan. The third and last division concerns modern Asia as a whole—since World War II—with the major stress upon internal problems and thinking, and external relationships with each other and the world, including foreign-aid and technical-assistance programs.

"Resources for Teaching and Further Study" will be exceedingly helpful to leaders and teachers.

The bibliography is far from exhaustive but is meant rather as a guide for further reading and assistance in building up a somewhat modest library. In general few brochures or pamphlets have been included. Economical paperbacks have been indicated wherever possible.

It is the sincere hope of all who made this book possible that it will constitute the opening of the door into a larger world "just around the corner" and that the study of a non-Western civilization will not only familiarize the student with a civilized tradition other than his own, thus permitting him to glimpse the world and his own civilization as others see them, but will also enable him to understand better his own cultural heritage by comparing it with another.

Contents

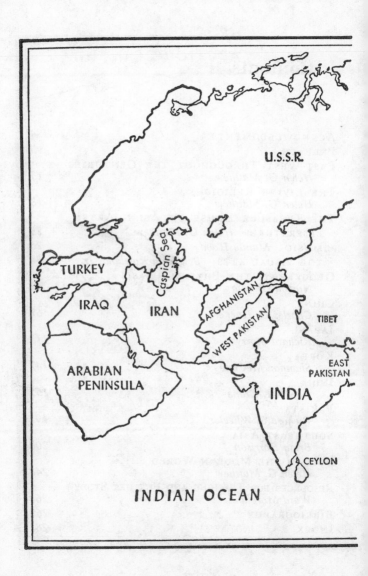

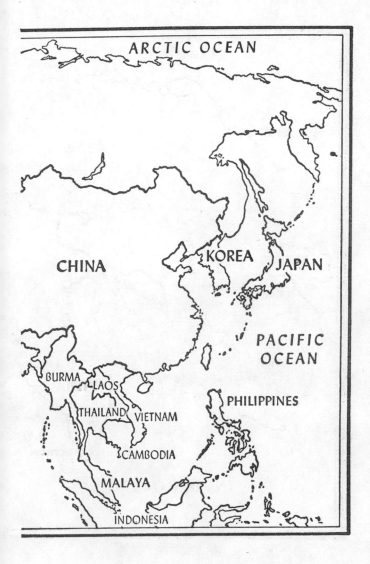

East-West Throughout the Centuries

THE CONTACTS between the East and the West have been constant and many for over two thousand years. At no time has Asia been entirely isolated from the West, despite popular belief. What is more important, even during the periods when contacts were slight, it was Europe, not Asia, that was undergoing a "dark age."

Magnificent civilizations existed in India and China long before the Christian era in the West, and like all highly developed civilizations, they depended upon exchange with the outside world for some of their goods and raw materials.

The lure of the East has always been strong in the West, no less in ancient times than in modern, and intrepid men were willing to undergo hardship and danger in order to reach it both for trade and out of curiosity.

The earliest contacts between the East and the West generally came about through tiny groups, through individuals acting on their own initiative, through semi-official enterprises: They were merchants, travelers, special envoys, philosophers, missionaries, pilgrims, scientists, soldiers, thieves, brigands, and even jugglers and acrobats. The adventures, perils, astonishment, and delight found in the letters they wrote, the diaries they kept, and the reports made to their chiefs, emperors, and friends are fascinating beyond words—long before the days of Marco Polo. Marco Polo was indeed a latecomer, in the thirteenth century, whose friends discounted his fabulous tales as "figments of the imagination."

The use of silk had been known in China as early as

1300 B.C. and the old silk road was already a well-organized highway, divided into four sections, by 106 B.C. and was the main overland route between China and Iran. A flourishing trade in Chinese silk kept the highway open, bringing the bolts of precious fabric to Samarkand, to Bagdad and Damascus, Tyre, Caesarea and Antioch, and thence to the farthest reaches of the Roman Empire. Silk had become so popular by the first and second centuries A.D. among Rome's luxury-loving upper classes that the authorities finally prohibited its use in order to stave off economic collapse and moral degeneration. The flow of trade was so great that in a single year the balance of payments in favor of China was more than a million pounds sterling.

Sea routes flourished too in spite of pirates and monsoons. In the time of Darius the Great, established routes linked the cities of the Ganges delta with ports on the Mediterranean and the Black Sea, using overland portages at Suez. Maritime expeditions of the Romans, manned chiefly by Greeks, pushed eastward to Cambodia, Tonkin, and the South China coast. After the third century A.D., Constantinople for almost a thousand years served as a link in the East-West trade until its cosmopolitanism became a byword throughout the European provinces. After the eighth century the floodtide of Islam swept across Asia Minor to the Java Sea and beyond, and the Muslims, who were vigorous traders, established merchant colonies and a vast banking network along the shores of most of Asia, even as far as Canton. With the Arabic-speaking traders went their scholars and scientists, eager to appropriate Eastern lore.

With the breakup of the hugh califates and the disintegration of Muhammadan politics and the closing of Constantinople by the Turks, traffic between East and West declined. But the fascination of the East, with its great riches and high civilization, whetted by the Crusades, led to ambitious attempts to find new trade routes. In the fifteenth and sixteenth centuries, expeditions of Portuguese, Spaniards, Italians, and English performed daring feats of seamanship, and their voyages opened the way for renewed trade with the Indies and the Moluccas. With the traders went missionaries, some of them remarkably successful. Matteo Ricci, who established a Jesuit mission in Peking in the seventeenth century, was so well received that for two hundred years his followers enjoyed extraordinary prestige among officials of the Manchu dynasty, some of them holding important posts. The great East India trading companies of the English, Dutch, Portuguese, and French were pioneers in organizing the exchange of goods between East and West, and from their trading posts, colonial empires were built.

The gifts of China and India to the West are impressive. During the first thirteen centuries of the Christian era, there was a steady flow of Chinese inventions into Europe. Tea was used in China long before it was known in Europe, and the exquisite vessels from which it was served are still called chinaware, the most delicate porcelain in the world. These articles became a major Chinese export by the ninth century. Paper was manufactured in China as early as A.D. 105, and its use spread rapidly through the East, through the Arab world, and into Spain in the twelfth century.

The oldest book printed from type is a Buddhist sacred text dated A.D. 868, beautifully done in Chinese characters. Paper money was printed in China as early as the tenth century, reaching Europe much later. Gunpowder, as is well known, derived from the Chinese, who used it at first for ceremonial purposes but from A.D. 1000 for military purposes as well; its application to cannons seems to have originated in China, and to have been introduced in Europe later, perhaps via the Mongols. The magnetic compass was employed by Chinese mariners early in the twelfth century. Interestingly enough, their primary direction was south so that when the invention reached Europe, compass reading had to be changed to conform to the usages of European mapmakers. Some of the commonest plants and fruits in our gardens today were imported centuries ago from China, including the apricot and peach, oranges, lemons, chrysanthemums, and many others. Lacquer and lacquerware were Chinese inventions, which reached Europe in the seventeenth and eighteenth centuries, although they had been used in China before the first century A.D. Many amusements that became popular in Europe were imitated from the Chinese, including dominoes, kite flying, the shadow play, and probably playing cards. The folding umbrella came from China, also the wheelbarrow, the rotary fan, the winnowing machine, and various machines for spinning and weaving silk fibers.

Of equal importance have been the Orient's artistic, philosophical, and religious contributions to world culture. A tale written in China in the ninth century is the world's first version of the story of Cinderella.

The practice of alchemy was common in China more than two centuries before the Alexandrians began their serious experiments. A civil-service system based on impartially administered examinations was in operation in the Chinese administration of public affairs as early as 165 B.C., and was to have a great influence on the establishment of the civil-service systems in Europe, particularly in England. One of China's great cultural achievements was the body of thought and poetry associated with Confucius. His teachings reached Rome in the second century, and have fascinated Western-ers ever since. Many translations of the Confucian *Odes* and *Analects* have been made into all European languages.

In the case of Indian philosophy and religion, there can be no doubt that both Hinduism and Buddhism have exerted a profound influence upon Western thought. Such concepts as nirvana, dharma, and the divine personality of the uni-verse have appeared strikingly in the works of the European romanticists, Schopenhauer, the American transcendentalists, Walt Whitman, Nietzsche, and many later writers. But it was not only the romanticists who seized upon Oriental thought. Voltaire and other intellectual rationalists of the eighteenth century, to say nothing of the royal court at Versailles, were devoted to *chinoiserie*, and the physiocrats derived considerable inspiration for their own political be-liefs from their study of the Chinese economic and po-litical institutions, which they so greatly admired.

Western artists too have gone to the Orient, particularly China and Japan, for inspiration, notably the French im-pressionists. Poets like Yeats and Ezra Pound have used the forms of Chinese and Japanese poetry in their own experiments; Yeats introduced the principles of Noh drama into his plays on Irish folk themes, and Pound translated the poems of Li Po and based much of his aesthetic theory on the concept of the ideogram. Other modern writers in every Western country have drawn liberally from Oriental literature.

America's indebtedness to Asia is great. Indeed, it was the search for new trade routes to the East that brought Magellan and Columbus to America. The lucrative China trade during the critical half century after the American Rev-olution helped our great Atlantic seaports to flourish and created many a New England fortune. Trade and manifest destiny led us into the Pacific, where we acquired territory, and our foreign policy has been often determined by our interests in Asia.

The West's contributions to the East are equally impres-sive. The conventional face of Buddha was an invention of Greek sculptors in Kabul before the birth of Christ. The screw, the clock, the piston, and many other Western inven-tions found their way into Asia centuries ago, and in recent times the flow of technological and scientific knowledge has been exceedingly rapid. Similarly, the culture, philosophy, and political and social institutions of the West have profoundly influenced Asian life, and many of the major upheavals now taking place in Asia are largely a result of this influence.

Western colonial powers, in the areas under their control, established new administrative systems, codes of law, schools and colleges, hospitals, public health services, and social services. A majority of the leaders in most Asian countries received all or part of their education in the West.

The Living Religions

RELIGION AND philosophy permeate the history and culture of every Asian nation, today as well as in centuries past. The phrase "living religion" is used over and over again by Asians, who take pride in the spiritual emphasis to be found in every phase of their existence.

It is impossible to understand Asian civilizations without knowing about the great religions that inspired them. Art, architecture, literature, drama, music, and even the dance have been deeply influenced by religion.

All the great religions of the world today were founded, centuries ago, in Asia, including Judaism and Christianity. Some are so old we do not really know exactly where and when they began. It is difficult to determine how many adherents may be claimed by one religion because in Asia it is often possible to "belong" to two or more religions at the same time without being inconsistent. Religion is personal and individual to an Asian.

Westerners have always been interested in the religions of the East, today more than ever. The number of inexpensive but well-edited and well-translated paperbound editions of Asian scriptures and scriptural commentaries that may be found on almost any book rack is evidence of our growing awareness of the spiritual life of Asia. *The Teachings of the Compassionate Buddha, The Glorious Koran, The Bhagavad Gita,* texts on Zen, translations from Confucius and Lao-tzu—these and many others are available to students and general readers. The importance of religion as a basis for any study of Asia today cannot be over-emphasized. Daily life, whether it involves one man or a million, whether political, social, or cultural in nature, is imbued and animated by deep religious feeling.

Of all the organized religions in the world today, Hinduism is almost certainly the oldest. Its origins lie in prehistory, perhaps in the animistic cults of the pre-Dravidian inhabitants of the Indus delta. Hinduism has no individual founder. Over thousands of years it has changed greatly, ramified, refined itself, divided into various branches; and it has given birth to two other major religions (Buddhism and Jainism) and to many minor ones. Today there are well over 300,000,-000 Hindus, mostly in India, but also in Ceylon, Bali, and Thailand. Hinduism is all-embracing, tolerant of all beliefs. Hinduism has many sacred books, including the Vedas, the Brahmanas, and the Upanishads—all of very ancient origin —and the two great epic poems called the *Mahabharata* and the *Ramayana,* which were written just before the beginning of the Christian era. The best known Hindu text in the West, however, is the much shorter *Bhagavad-Gita,* a lyrical dialogue between Krishna and Arjuna that is *The Song of God* taken from the *Mahabharata.* It is philosophical in nature, and is considered the best source of Indian pantheistic and devotional teachings. Hinduism celebrates many deities and its literature contains a large body of myth and legend. Hindus believe there is one Universal Spirit, without beginning or end, a World Soul, who is personified in Brahma, the creator; Vishnu, the preserver; and Shiva, the destroyer. Like other religions, Hinduism has its temples and its priesthood, the Brahmans, but much of the special quality of Hindu life derives from the informal organization centered around the *gurus,* men noted for their wisdom and holiness who undertake to guide students and disciples in their religious aspirations. Hinduism is a very personal matter and involves a wide range of beliefs and practices.

Buddhism, which is often called the Religion of the Enlightened One, arose in India in the sixth century B.C. within the general concept of Hinduism. A young Hindu prince, Siddhartha Gautama, became deeply concerned about the apparent emptiness of human existence and set out in the search for wisdom (dressed as a beggar), having given up his princely inheritance. He traveled far and wide, listening and meditating, until finally while he was sitting under a huge banyan tree one night he came to the end of his search for the truth and wisdom that would end human suffering. Buddhists believe that the fundamental aim of the religious man is to eliminate self-centered desire and to follow the "eightfold path," which will lead to Nirvana. Gentle-

19

ness, serenity, meditation, and compassion are a fundamental part of Buddhist teachings. Buddhism spread quickly and today flourishes in China, Japan, Burma, Mongolia, and Southeast Asia, but virtually died out in India during the tenth and eleventh centuries. In Thailand it is the state religion, and the law requires every young man to spend at least six months as a monk, shaving his head, donning a saffron robe, and living in a monastery. Later in life many Thai men return to the monastery for periods of meditation and spiritual refreshment, as Premier U Nu of Burma did not long ago.

In recent years the Zen sect of Buddhism has attracted an extraordinary interest among Western artists, writers, and intellectuals. Zen originated in China in the sixth century A.D., incorporating various aspects of Confucian and Taoist thought. It spread quickly to Japan—the name comes from *zazen*, the Japanese word meaning "to sit and meditate"— where it enjoys much prominence today. The qualities that distinguish Zen from other types of Buddhism are somewhat difficult to define, but in general the Zen believers have attempted to strip away the formal or symbolist elements of Buddhist practice and to concentrate upon a simple, direct, practical approach to truth. In effect, this approach is made through meditation and self-analysis, and the truth is transmitted from master to pupil rather than through scriptures. Full self-awareness, or self-realization, in the world of natural things is the objective of the disciple, who then understands Zen as all life—poetry, philosophy, morality, and action.

Islam is the third great Asian religion, and is practiced by a very large number of followers—some 320,000,000 altogether. It is particularly strong in Arabia, North Africa, the Middle East, Asiatic Russia, parts of China and India, Indonesia, and of course Pakistan, which split from India on religious grounds and established its constitution on the basis of Islamic law. Islam means "submission." The religion was founded by the prophet Muhammad in the seventh century A.D. in Arabia and very quickly spread through North Africa and the Asian continent. The Koran, the sacred book of Islam, contains Muhammad's prophecies, and a large body of critical work has been based upon it. There are a number of sects, but in general Islam is a remarkably close-knit religion, strongly permeated by nationalistic and militant concepts. Modern Islam is far more than a religion in the ordinary sense; it is a political movement, a social development, and a philosophical program that today is undergoing a vast resurgence.

Confucianism is not a religion but rather an ethical code to morals, conduct, and manners. Confucius, who lived in the seventh century B.C., is revered as the First Teacher, the first great moralist, and the founder of a great ethical code. His codes for the relationship between ruler and subject, father and son, husband and wife, elder brothers and younger brothers, and friend and friend became the guides to moral life and courtesy. Moderation and balance, inner virtues, and external polish were emphasized. The *Analects* and the *Five Kings* have preserved his sayings.

The influence of Confucianism as a way of life in China cannot be exaggerated. There are probably almost one half billion Confucians in China today, and the modes of conduct typically attributed to all Chinese in their courtesy, their formality, and their love of beauty, art, and music probably have their origin in the teachings of Confucius.

Confucianism has spread into many other parts of Asia, wherever Chinese have migrated.

The followers of Taoism are far fewer in number, but the influence of Taoism has been particularly strong among Chinese intellectuals and artists. Lao-tzu (the Old Philosopher) lived in the sixth century B.C. His sayings, difficult to interpret, are contained in one short book of some 5,000 words and are primarily mystical and impressionistic. Nevertheless, Taoism has kept its place in Chinese culture for more than 2,500 years and has spread successfully into Manchuria and Korea.

Shintoism, the native religion of Japan, is prehistoric in origin and was at first nameless. Shinto means the "Way of the Gods" and is Chinese in origin. Shinto is essentially a primitive religion without an organized philosophy and a clear moral code. It is basically a simple nature worship with many mythological gods, among whom the Sun Goddess, from whom the emperor was supposed to have descended, was the greatest. It is in reality not so much a religion as a set of rituals, customs, traditions, pilgrimages, and shrines. For centuries Buddhism, Confucianism, and Shinto were so involved together that in 1871 they were separated by imperial decree. There were so many Shinto sects that a state Shinto was established, which lasted until its dissolution was ordered in 1946, and all the others remained as secular sects. Shinto beliefs, attitudes, and practices have played an important part in the determination of the Japanese character and in Japanese politics.

Christianity has never had a large number of adherents in Asia. Today Christians number only between one and three percent in most Asian countries except in the nominally

Catholic Philippines, but the influence of Christianity has been tremendous and far-reaching, far exceeding the number of converts. Among other things, Christianity was responsible for the establishment of schools and medical services, the inauguration of social-welfare programs, and the improvement of agriculture. A large number of non-Christians who are leaders in their respective countries today were educated in mission schools and colleges and are building upon the foundations established earlier by Christian missionaries.

In addition, many minor religions flourish in parts of Asia still untouched by the larger civilizations. Primitive cults may be found in Borneo, the Philippines, inland areas of Southeast Asia, and the Himalayan uplands. Many of these local religions are extremely valuable to anthropologists who wish to reconstruct the early stages of religious development, and many also have contributed significantly to our concepts of primitive art.

Asians often affirm that spiritual values receive greater emphasis in their countries, whereas the West is considered to be more materialistic. In fact the civilizations and cultures of both East and West have been profoundly influenced by religion.

The Treasure House of Asian Arts

Literature

LONG AGO Francis Bacon said, "Reading maketh the full man." If we seek to know and understand another people, surely one of the best methods to do so is to read their literature. How much of our knowledge of England derives from Chaucer and Shakespeare and Dickens? Our vivid sense of the great world of the Greeks a few centuries before Christ owes as much to Sophocles and Plato and Aristophanes as it does to the research of historians; and the stranger can find an introduction to America in the writings of Franklin, Twain, Hawthorne, Whitman, Frost, Fitzgerald, Salinger, and Faulkner.

Asia had created a considerable literature centuries before the age of Pericles; Confucius, the single greatest name in Chinese literature, died about 479 B.C. The Vedic hymns of India go back to at least 1000 B.C., and probably earlier. Japan produced its greatest novel, Murasaki Shikibu's *Genji Monogatari* (*The Tale of Genji*), several hundred years before Europe produced anything that can be called a novel. It was the Jesuit missionaries in the Mogul palaces in India and at the courts of the Ming emperors in China who first began to translate Oriental literature and send it back to Europe. Later generations of civil servants, missionaries, and traders learned the languages of Asia, became interested in the thought of the Orient, and provided European versions of Oriental classics. More recently, World War II has served as a stimulus, and men who learned Japanese as an enemy language have subsequently become interpreters of Japanese civilization to the West.

China

China's great religions have contributed books that are among the great monuments of world thought. The *Analects* of Confucius, available in numerous translations, is a puzzling, haphazard, and often obscure collection of unrelated sayings; but it has been treated as gospel by generations of Chinese, and maintains even now the ability to speak with human directness. The *Tao Tê Ching*, the basic book of the Taoist faith, is even more baffling at first glance, but its elusive and sophisticated unworldliness goes far toward explaining the impressionistic, suggestive quality of much Chinese art. Chinese thought is not, however, all unworldly: the *Han Fei Tzu*, parts of which are translated in Arthur Waley's *Three Ways of Thought in Ancient China*, is a ruthlessly practical handbook of politics that ranks with Machiavelli's *The Prince*.

Poetry is a part of life to the Chinese in a way that it has rarely been to Westerners. Mao Tse-tung, for instance, is a poet as well as the ruler of Communist China, and men of affairs have never found anything odd in writing poetry in unofficial moments. Despite the inherent difficulties in translating poetry, Chinese lyrical poetry has had a wide influence on English poets and readers. The ancient collection *Shih Ching*, popularly believed to have been made by Confucius, has been memorized by Chinese schoolboys for centuries; these are comparable to folk songs and tell with direct passion of love and separation, fighting wars, and tilling the soil. Similarly universal themes appear in the eighth century in the poetry of Li Po and Tu Fu; even in translation their poems have wit, color, and tenderness.

The Chinese have been great tellers of tales, too, and although it is only in recent years that the Chinese have taken their novels seriously as literature, nowhere will the Westerner get a more vivid sense of Chinese literature than in two massive novels: *Hung Lou Mêng* (*The Dream of the Red Chamber*), a wise and tender portrait of a great family in decline, and *Chin Ping Mei* (*The Golden Lotus*), a ruthless study of merchant life.

The present century has found Chinese literature much affected by that of the West. Perhaps the most significant of the twentieth-century writers is Lu Hsun, whose moving tales picture clearly China's old civilization in conflict with new practices and ideas. Lu Hsun died in 1936; since then China has been so torn by war, both civil and worldwide, that little literature of any sort has reached the outside: Peiping issues propaganda novels of no distinction, and literary efforts in Hong Kong and Taiwan are chiefly characterized by a nostalgic harking back to a vanished past.

India

The literature of India is many literatures, for there are still about twenty major languages spoken in the vast area that we call India. Its classical literature is written in none of these languages but in Sanskrit, which is no longer spoken. Perhaps the most influential of Sanskrit works is the *Bhagavad-Gita,* many times translated into English and the most important source of inspiration for the many Westerners who have been influenced by Hindu beliefs. The *Bhagavad-Gita* is in fact a portion of the *Mahabharata,* one of the two great epics of India. The *Mahabharata* is a partly historical account of the tribal wars of India's past. Like the *Iliad,* it gives us an idealized picture of a way of life long vanished. The other epic, the *Ramayana,* is the tale of a single hero, Rama.

The drama in India is an ancient and highly developed art, elaborate, spectacular, and full of lyrical passion. Kalidasa's romantic play *Sakuntala,* though far too long for the endurance of a Western audience, is the most famous example.

Perhaps India's most direct influence on Western literature has been through the sprightly animal tales, religious and didactic in intent but comic and imaginative in their telling; there are many of these tales, and they have spread throughout the world.

Because so many of the Indian intelligentsia have been educated in British universities, English has become one of the major languages of India; one of the best ways to experience modern India from afar is to read some of the novels written in English by Indians, particularly R. K. Narayan's *The Financial Expert, The Man-eater of Malgudi,* and *Waiting for the Mahatma,* gentle comedies of village life. More serious in tone is *Nectar in a Sieve,* by Kamala Markandaya, an account of the struggles of a peasant family. India, too, is the only Asian country to have produced in Rabindranath Tagore a writer who has had enough impact on the West to win a Nobel Prize.

Japan

Japan's culture and literature are far younger than those of China and India. Perhaps the nature of the Japanese language makes translation easier; Arthur Waley's translation of *The Tale of Genji* is possibly the greatest single work of translation from the Oriental languages. This vast panorama of life at the Japanese court is witty, sentimental, and exquisite in turn; its delight in the shimmering surface of life strikes a note that many people feel to be the dominant tone in Japanese art.

The Japanese excel in many literary forms. Their Noh play is a curiously impressive fusion of poetry, music, and dance. The Japanese three-line verse form known as the haiku is, at its best, a demonstration of the magical suggestion and evocation that can be achieved in a mere seventeen syllables. Even the popular novels of the seventeenth and eighteenth centuries by Saikaku and others, with little more literary pretension than that of the modern comic strip, provide a portrait of an age brimming with life and sparkling with wit.

Twentieth-century Japanese literature is often concerned with the conflict between Western thought and Japanese tradition, reflected in Junichiro Tanizaki's *The Makioka Sisters* and *Some Prefer Nettles* and in Yasunari Kawabata's *Thousand Cranes*.

Music

The beautiful simplicity of the Chinese pen-and-ink drawing, the intricate and rich details of an Indian miniature painting, the grandeur of mountains or lakes rendered impressionistically on a Japanese screen—these objects have an immediate appeal for the Western observer. His appreciation will deepen, it is true, as he comes to know more about each of these art objects in relation to its own specific style and as he begins to understand more about the particular society that produced the object. The Westerner's satisfaction will be more complete when he is able to distinguish earlier styles that led to the development of the object under discussion and later styles toward which it contributed. But the most important point is the fact that Oriental art is immediately acceptable to him. This seems to hold true for architecture, sculpture, textile design, pottery, literature in translation, and many other cultural treasures from the East. In fact, the influence of these many artistic forms on Western society has been long and continuous. Housing, clothing, foods, fabrics, philosophies, games, hobbies, flower arrangements, and most of the commonplace aspects of our everyday life have been touched in one way or another by the cultures of the greater Orient, that is, those countries lying east of the Mediterranean.

But what about music?

The average concertgoer who enjoys the symphony orchestra, opera, or chamber music has probably heard little or no Chinese, Indian, or Japanese music. Why have so many of the other art forms from the Orient touched, influenced, and refashioned our own cultural expressions, whereas music from the East seems to have remained foreign and inaccessible? The question becomes even more perplexing when we realize that the musical instruments of the Western symphony orchestra developed, through the course of many centuries, from prototypes that originated in the Orient. And further, that the musical practices of the early Christian church were strongly influenced by the music of the Near East.

The symbols of communication on which the visual arts depend, as well as the abstract ideas that people the world of literature and philosophical thought, begin to accumulate from the earliest days of perceptive childhood. Representational shapes in the form of houses, buildings, tables, chairs, wheels, wagons, animals, trees, insects, clouds, and birds form a vocabulary of visual objects, even though they differ in detail, that are recognizable throughout the world. Abstract forms such as the square, the sphere, the triangle, the cone, the cylinder, and their variants, in combination or individually, are another part of the visual vocabulary. The world of ideas must be referred to experience: the experience of childhood and adolescence, of young adulthood and maturity, of wisdom and old age, of birth and death, of marriage and separation, of war and peace, of religion and agnosticism. The accumulation of this vocabulary, too, begins with early childhood. This process of conditioning and experience accounts for the relative sophistication of the individual's visual perception and familiarity with abstract thought.

But what about his perception of sounds?

Anyone who has studied a foreign language will remember the first time he heard the strange tongue spoken. Except for occasional hints of emotional content, perhaps suggested by facial expressions or movements of the hands, the beginner is unable to differentiate the stream of sounds into words, phrases, or sentences. As his ear becomes more familiar with the sounds through repeated exposure, he is able to understand an occasional word or phrase. Finally, after many years of practice, he begins to enjoy the beauty and finesse that any language affords in communication. Sounds that were once so strange to his ears he may now manage with no more than a minimum of accent.

One might question whether the foreign spoken language is analogous to "foreign music." A lover of opera has a little difficulty in accepting French, Italian, or German forms of this musical genre. The symphonic repertoire of the New York Philharmonic is not too dissimilar from that of any major orchestra in Europe. And although there are many different spoken languages in the Western world, the musical language of the West is reasonably unified, that is, if we speak of art music. In the traditional literature of European art music, it is possible to distinguish certain national characteristics, but these minor differences only increase the richness of the European art tradition. For the last several hundred years, the same tuning system, scales, musical instruments, and the fashion of influence and counterinfluence from one European country to another have resulted in a unified musical language.

The folk music of Europe and the Americas, however, is marked by national, regional, and even local diversity. And in the Orient, art music and folk music are inseparable from the context of the societies that they, in no small measure, help define. Therefore, we may say that the Orient has many different musical languages.

The problems of learning a foreign spoken language are similar to those encountered in learning a foreign musical language. Even in the West, the music lover who has heard only the literature of the nineteenth century may say that the music of Bach "all sounds alike." Such an observation is also likely to be made on a first hearing of Chinese, Indian, or Japanese music. Such a reaction to the music of Bach is not prompted by any essential differences in the musical materials employed, but by an unfamiliarity with the style characteristics of the eighteenth century. Repeated exposure to these masterworks of the baroque period will enable the newcomer to perceive the several streams of melody that together make up a polyphonic texture. Therefore, even within the reasonably unified musical tradition of the West, "acceptability," or in other words understanding, is relative to the degree of familiarity that the listener has with a particular idiom.

One other essential difference between the music of the European tradition and the many musics of the Orient is the manner in which the most basic elements of music have been emphasized. In the past two hundred years, music in the West has developed such a rich harmonic vocabulary that melody and rhythm have been relegated to a comparatively minor role. In the Orient, on the other hand, it is precisely the element harmony that has been neglected, whereas melody and rhythm have developed refinements and a degree of sophistication as yet unknown and untried in the European art tradition. Once this fundamental difference between East and West is understood, it becomes apparent that musical interest in the Orient, with a few notable exceptions in Southeast Asia, does not lie in the amassing of large sounds associated with the Western orchestra, but rather in the sensitivity of a few performers as they carry melody and rhythm to artistic heights not found in the literature of European tradition.

China

The oldest historical accounts of music come from China. Semilegendary sources credit Emperor Fu Hsi as the inventor of music in 2852 B.C. and Emperor Huang-ti, the "Yellow Emperor," as the one who established the *huang chung,* or yellow bell, in 2697 B.C. This was the fundamental note of a twelve-tone theoretical scale known as the twelve *lüs.* The huang chung was preserved in the form of a bamboo tube, or in later times a tube made of jade or other more permanent material, and its volume and length served as the standard for weights and measures. The odd-numbered lüs, 1, 3, 5, 7, 9, and 11, were considered as *yang,* or male; the even-numbered lüs were termed *yin,* or female. Comparison was drawn between the twelve lüs, the twelve Chinese hours, the twelve moons, and other extramusical concepts.

In these very ancient times, music was exalted as an art, practiced by philosophers and mathematicians, in fact considered essential to the welfare of the state and the well-being of the individual. It is said that each new dynasty immediately assigned the mathematicians and philosophers to the problem of recalculating the precise pitch of the huang chung in the belief that the preceding dynasty had failed because this fundamental pitch had been erroneously determined. In the teachings of Confucius, music was considered essential to the best conduct of man and the ideal operation of the state.

During the span of centuries before the Christian era, Chinese music was subjected to countless influences and modifications from contacts with foreign cultures in the form of invasion and conquest. In 246 B.C. Emperor Shih Huang Ti ordered the mass destruction of all books except those concerned with medicine, agriculture, or divination. In his attempt to eradicate any remembrance of earlier centuries, the mad emperor all but destroyed the art of music and dance. Beginning with the Han dynasty, however, ancient books and musical instruments were recovered from places where they had been hidden during the time of Shih Huang Ti, and slowly the art of music was reconstructed.

Music, dance, and poetry were an inseparable part of the important ritual of the courts and temples. Every aspect of a particular ritual in this connection was closely controlled so that the precise number of instruments, players, positions, costumes, dance steps, ritualistic words, and poetic texts was precisely specified. After the destructive reign of Shih Huang Ti, the status of the musician never again reached any appreciable height in society. A few instruments, however, continued to be associated with the achievements of the intellectual. The *chin*, a zither with seven silk strings, had been a favorite instrument of Confucius, and up to modern times continued to be the favorite instrument of the intellectual. A plucked lute known as the *pi-pa* introduced into China around A.D. 500 developed into the favorite instrument of the courtesan by the sixteenth and seventeenth centuries. About this same time, the classical lute in Europe achieved a similar popularity. The music of the chin is introspective in character, requiring great sensitivity on the part of the musician and the mastery of many difficult techniques to express an infinite variety of nuances. The pi-pa, in the hands of a virtuoso, can be played in a flamboyant and energetic style or, by contrast, in a relatively simple and delicate manner.

In a great variety of forms, music, dance, and poetry are closely associated with calendrical rites, such as birth, death, marriage, etc. Instruments such as the *erh-hu*, a two-stringed, bowed lute, and several types of plucked lutes, flutes, drums, cymbals, etc., form the more popular types of instrumental ensembles. Every kind of festival, big or small, includes music, and although the intellectual developments of music theory that abound in Chinese treatises may not be known to the average Chinese, music lies close to his heart as one of the essential attributes of life.

The most stylized form of music, dance, and poetry occurs in Chinese theater. In the traditional form of opera, the actors perform within the conventions of stereotype roles so that costume, makeup, masks, movements, style of voice delivery, and singing define the stock character. A similar style of theater known in Europe was the *commedia dell'arte*. The tradition of male actors performing female roles, the classical mannerisms of voice delivery, the stylized movements, and the dramatic commentary supplied by the instrumental ensemble account for the initial difficulty of the Westerner in appreciating this art form. In modern China, although the classical Chinese opera appears to be continuing in a modified form, Yangko theater, originally a folk dance utilized by the Communists as a propaganda vehicle, has become a major development.

Japan

Many of the important musical instruments and musical forms of China had a profound influence on the development of music in Japan. One of the most remarkable of these forms is Japanese *gagaku*. This instrumental music has had a continuous tradition in Japan from A.D. 700 to the present. The stately and "elegant" style of the music, as well as the highly abstract movements of the dance form associated with it, *bugaku*, are relatively unknown to the large populace of Japan because its usage for many centuries has been confined to the imperial household and shrines. Although an important part of this musical literature derives from China, a similar tradition in Korea has also enriched the Japanese literature. The complete instrumentation of the ensemble is: three flutes (*fué*), three oboes (*hichiriki*), three mouth organs (*shō*), two plucked zithers (*koto*), two plucked lutes (*biwa*), two types of drum (*taiko* and *kakko*), and a small hanging gong (*shōko*). The stringed instruments are omitted from the ensemble during the performance of bugaku.

Gagaku musicians in the imperial household are required not only to become masters in this Japanese tradition of music and dance but also to become proficient on some musical instruments of the West, forming an orchestra that emphasizes the classical tradition. Japan, more than any other country in the Orient, has felt the impact of European art music. In modern times, a Japanese musician is characteristically schooled in either Western music or one of several types of Japanese music—but not both. The musicians who accompany the *kabuki* drama are usually specialists in this type of dramatic music only. The dramatic action is underscored by three drums, supplemented by drum calls from the principal player; and several plucked lutes (*samisen*) and two flutes add relatively independent melodic variety. The plots of the kabuki play are based on the literature of the Noh drama and the puppet theater, *bunraku*. Probably because of the great amount of action and variety characteristic of the kabuki theater, it enjoys the greatest popularity in Japan today. Fairly elaborate staging, rich costumes, and relatively fast-moving stories typical of this form of theater are unmatched for their display of pageantry and variety. The Noh drama, on the other hand, utilizes a simple and very beautiful abstract staging with only the minimum of stage properties. The movements of the Noh dancer are more restrained, and the substance of the drama itself appeals less to popular taste. Some of the finest actor-dancers, however, are found in the Noh theater. The puppets of the bunraku theater are about two thirds life-size, and are manipulated by three persons, one principal dressed in an elegant costume of the sixteenth century and two assistants dressed in black, therefore, "invisible." The former popularity of bunraku began to decline in the seventeenth century with the rise of kabuki, until today it may be seen only in Osaka.

Among the many types of Japanese instrumental ensembles, the form known as *sankyoku* is immediately attractive to Western ears. This is a trio of instruments: the samisen, the koto and the *shakuhachi*, an end-blown flute that derives originally from China. In recent times, there has been a great revival of interest in the study of koto. Among the popular traditions of Japan, the performances of the geishas on koto or samisen and voice are well known. Although in modern Japan, especially in metropolitan centers like Tokyo, many of the traditional uses of music seem to be falling by the wayside, a wide variety of folk traditions continue in less urbanized areas.

India

The music, dance, and poetry of India are perhaps better known than any other form of Oriental music to Westerners. Like the music of China and Japan, the beginnings of Indian music may be traced to ancient times; in fact, it exerted a profound influence, directly or indirectly, on the musical cultures of both China and Japan. But in modern times, most of the art music heard today is based on the reconstruction of former traditions that had died out. The art music of India has a relatively small but devoted intellectual audience, which is highly sophisticated in its appreciation of the art of improvisation. Traditionally, the professional musicians who perform this music were supported by patrons. The study of either music or dance is long and arduous, and the high standards demanded of the performers require all of their time and energy so that some kind of patronage was essential to the successful continuation of these art forms. Mastery of an instrumental, vocal, or dance style represents a real intellectual attainment as well as an extraordinary technical skill. It is not surprising, therefore, that the great musicians and dancers of India have passed on their achievements to immediate descendants so that one might speak of family lines of performers. In contemporary times, however, patronage is rare, and the artists of today depend on concert tours and radio appearances for support.

Under the old *guru* system, a young boy pledges his life and devotion to the master, who in exchange accepts the responsibility of passing on to this selected aspirant his total knowledge. The young disciple literally becomes a servant in the house, attending to all kinds of menial chores for the privilege of sitting at the master's feet while he performs or instructs other pupils or devotes his attention to the disciple himself. The guru is a severe taskmaster, rewarding excellent progress of the young musician with a nod, or one mistake in a lesson with a severe beating. Between the dread of physical punishment and the awesome respect for the musical artistry of his master, the young pupil drives himself with unremitting concentration until one day he is invited to perform in public with his guru. During these difficult years of development from awkward apprentice to accomplished performer, an extraordinary bond of loyalty and admiration develops between the man and the boy. Eventually, after the young musician himself has won acclaim as a performer, he in turn will become a guru, accepting with the pledge of his young disciple a responsibility to teach him all that he has learned, and the further obligation of producing a finished young performer who will be a better musician than he himself. With this highminded purpose guiding the best of musicians in India, it is not surprising that the outstanding artists of the past have achieved sainthood. Of the many paths leading to Nirvana, music is the most direct.

The art of melodic invention as it flourishes in the Indian concept of *raga* and the vitality and subtlety of rhythmic development based on the *tala* system afford the Indian musician an incomparable basis for improvisation. There are stylistic differences between the music of north and south India, as well as some superficial contradictions in terminology. The principal instruments of north India are the *sitar* and the *tabla*. The sitar is an elaborate plucked lute made of teak and well-seasoned gourds that has six or seven principal strings and thirteen sympathetic strings. Subtleties in melodic invention can be realized by slightly raising or lowering the pitch of the principal tones of a given raga and by the employment of microtonal ornaments. The melodic subtleties of the principal instrument are brought into sharp relief as they contrast in pitch to the steady sounds of another plucked lute known as the *tamboura*. This instrument simply repeats over and over a drone of several constant pitches. The tabla and *baya* are a pair of hand drums that furnish elaborate rhythmic patterns superimposed over a basic *tala* and also reinforce the drone. In south India the two equivalent principal instruments are the *vina*, a plucked lute, and the *mridangam*, a double-headed hand drum. The tamboura is also used for a drone instrument. The style of sitar and the tabla is more flamboyant than that of the vina and mridangam. In both north and south India the vocal performer shares an equal importance with instrumentalist and frequently appears as an important member of the ensemble.

Sharing the same basic music principles as the art music of India is an immense folk tradition, which differs remarkably from region to region. In this sphere of musical activity, a great variety of instrumental forms are found, and unlike the art tradition, folk music is enjoyed by an immense public. Fairly recent are the products of the motion-picture sound track, which, although they enjoy great popularity, are uniformly disapproved by the serious musician.

The Visual Arts

Except for the work of some of the later periods in China and Japan, it could be said as a generality that Asiatic art was almost exclusively dedicated to religion. It was the function of art to make credible, in visual terms that all could understand, the deep, mysterious concepts of Hinduism, Buddhism, or Taoism. In such an art the artist's primary concern is not with realism or the representation of things as they are because the things he represents exist not in the human but in the divine world. For this reason the Asiatic artist's representation of gods and demons will often have an abstract or even grotesque form. This form, sometimes arrived at by elaborate systems of mathematical measurement, is intended to suggest, by being abstract and having nothing naturalistic about it, that the object portrayed is supernatural or divine and, by the same token, a proper object of worship.

Asiatic art has never had any interest in the scientific problems of representing reality in the way that painters of the Renaissance gradually solved the problems of perspective and light. Science, as we understand it in the West as an investigation of the phenomena that surround us, has never played a part in Eastern civilization until relatively modern times. For the Asiatic artist the problem was to represent a symbol of gods or animals or flowers; thus what he shows us is a kind of symbol in which only the most essential, or conceptual, aspects of the subject are clearly defined, without regard for the scientific conditions that govern its existence as a solid form in space. Oriental artists have never been interested in the beauty of the human form as we think of it in connection with the Hellenic tradition in the West. Man was never the center of the universe as he came to be in the Renaissance, and his body at best was only the temporary home of the soul in its long journey to union with divinity.

From the aesthetic point of view, the artist in early India or China was governed by certain principles, or canons, systems of measurement for laws of gestures and poses, that were intended to ensure that he represented his themes in the most ideal rather than the most real manner possible. Generally these aesthetic guides, often in the shape of manuals, stipulate above everything else that the artist must suggest the feeling of life and movement appropriate to a given subject; that is, even if an Indian or Chinese artist's representation of a horse lacks the anatomical accuracy of a drawing by Leonardo da Vinci, it must suggest the universal idea of "horse" and suggest the qualities of fiery spirit and strength that we associate with this animal. In the same way, a landscape painting need not necessarily have anything to do with a recognizable spot, but it should evoke something of the feeling that we have of the dwarfing majesty and vastness of a great expanse of mountains and rivers, even though the elements of nature in the picture are represented by a kind of symbolical shorthand of brushstrokes that have nothing to do with the structure or texture of a real landscape.

Asiatic art through the thousands of years of its existence has been under the spell of tradition in much the same way that Western art has always been attached to the classical tradition of Greece and Rome as a source of inspiration. In the East this attachment has been partly what we would call a reverence for the past and its authority, partly a recognition of the fact that artists of earlier periods had solved certain problems in the portrayal of themes so satisfactorily that their performances were recognized as models of perfection to be emulated by later ages. This does not mean a stagnation in the sense that Egyptian art remained frozen in convention for thousands of years, but rather that the models of antiquity and the ways of their making served later generations as a source of inspiration, as a point of departure for their own artistic invention within the self-imposed rules of their craft.

We shall find, too, that Asiatic art of the traditional periods in which we are interested has always expressed itself in a series of accepted themes imposed by religion or aesthetic convention. This is as true of the purely religious art of India as it is of secular painting in China. Although there might seem to be a monotony in these hundreds of images of Buddha or Siva or of Chinese views of mountain scenery, we must remember that variety and creation exist in the performance rather than in the theme, in much the same way that every performance of a Shakespearean play is different and affords the actor an opportunity for his own creative interpretation.

As in the West, so too in the Orient, art styles or ways of representing things divine or earthly change with the tastes and requirements of a given time, so that in ages of implicit belief we can expect idols of a formalized abstraction, which suggest that the gods in their perfection are above and different from imperfect mortals; in periods of materialism the divine assumes a more realistic or sentimental aspect, an icon intended to evoke belief because of its suggestions of human feelings and human prettiness.

The civilizations of Asia are immensely old in art, antedating the beginnings of Mediterranean culture by thousands of years. Not only that, but the traditions that have sustained man and his art for so long a time are still alive in many parts of the Indian world and the Far East. It could be said as a generality that in the great periods of artistic expression in India, China, and Japan, art was traditional in the same sense as medieval art in the West. Its beauty depended on the integration of craft and purpose, the appropriateness of material and the artist's vision directed to producing works calculated to reveal the beauty of unseen beings in a style symbolizing rather than representing realistically their supernatural powers. A visit to the collection of Oriental art in any one of the great American museums will reveal to the visitor the power of these arts that rival some of the great masterpieces of Western art in their formal beauty and that have, in their meaningful abstraction, a direct appeal to our modern aesthetic point of view.

India

The art of India began some 2,500 years before the Christian era in the civilization of the Indus valley, a culture related to the ancient monarchies of the Mesopotamian world. In certain statuettes of this remote time we can already discern the Indian sculptor's tremendous feeling for mass and volume; there is also present the expression of a breathing inner life in human forms that reappears in some of the great sculpture of the historical periods, such as the famous trinity in the Cave of Elephants. Even in the beginning of this tradition, Indian artists suggested a union of the sensual and the divine in human forms and something of the dynamic energy of the divine being; these we can observe in the great bronzes of Dancing Siva of the Chola period. Throughout the history of Indian art we may note a balance between the expression of self-contained serenity, as expressed in the spheroidal volumes of the Buddha images of the Gupta period, and a bursting vitality of movement and inner sensuous power in the statues of the deities of the Hindu pantheon. These forms are as exciting and compelling as the most modern experiments in sculptural form by Henry Moore.

Indian art, especially in the sculpture and painting of the later centuries, has an epic quality, something of the titanic sweep and metaphor of the Indian classics the *Ramayana* and the *Mahabharata*. A romanticism, even a sentimental quality appears in later Indian painting as a reflection of the cult of the loves of the god Krishna. It is not surprising that Indian representations of the epic loves and struggles of the gods and heroes have something of the dynamic and formalized quality of the Indian theater and the Indian dance since undoubtedly the language of gestures codified in these public arts found their way into the idiom of painters and sculptors. Indian art is frequently sensual both in subject matter and in the often provocative and erotic presentation of the human figure. This is because since very early times the idea of the soul's union with the divine had been symbolically alluded to in the sexual union of human beings.

Certain symbolical devices of Indian art, like deities with many heads and arms, must be accepted as parts of a sacred visual language intended to instruct the believer in the truths of religion in the most explicit way. The multiple arms of the Dancing Siva are not intended to portray a biological monstrosity: these extra limbs are necessary so that the god may simultaneously display the various attributes of his power in a single concrete image.

China

Like the civilization of India, Chinese art is one of the oldest continuous traditions in the entire world. Certain features, like the artist's capacity for animating his forms within a self-imposed discipline of abstract, essentially linear design, have remained unchanged from the period of the archaic bronzes to the paintings of the Ching dynasty. One of the lessons of Chinese art is economy of means and a feeling for the material. Visit any collection of Chinese art and you will be stirred by the strange, dynamic organization of shapes in the ancient bronze vessels of the Shang and Chou dynasties. For the Western eye some of the landscapes of the Sung period and later in these same collections may remind the student of the succinctness of statement and poetic suggestion of the vastness of nature that we encounter in the drawings of Rembrandt and Claude.

The real classical religion of China that might be called Sinism was based on ancestor worship and subservience to the will of heaven. Even though the Chinese in these traditional periods were an essentially practical people, there was at the same time a mystical side to their nature that was fascinated by ritual and auspicious numbers.

The Chinese from the very beginnings of their civilization have had an intense awe and awareness of the vast, mysterious forces of the universe. The aim of man in this cosmos was, as Confucius expressed it, to be in harmony with heaven and earth in order to attain a measure of happiness in this earthly life. The attainment of such an order required a submission to correctness and good form in every action. Opposed to this Confucian doctrine of regularity and conformity were the spontaneity and mystery offered by Taoism. In this natural, more undisciplined philosophy was the idea of retreat into the enfolding wonder of nature, the contemplation of the beauty and mystery of nature as a path, or way, to final absorption in the Tao itself.

Chinese art has never, strictly speaking, been anthropomorphic. Although obviously the illustration of Confucian principles and actions and the worthy deeds of legendary personages demanded a style of figure painting, the Chinese awareness of cosmic forces from earliest times found expression in an essentially creative abstract ideation of cosmic forces, first in the mysterious brooding emblems of celestial and terrestrial elements that inhabit the bronzes of archaic times, and later in the figuration of the awesome beauty of universal nature in terms of landscape.

In Chinese literature as in Chinese painting we have the concept of nature as an escape from the machine of society, a passionate ardor for the wild beauties of our world, that has its parallel in the poetic ideas of the romantic period in the West. Nature is thought of as a reflection of a loftier reality.

Chinese art is no more concerned with the idea of realistic portrayal as the be-all and end-all here of artistic creation than Indian art is. More important for the Chinese artist than the recording of the superficial exact appearance of particular things is the aim to suggest the dynamic inner life that possesses the forms of all things. The Chinese painter is, then, more concerned with expressing a feeling of the appropriate growth and essential structure of things in order to communicate their life movement—the very breath of the life possessing them—in pictorial terms.

What might be described as an innate Chinese feeling for expression in an essentially abstract or symbolical artist language manifests itself first in the linear shapes that portray the totemic beasts of the archaic bronzes and later in the unifying language of brushstroke that is the whole basis of Chinese painting. Chinese painters of the historical periods develop a specific vocabulary of strokes for the portrayal of things in nature that in the feeling for the rhythmic organization of these touches of the brush and the coloristic richness of the ink has an obvious relationship to the Chinese calligraphy that employs essentially the same technique and the same symbolical approach in the tracing of the ideographs of the Chinese language.

Japan

The history of art in Japan divides itself into periods when the arts were strongly influenced by currents from the Asiatic mainland, chiefly China and Korea, and eras when the Japanese for various political reasons were cut off from the outside; in these periods of nationalistic seclusion they developed a peculiarly Japanese aesthetic mode of expression. The qualities of patternization and realism balance one another throughout the history of Japanese art. At the same time, certain other specifically Japanese traits are present even in the times of strongest foreign influence: for example, the earliest grave figures, or *haniwa*; the Buddhist icons of Japan's Middle Ages; and even the forms in the Japanese prints are characterized by the quality of *heimei*, of *meikaisei*, meaning "radiant flatness." This quality reveals itself in the peculiarly ingenuous, sweet, and childlike serenity of expression and in the feeling for composition essentially in flat, decorative forms. These terms and their definitions could be applied to the Yamato-e style of painting in the thirteenth century and later with its sensitively drawn, weightless figures in settings of gold and silver foil. In certain periods Japanese sculpture has a quality, described by the word *ryo,* of voluminous expansiveness and feeling for weight and mass that rivals the character of Indian carving of the great periods.

In view of the close contacts between Japan and China for many centuries, it is not surprising that many techniques and modes in Japanese art are a translation of continental Asiatic forms into Japanese terms. The greatest Japanese landscape painter, Sesshu, transformed his models of Chinese painting of the Sung dynasty into his own peculiarly Japanese decorative formula, in which brushstrokes give more of an impression of vibrant surface ornament than spatial or textural definition. When Japanese artists turn to realism in portraits, in religious images, or in caricature, they achieve something far above the usual definition of realism as a description of the outward appearance of forms; they achieve the most powerful spiritual characterizations in terms revealing the specific psychology of the subject, with a suggestion of inner fervor, serenity, or aliveness that transcends the naturalistic mode. In a way this is a realism of universals: some of the famous portraits of Buddhist priests are more symbols of priesthood than likenesses of individual holy men, and Sharaku's prints are really portraits of the role rather than the actor.

Insofar that it is possible to point in generalities to the universal contributions of the arts of different countries, it could be stated that Indian art, like the Indian religions, has been more concerned with the absolute than the particular, and this in itself will serve to explain the unfamiliarity of its expression. This expression in the great centuries of Buddhist and Hindu art was dedicated to embodying in appropriately abstract terms a symbolical figuration of the gods: as embodiments of the sublime self-contained serenity of Buddhist deities, or, in dynamic supernatural terms, portraying the cosmic power of the Hindu titans. Added to this is a wonderful awareness of the sensuous beauty of the human body and the specific aliveness of all of nature's creatures.

Art in China from earliest times was concerned with an evocation of the mysterious, magical elements of nature and the cosmos. In the beginning the cosmic powers were symbolized on the archaic bronzes in fabulous monster shapes of tremendous decorative, as well as dynamic, value. In the later historical periods we witness in painting, China's greatest art, a similar concern with a romantic and lyric evocation of the mystery of nature in a self-imposed vocabulary of calligraphic drawing that stems from the age-old formal beauty and abstract organization of Chinese writing.

One of the qualities of Japanese art that appeal most strongly to the Western observer is the feeling for the beauty of natural forms and their specific growth, so that the flowers in a screen of the Tokugawa period, arranged with a great feeling for decorative design on a flat surface, suggest the same vibrant, pliant growth and fragility of floral forms that we admire in Botticelli. In addition to their wonderful expressiveness in surface pattern, Japanese artists have always had a sensuous feeling for the intrinsic beauty of texture and material. This is something we can discover in lacquer boxes by Korin and in the beautiful and appropriate suggestion of the grain of the wood block in some of the superlative prints made by artists in Japan today. The very negation of naturalistic space and perspective, completely consistent with design conceived essentially in two dimensions, has exercised a powerful influence on modern artists in the Western world. Men like Whistler and Degas were tremendously moved by the lessons in abstract design to be learned in the prints of Utamaro and Hokusai.

Through the whole fabric of the art of Japan there run the twin threads of realism and pattern, both dedicated to an expression of the inimitable Japanese sensibility to the beauty of all things great and small in nature. In those periods when Japan is isolated from foreign influences, we encounter an extraordinary and sensitive organization of unreal decorative shapes. Sometimes, as a marvelous foil, the simplicity of statement and ornamental abstraction of natural forms are set off by the sensuous gorgeousness of the material in which a fan, a screen, or a print is wrought. More than any other Asiatic artists, the Japanese, when they cultivated realism, achieved amazing psychic as well as physical characterizations of their subjects, but always contained within a framework of formal patternization.

Geography,
the Physical Basis

IN ASIA, largest of the continents, live sixty percent of the people of the world, not evenly distributed throughout the vast Asian territory, but localized in certain major concentrations that form the core lands of the various Asian states. Size and diversity, both of physical elements and populations, are two distinctive qualities of Asia nowhere else in the world evidenced on so grand a scale.

Nevertheless, the history of the past few hundred years has been drawn in large part with Asia as an appendage of Europe, in effect a backwash area in the stream of international affairs. The cultural will of the West was affirmed in Asia; what Asia willed had little consequence in the Occident. Indeed, it may be held that Asia had no will, that it was subject to the control and manipulation of the West, and that it lacked in whole or in part the cohesiveness and integrated organization that are prerequisite to independent survival in a highly competitive and increasingly interdependent world.

Within the past half century, however, an Asian will has come into being, though most often amorphous and sometimes ephemeral. The culmination of this gradual growth of Asian self-consciousness followed the launching of the Pacific War by Japan in 1941. The previous seventy years had been characterized by a series of wars that facilitated

Much of the material in this chapter originally appeared in "Asia, the Physical Basis" and "Asian Asia, Patterns and Problems," by Norton Ginsburg, in *The Pattern of Asia*, © 1958 by Prentice-Hall, Inc. Used by permission of the publisher.

Japan's expansion onto the adjacent continent, and were accompanied by a channeling of vigorous nationalism, organized social effort, and natural resources into the development of an expanding economy and an ambitious plan for dominating much of East Asia. Although Japan's military program ended in failure, her professed intention of freeing Asia from Western domination and her early military successes, especially in Southeast Asia, fed fuel to the fires of Asian nationalism.

After the close of World War II a number of newly independent countries made their appearance on the map of Asia, and in other places where Europeans and Americans had been politically and economically dominant there followed a further and sometimes drastic loosening of the ties with the West. Thus, since the war there has come to be not only a more diverse Asia but also a new Asia. It is with the new Asia that we are concerned, for the social, economic, and political landscapes of Asia are in flux, and the changing problems of the various Asian states and regions must be assessed within new frames of reference.

The Situation of Asia

What is known as the Asiatic continent is the northeasterly component of the Eurafrasian landmass. It is roughly quadrangular in form and covers approximately eighteen million square miles, one third the land surface of the earth. From north to south this quadrilateral ranges from 85° N. to beyond 10° S. latitude; its west-to-east dimensions, from the western margins of Turkey eastward to the Bering Strait, extend from 25° E. to 170° W. longitude, almost halfway around the world.

In modern times, access to Asia has been mostly over the seas and oceans that rim its more southerly coasts, and it is in the regions accessible by sea that European influence has been most important. The opening of the Suez Canal in 1869 provided a convenient western gateway to much of coastal Asia; after 1860 the opening of Japan to foreign trade and the establishment of regular transpacific steamship services provided an eastern entrance, but only over a sea of more than continental dimensions—the Pacific. Foreign access to much of Asia is still chiefly maritime, but the improvement of land transportation in the Soviet Union has increased the landward accessibility to Central Asia and to northern and western China; and air transportation, with its possibilities for transpolar connections between North America and Asia, may further alter the established patterns of accessibility.

Economically and politically, Asia has begun to occupy, relative to the rest of the world, a position more in keeping with its area, resources, and population. The European "tail" no longer wags the Asiatic "dog," although it remains remarkable that so seemingly minor an appendage of the great continent should continue to exert so important an influence upon Asian affairs. The position of the Soviet Union has also focused attention on Asia, where Russian political imperialism and pressures seem to be most intense and potentially most effective. Thus many of the Asian countries have gained the special attention of the United States, whose clear interest it is to maintain them as "going concerns" within which political decisions can be made without excessive interference from foreign powers, especially the Soviet Union. At the same time, Asia, apart from China, has been acquiring a transpacific world view, which has come to balance the traditional orientation westward toward Europe.

The increasing concern of the West with Asia and of Asia with the West must be viewed together with the expansion of Occidental values and technologies throughout the world and the emergence of a closed world order in which the best of the "empty spaces" have long since been occupied. Each of the Western powers, with the possible exception of the Soviet Union, is finding necessary a global view of physical resources and the problems of their development, both of which Asia possesses in abundance.

The Environmental Pattern

Much of Asia appears singularly inhospitable to human occupance. Yet, within Asia live 1.8 billion people, over three fifths of the population of the earth. What physical basis underlies this apparent anomaly?

Asia, unique among the continents, is characteristically mountainous. Amidst its great mountain ranges appear extensive plateaus, some expressionless and featureless, some severely broken into badlands of forbidding aspect. Nowhere in interior Asia is there a great fertile lowland comparable with that of the South-draining Mississippi basin, which would permit the entry of tempering winds from lower latitudes into the heart of the continent. Nor are there great river basins that provide access to the interior, as do the Amazon in South America and the Congo and Zambezi in Africa.

The core of the Asiatic mountain system lies in the vast complex of young mountains and plateaus focusing upon Tibet and bounded roughly on the south by the sweeping northwest-southeast arc of the Himalaya; on the west by the knotted Pamirs, the roof of the world; on the north by the Tien Shan of China's Sinkiang province; and on the east by the mountains of southwestern China. To the west, a chain of mountains and plateaus extends well into southwestern Asia and dominates the landscape in Iran, the Caucasus, and Turkey. To the north, the Tien Shan are connected with a parallel-trending chain, the Altai mountains of Mongolia, which are structurally related to and form part of the series of complex ranges in northeastern Siberia that continue into eastern Manchuria and Korea. In the far east appear the mountains of Japan, part of the zone of volcanism rimming the Pacific through Taiwan, the Philippines, and the East Indian archipelago.

If all the main ranges and plateaus on the mainland of the continent are considered together, they extend generally east-northeast and west-southwest for some five thousand miles and constitute the largest body of highlands in the world. Within that upland mass are some of the world's highest mountains; these, when combined with the deserts that lie between certain of the ranges, form a continental barrier of unmatched impenetrability. Around the high uplands there also are great stretches of hill lands—as in southeastern China and part of geologically ancient peninsular India—where elevations generally are lower but where high relief limits opportunities for both occupance and communications.

The mountain core acts as the hub of a colossal wheel, the spokes of which are formed by some of the greatest rivers of the world, spiraling outward from the rain-catching and snowcapped slopes of the ranges of the highland core. Not all of these rivers reach the sea, however. Within the continent are some five million square miles of interior drainage. Numerous rivers rising within or on the margins of the core complex flow without tributaries for hundreds of miles across deserts and steppes until they disappear into often saline lakes, swamps, or wastes or into the Aral or Caspian seas. In general, these drainage systems offer limited opportunities for livelihood, and it is only in relatively small irrigated oases of intermontane basins that settlement is found.

Yet the arid and mountainous heartland of Asia cannot be considered "dead." In the past it was from this heartland that nomadic peoples spilled over into Europe, the Near and Middle East, India, and China and brought under their sway vast empires, comparable in size and power to the largest the world has seen. Today, however, the direction of power flow has been reversed, and instead of invasions outward from Central Asia, the invasions, on a smaller scale and less violent, are inward. These take the form of the development of irrigated cotton agriculture in Soviet Turkestan and mineral explorations and exploitation and increased agricultural activity in Sinkiang and Mongolia. For the time being at least, the self-generation of political and military strength that characterized interior Asia in the past has ceased because the tractor, truck, and airplane have made obsolete the mounted mobility of the nomad.

The Asian rivers that flow northward—the Ob, the Yenisei, the Lena, and lesser streams—rise in the mountains of northern and northeastern Asia and cross extensive coastal lowlands before they enter the Arctic Ocean. For the most part these northern lowlands are too cold for large-scale, permanent human occupance. Only in the northern latitudes of North America are there comparable areas of lowland in which cold forms so great a barrier to human habitation.

The great rivers flowing eastward and southward define the Asia that is populous and developed. From a highly restricted area within the interior mountain core flow such rivers as the Indus, the Ganges, the Brahmaputra, the Irrawaddy, the Salween, the Mekong, the Yangtze, and the Hwang Ho. Between and beyond the major river basins flow such lesser yet large streams as the Narbada, Cauvery, Kistna, and Mahanadi of peninsular India, the Chao Phraya of Thailand, the Red and Black rivers of Indochina, the Si system of South China, the Hwai of North China, and the Liao and Amur-Sungari systems of Manchuria and the Soviet Far East. Within the valleys of many of these rivers have developed the cultural cores of lasting civilizations and modern nations, and it is in them that most of the peoples of Asia live.

Climatically Asia is as varied as it is orographically and hydrologically. The primary climatic quality of Asia is continentality. The seasonal heating and cooling of this, the world's largest landmass, makes for major seasonal variations in climate. In winter, when the interior regions are cold, a semipermanent high-pressure belt forms within the northern interior of the continent, and polar continental air masses, outflowing as strong, cold northerly winds from the anticyclones within the belt, bring winter to most of the continent. In summer the rapid and continuous heating of the interior results in lower pressures and in the inflow of tropical maritime air from the continent's margins. Since the outflowing winds are land-originated and usually do not pass over large bodies of water, they are dry, and the winters also tend to be dry. Conversely, in summer the generally weaker inflows of air from the eastern and southern seas are humid and carry with them the moisture that for much of Asia makes summer the rainier season.

Each continent exhibits this seasonal reversal of winds and rains, known as the monsoon effect, but nowhere else are these reversals as notable as in Asia. In North America there is a smaller landmass in which cooling and heating takes place; in South America only a small part of the continent lies in the higher latitudes, and the winter monsoon effect is minimized; as for Africa, no part of that continent lies within the higher latitudes, and the monsoon effects are restricted to relatively limited areas along its eastern littoral. Europe, as a westward-facing, ocean-fronting area, is most strongly influenced by the westerly winds of the upper-middle latitudes, and the climate of Europe is predominantly maritime all the year round, except in the Mediterranean region.

In terms of temperature, the alternation of seasons means little in the southern Asian peninsulas and archipelagoes. These lie on or near the equator, and daily and monthly mean temperatures vary little from season to season. Diurnal variations in temperatures also are relatively slight except in drier regions such as those of southwestern Asia. India and to a lesser degree southeastern Asia and parts of southwestern Asia are protected from these cold, dry winds of the interior by the mountain core and its major outliers. North of India the mountain barrier prevents the flow of maritime air from the Indian Ocean into the interior, and in summer a secondary low-pressure area appears over the hot deserts of northwest India.

The interior regions, isolated as they are from the sea by great distances and mountain barriers, are dry and exhibit the extremes of seasonal and diurnal temperature variations that tend to characterize middle-latitude deserts. In eastern Asia temperatures vary primarily with latitude, and in this respect the east coast of China may be likened to that of eastern North America. Temperatures also vary notably with altitude. The Tibetan highlands, for instance, are well over ten thousand feet; thus winters are cold and summers cool. Even at much lower elevations, mean temperatures are far below those in the coastal lowlands, especially in southern Asia and parts of eastern Asia where the "hill station," or mountain summer resort, is a distinctive occupance feature, developed usually by Europeans seeking relief from the high temperatures and humidities of the steaming lowlands of, for example, India or Java.

Although the greater part of Asia receives most of its

rainfall in the summer, there are several major exceptions and many minor ones. Much of the rainfall of southwestern Asia comes in the winter, and the summers are dry. Along eastward-facing coasts in southern Asia north of the equator, rainfall is heavy in the fall and winter when northeasterly winds of continental origin strike the coasts after passing over large bodies of water. This is the case in southeastern India and along the east coasts of Malaya, Indochina, and the Philippines. South of the equator, Java and the Lesser Sunda Islands receive more rain in summer, which is the northern winter. In Japan, the west-facing coast of Honshu also receives its heaviest precipitation in winter.

Precipitation varies markedly everywhere owing to orographic factors. Exceptionally heavy precipitation in summer characterizes the west coast of India, for example, where the Western Ghats rise precipitously from a narrow coastal plain, but on the plateau just to the east of the Ghats is a rain-shadow zone where summer rainfall is scanty and irregular. On a grand scale there is no better example of orographic influence on climate than Tibet, which displays a tundralike climate similar to that of northern Asia but at over thirty degrees of latitude farther south.

In the case of India, the barrier of the Himalaya has created what may be considered to be an autonomous climatic region, separated from the rest of Asia. Here is experienced the true summer monsoon, the sudden onslaught of winds from the southwest and south, which comes with triggerlike suddenness, though not always with temporal regularity, and carries warm maritime air across the parched face of India. Conversely, in winter, cold winds from the continental interior are largely blocked by the mountain wall, whereas the cyclonic depressions that cross northern India in winter from southwestern Asia are shallow and weak.

Among natural factors other than climate, soils are most important in limiting the usability of the land. The most important soils are those relatively immature soils of alluvial origin that are found in river valleys. Especially in the lower and middle latitudes, these are the soils that are richest in plant nutrients, in many cases maintain their fertility through periodic inundations by silt-bearing water from rivers in flood, and in large measure provide the peoples of Asia with their sustenance. Yet not all of these soils are equally fertile, and many have been so long utilized for agriculture that their natural fertility has been drastically reduced.

Certain other immature soils also are locally important, especially in southeastern Asia where soils have formed over recently deposited volcanic materials. Where the parent volcanic materials are basic rather than acidic, the soils may be very rich and may retain their fertility for long periods. Such soils help explain the enormous densities of rural population in Java.

In sum, Asia possesses a limited agricultural resource base, and the continent therefore offers fewer opportunities for productive agriculture than its size might indicate. It is doubtful whether with present technologies more than twenty percent of the total land area of Asia is suitable for agriculture, and at least a quarter of this percentage consists of marginal land. In fact, not only is most of Asia unattractive to settlement but also much of it is virtually unoccupied, although it does have more people and greater concentrations of people than any other continent of the world.

The Pattern of Resources

Possibilities for the economic development of national states and regional economies depend to an increasing degree on resources other than those of agricultural significance: forests, power resources, and minerals.

One of Asia's major resources is found in its forests, but many of these are remote and too inaccessible for immediate exploitation. In addition, those in the Soviet Union are for all practical purposes of little significance to the rest of Asia. In the mountains of west China and interior Asia are considerable reserves of timber, but these also are relatively inaccessible and of little general commercial importance. In Japan, Korea, and Manchuria, middle-latitude forests of mixed and coniferous types cover wide areas, but none of the East Asian countries is adequately supplied with wood for fuel, lumber, and pulp, although they conceivably could be made self-sufficient with afforestation and proper forest management and control. In southern Asia vast areas are covered by stands of tropical and subtropical forests within which are trees of high commercial value, such as teak and Philippine mahogany, but many of these forests are difficult of access, consist primarily not of homogeneous but of heterogeneous stands, and in general are far removed from the major consuming centers in India, Japan, and China. On the other hand, the growth rate in regions of warmer climates is much higher than in the middle and upper latitudes, and the use potentials of these forests are higher than those in the north, especially if the problem of the economical conversion of tropical hardwoods to pulp for paper and rayon is fully solved.

Of greater significance are power resources, which, in addition to fuel wood, the chief fuel in Asia, consist of coal, petroleum, natural gas, and water.

Coal is found in many parts of Asia. In Soviet Asia are found some extremely large, high-quality coal measures, but on the whole these are of little consequence to most of Asia. China has in Shansi and Shensi provinces some of the largest coal reserves in the world, but since these are not easily accessible, most of China's production comes from substantial but lesser deposits in northern China and Manchuria. Korea also possesses important coal deposits, chiefly anthracite, especially in the north, but the most fully exploited coal measures in eastern Asia are the modest deposits of Japan, the main fields being in northern Kyushu and western Hokkaido. Most of southeastern Asia is coal-poor, but northeast Vietnam possesses large deposits of anthracite. India's coal reserves are somewhat larger than those of Japan and are localized primarily in the northeast, but Pakistan's reserves are very small and of poor quality.

Petroleum is far less well distributed than coal. The most important known reserves are in southwestern Asia, at or near the head of the Persian Gulf. In southeastern Asia are a number of much smaller fields, chiefly in eastern Sumatra, coastal Borneo, and Burma. Minor fields also are exploited in Japan, and some production takes place in Assam and Kansu and Sinkiang provinces of northwest China, where large reserves have recently been reported, but exploration of most of the rest of Asia has not reached the point where the extent of petroleum resources can be determined. Deposits of oil shales have been discovered and partially utilized, especially in Manchuria, but natural gas is as yet of little importance in the energy-producing pattern of Asia.

Asia's waterpower potential exceeds that of the other continents; it is more than twice that of the next largest continent, Africa. Yet in terms of developed waterpower resources, Asia ranks low on the list. Only in Japan and to a lesser extent in India, Korea, and northern China has this inexhaustible resource been exploited significantly. However, large-scale hydroelectric development is now under way or contemplated in many Asian countries, and it usually is tied in with multipurpose projects in which flood control and irrigation are important elements.

To summarize, the power potential of Asia is high, but has been realized only in small part. Mineral fuels are unevenly distributed among Asian countries, and although waterpower resources are abundant, they also are highly localized and present engineering as well as fiscal problems that can be met only with difficulty. In terms of actual energy consumption, Asia, apart from the U.S.S.R., utilizes only twelve percent of the world total, and in terms of per-capita energy consumption lies at the bottom of the list of continents.

The situation with regard to Asian nonpower minerals is similar. On an absolute basis, Asia is mineral-wealthy; even on a per-capita basis it is far from poor; but in terms of production it ranks low on the world scale, although not so low as in its production of power. The locations of many of its minerals are disadvantageous, and even in the more densely populated countries there are vast areas that never have been mineralogically surveyed.

In general, all key metallic minerals are found in quantity in Asia, even apart from Soviet Asia. Iron-ore deposits among the largest and richest in the world are located in the Indian peninsula, occurring in the northeast in happy conjunction with limestone and coals of coking quality. China possesses iron ore in moderate quantities in its central, northern, and northeastern regions, although its Manchurian ores are not of high grade; and northern Korea also possesses sizable deposits. Lateritic iron ores are mined in the Philippines, Indochina, Malaya, and Indonesia; and although few of these deposits are of world importance, all are of great interest to Japan, whose deposits are quite small.

Bauxite is mined in southeastern Asia in considerable quantities. Tin and tungsten are found in southwest China and in the southeastern countries, especially Thailand, Malaya, and Indonesia. India possesses the world's second-largest deposits of manganese, and copper is found in marketable quantities in the arc of countries from India to Japan. The Philippines and Turkey are rich in chrome ores; lead and zinc are scattered widely, one of the major Asian sources being prewar Burma.

Nonmetallic minerals are widely scattered. Salt comes primarily from the evaporation of seawater, although there are exceptions in the salt wells of southeastern China. India is noted for its mica, Ceylon and Korea for their natural graphite. Potash is the distinctive product of the Dead Sea, but natural nitrates and phosphates, the bases for fertilizer industries, are not plentiful in Asia. Sulfur is abundant in Japan, and is found elsewhere in association with volcanic activity. In general, building stone, limestone, sands, and clays are abundant.

As with fuels, the problem Asia faces with regard to minerals is in transporting them from their natural sites to the centers of demand. Because Asia itself, apart from the

Soviet Union and Japan, is not as large a consumer of minerals as are Europe and North America, it ranks very high in terms of its mineral exports to the rest of the world. At the same time, the flows of these raw materials within Asia itself are by no means inconsequential. Persian Gulf oil moves to India and Japan; Indian and Japanese coal goes into southeastern Asia; iron ore from India and southeastern Asia moves to Japan, as do smaller quantities of bauxite and the less important metallic minerals. Significantly, the chief Asian mineral importers are countries such as Japan and metropolises such as Singapore and Hong Kong, which reflect or symbolize industrialization and the Western world rather than traditional and indigenous Asia.

Patterns and Problems of Asian Asia

Asia's physical diversity is matched only by its cultural heterogeneity. Just as there are several Asias definable in physical terms, so there are several Asias that can be distinguished on the basis of cultural differences. Most significant among these is the paradoxical division between the Asia that is Asian and the Asia that is not.

What Is Asian Asia?

To a degree Asian Asia is a negative concept: it may be defined as that part of the Asiatic continent not fundamentally European or Mediterranean in civilization. It does not include, therefore, most of Soviet Asia, which is culturally non-Asian, which is separated by vast distances from the parts of Asia that are, and which operates entirely as an appendage to the Russian heartland in Europe, spilling over into the western part of the Siberian plain and continuing eastward as a slender ribbon embracing the steel thread of the Trans-Siberian Railway. Although the greater part of the Soviet Union lies in Asia, its traditional patterns of culture, whether Christian or Marxist, have long been oriented to and identified with Europe despite the exotic overtones given to Russia long ago by Mongol conquerors. However, the fact that the Soviet Union borders upon most of the rest of the Asian continent and many minority groups are split by the 8,000-mile-long international boundary is exceptionally significant in Asian Asia's affairs. No discussion of the political and economic geography of the rest of

52

the continent can help but return repeatedly to the political—and to a certain extent the cultural—influences that the Russian empire can and does bring to bear.

A somewhat less forceful but still effective argument can be made for excluding most of southwestern Asia, that great region of deserts and steppes that looks primarily to the Mediterranean and within which lies the cradle of Western civilization. This area belongs most appropriately to the Near and Middle East, a pastoral and oasis-dotted region that historically has acted as a crossroads between Asian Asia and the West but has evolved civilizations, economies, and world views substantially different from those found elsewhere in Asia. Nevertheless, it was from southwestern Asia that Islam moved into southern Asia, the Indian subcontinent, and the Malaysian archipelago, and it was Arab seamen who contributed significantly to early Western knowledge of and commercial and political relations with the so-called "Far East." Furthermore, the countries of southwestern Asia share with other Asian countries proximity to the Soviet Union and the problems of new nationhood and economic development, giving them an additional commonality with the rest of Asia.

On the other hand, Asian Asia also is a positive concept. It is the Asia that rims the southern and eastern margins of the great continent. This is the Asia that is populous; this is the Asia that is non-European, even if European-influenced. Here, in what is termed the Asiatic Triangle, in the valleys of the great rivers, are the cores of lasting civilizations and modern nations. Very often these are separated from one another by expanses of largely unoccupied land—deserts, steppes, barren or forested mountains and plateaus—all of which singly or in association act as formidable barriers to communications. Here also, all within a distance of some 750 miles from the sea, are some of the world's more densely populated regions, where the basis for livelihood is subsistence agriculture and where "vegetable" rather than "mechanical" civilizations predominate.

In terms of the problems and patterns of occupance and livelihood, Asian Asia displays in most of its parts similarities that provide a unity for geographic examination. This unity is further supported by the almost universal conflicts between nationalism and colonialism that characterize the area, providing the various countries within it with a uniformity of purpose and outlook that exist almost incongruously with the cultural diversity that otherwise is apparent. In almost all of the Triangle, also, a social revolution is under way, termed by some a "revolution of rising expectations," by which the Asian peoples have set their eyes on goals of economic as well as political freedom and on the material attainments of the Western world.

Despite these unifying qualities, the Asiatic Triangle presents a range of cultural differences that is perhaps unmatched anywhere else in the world. From its western tip in Afghanistan to its northeastern terminus in Hokkaido, its peoples present an astonishing variety of languages, religions, ethnic complexes, personality structures, and forms of government and political control. Their patterns of occupance, though in some ways similar, range from the nomadic herding and transhumance of the Tibetan herdsman to the earthbound solidity and permanency of the Indian village. Furthermore, as already indicated, the areal differentiation of natural conditions is fully as great from west to east as it is from north to south, and this is reflected in differences in numerous artifacts and cultural practices.

On the basis of these differences, it is customary to divide the Triangle into three great realms, or superregions: South Asia, Southeast Asia, and East Asia. In addition, a fourth and essentially negative realm, Central, or High, Asia, could be added, consisting of the associated high mountains, plateaus, and deserts that form the continental core lands. However, since it possesses no political individuality, it customarily is treated as part of China, under the hegemony of which most of it falls.

South Asia includes India, Pakistan, Afghanistan, Ceylon, and the mountain states of Nepal, Bhutan, and Kashmir. The latter three possess a natural affinity with the mountain core, balanced by a traditional political orientation toward India. Afghanistan might well have been assigned to southwestern Asia, but its traditional political ties also have been with India. Muslim Pakistan itself in its western portion is little more than an extension of the Middle Eastern arid lands as they blend into humid Asia, but it is divided into two parts, the eastern and more populous one of which is imbedded in a regional matrix that is in both physical and cultural terms predominantly Indian. Ceylon differs culturally from the other countries primarily in that its religion is neither Islam nor Hinduism, but Hinayana Buddhism. Yet in spite of these great differences, South Asia may rightly be defined in terms of its Indian center of gravity, its former integration under British rule, the present membership of its countries in the British Commonwealth of Nations, its isolation from the rest of Asia by formidable mountain barriers, and its subjection to the far-from-uniform sway of the seasonal monsoon regime.

Southeast Asia—Burma, Thailand, the states of the former Indochina, Malaya, Indonesia, British Borneo, and the Philippines—can best be defined initially in negative terms. It is neither Indian nor Chinese in culture, although it lies between the two and has been influenced substantially by both. It may also be identified by the strong maritime quality that its seas and its fragmented littoral impose, by its relatively less dense population and agricultural frontiers, and by its great diversity of ethnic groups, languages, religions, political systems, and states. Yet there are numerous connections with the other realms, ties for example with Pakistan and the Middle East through Islam in Indonesia and Malaya, and with South and East Asia by predominantly wet-rice agricultural lowlands that are not far different from those in much of India and East Pakistan on the one hand and southern China and Japan on the other.

East Asia, composed of China, Korea, and Japan, may best be identified in terms of two variables: a predominantly Sinitic culture and a largely middle-latitude position fronting the Pacific. However, Japan has long looked southward as well, and there are strong Malaysian influences apparent in Japanese cultural forms. China's interests in Southeast Asia, too, are noteworthy. Japan's relatively advanced industrialization also helps differentiate East Asia from the other realms, as does the fact that non-Asian influences in the East Asian countries have never taken the form of full political control. Again, much of the diversity appearing in East Asian landscapes may be explained in terms of a degree of latitudinal and climatic diversity that is not duplicated in the other Asian realms.

Accessibility and Communications

The Asiatic Triangle not only occupies the southern and eastern margins of Asia, but its commercial world view has been, at least since the middle of the nineteenth century, essentially maritime. This is true even though the indigenous Asian societies have by and large tried to maintain cultural isolation, as evidenced by the magnificent if ostrichlike reluctance of eighteenth-century imperial China to communicate with the West. With some exceptions, the pressures upon the countries of the Triangle to look seaward have greatly increased since the close of the Second World War, although the direct influences of the former imperial powers have declined substantially with the granting of political freedoms to their numerous former colonies and protectorates. At the same time, however, the rise of China as a major and aggressive power has created in its neighbors a new and singular awareness of its proximity.

Overland communications between the Triangle and the outside world are remarkably few. Accessibility to western and interior Asia and the Soviet Union to the north is limited by the barrier of the mountain core and its associated ranges, plateaus, and desert wastes. The only railways connecting the Soviet Union with the rest of Asia lie near the longitudinal extremes of the continent. In the east, a branch of the Trans-Siberian Railway enters Manchuria at Lupin. There is a break-of-gauge, and the line traverses Manchuria, terminating at Vladivostok. Several other Russian lines, parts of the Turk-Sib system, come close to the Persian and Afghan borders but do not cross them. There is only one major rail connection across interior Asia at any point: a spur of the Trans-Siberian that runs southward to Urga, the capital of Outer Mongolia, and thence to northern China, again with a break-of-gauge. The Chinese also are constructing a railway northwestward across Sinkiang province to connect eventually with the Turk-Sib system. To the southwest, although one line extends west from Pakistan across the Persian border, it does not connect with the sparse Iranian network.

Railway communications between the various realms are no less few. No railway pierces the Himalayan barrier into Pakistan, and there is no crossing of the difficult Burmese border ranges that separate India from Burma. Not only does Southeast Asia have no overland rail connections with South Asia but also its connections with China consist only of one meter-gauge line running from Hanoi in Tonkin into Yunnan province and a second line from Tonkin into Kwangsi province and thence into Hunan and connection with the main Chinese railway network.

Rail facilities between individual countries within each of the realms are more numerous, but are still few. In South Asia, however, India and Pakistan share a relatively dense railway net, one of the legacies of British rule. In Southeast Asia, Burma and Thailand have no operational rail connections; Thailand and Cambodia are linked by one operational line between Bangkok and Pnompenh; and Thailand and Malaya share a line that connects Bangkok and Singapore. Indonesia and the Philippines, as island countries, have no rail links with the mainland. In the East Asian realm there are three major rail links, one of them with double tracks, between Manchuria and Korea. Between Japan and Korea, differences in gauge prevent the operation of through-train ferries, although fast ferries could make transfer of passengers and goods quickly.

Highway communications between the Triangle and the rest of Eurasia are of even lesser dimensions. Several seasonal roads connect northern China with Outer Mongolia and Russia, the chief one trending northwestward through the so-called Kansu Corridor south of the Gobi. These and other routes through southern Sinkiang have for thousands of years been arteries of commerce between China and the West, but none of them can be regarded as a highway in the modern sense. No paved roads lead into South Asia from the west either, but even before the time of Alexander, the famed Khyber and Bolan passes allowed invaders and tradespeople to enter India.

The three realms also have poor highway connections with one another. Northward from India are numerous trails into Tibet and China, but none of these is suitable for wheeled vehicles; eastward into Burma there exist only the seasonal and neglected Ledo Road from Assam and a lesser route through the state of Manipur midway along the Indo-Burmese boundary. Between Southeast Asia and China there are but a few connections, chief of which is the little-used Burma Road between Lashio and Kunming, and two roads leading northward from Tonkin.

Within the realms, international highways may link several countries, but even when paved they usually feed into little-developed national road systems. Only in South Asia does a well-established highway system link the two main countries, and this is primarily the result of a division of what formerly had been an integrated system. In the Southeast Asian mainland countries, all-year roads connect northeastern Thailand with Indochina at three points, but there are no through routes between Thailand and Burma or between Thailand and Malaya. In East Asia the road links between Manchuria and Korea cannot compare with the railway connections, and neither country possesses well-developed internal road systems.

In recent years the rapid development of air transportation has to a small degree countered the paucity of external and internal overland communications. Several major airlines link the countries of the Triangle westward with Europe and eastward across the Pacific with the United States. Air services also are provided between Soviet territory and China, Korea, and North Vietnam. Most commercial services, however, tend to skirt the southern margins of the continent. The main routes from London and Western Europe to Tokyo do not follow the approximate Great Circle through Leningrad, Irkutsk, and Vladivostok, but instead follow a reverse arc through Rome, Cairo, Lydda, Basra, Karachi, Delhi, Calcutta, Rangoon, Bangkok, and Hong Kong. That political factors encourage this routing is at once apparent, but it is even more significant that the major air services tend to serve the Asia that is both populous and Asian. On the other hand, transpolar services also are maintained between Tokyo and Western Europe. In general, air services are locally important for the movement of passengers and especially valuable cargo and for the transport of mail and passengers from the outside world; they are of minute if increasing importance in most movements of commercial freight and in the transport of Asians within the Triangle.

The main transport routes to and within the Triangle are maritime. The coasts of the Triangle countries are rimmed with harbors of various capacities, among which are some of the world's major ports. Most of these latter are equipped with well-developed port facilities, and to them come regularly scheduled ocean liners not much smaller than those that ply the North Atlantic. Many of them also act as entrepôts, among which coastal vessels, both Western and native, carry on extensive cabotage. Singapore and Hong Kong are famous entrepôts, but Bombay, Madras, Colombo, Calcutta, Rangoon, Penang, Manila, Dakarta, Shanghai, Tientsin, Yokohama, and Kobe also have entrepôt functions. To a large degree the great port cities act as the centers of commercial and industrial activity; to a lesser degree they are centers of political activity and control.

The eastern maritime approaches to Asia follow two routes across the Pacific. One is near a Great Circle route, that crosses the North Pacific from the Pacific coast of North America to Yokohama, Shanghai, Hong Kong, and Manila. The southern route via Honolulu is followed by most vessels that sail from North American Atlantic and Gulf ports and that enter the Pacific through the Panama Canal.

The approaches from the west are through the maritime gate at Suez, and the Indian Ocean is in shipping terms a European sea, as evidenced by the European flags that predominate within it. Singapore, overlooking the eastern entrance to the Indian Ocean, the Strait of Malacca, acts as a convenient point of division between the essentially European Indian Ocean and the predominantly American North Pacific, although European, and particularly English, companies are engaged in trade along the Asian coasts east of Singapore to a degree symbolized by the commercial wealth and maritime importance of Hong Kong. In addition, Japanese shipping, after a near-shattering decline at the end of the Second World War, has regained much of its previous importance in the Asian and, to a lesser degree, transpacific trades.

The shipping routes that gird the Asiatic Triangle coasts extend for thousands of miles. The arterial route between Suez and Kobe covers 8,100 nautical miles by way of Aden, Colombo, and Singapore, nearly twice the distance from Seattle to Yokohama. The sea-route distance from Singapore to Kobe alone is about 3,100 nautical miles, approximately the same as that of the transatlantic crossing from New York to Liverpool. The route from Suez to Bombay covers a similar distance, and the coastal route between Bombay and Calcutta measures 2,150 miles.

These great distances mean that the movement of freight even by sea, the cheapest medium of general cargo transportation, is costly and that freight rates within the area often are higher than those elsewhere. Thus, the costs of commodities produced in the Western world frequently are higher to the Asian consumer, whose purchasing power is low to begin with, than to the consumer in Western Europe or in the United States. Because of these great distances, also, vessels on the Europe-Suez Indian Ocean-Far East route or the North America-East Asia-Transpacific route usually make numerous stops along the way, in contrast to vessels on the North Atlantic run, and numerous round-the-world services serve Triangle ports. In this connection it is important to note that the distance from American east-coast ports to Hong Kong is about the same by way of the Atlantic and Suez as by way of Panama and the Pacific.

The Patterns of Culture

The theme of diversity and complexity that applies to the Asian Triangle is well displayed in the distribution of ethnic, religious, and linguistic groups within it. In South Asia the terms "Indian" and "Pakistani" refer to two nationalities rather than to ethnic entities, since each country contains numerous peoples having significant and broadly cultural distinctions: Afghans, Punjabis, Rajputs, Sikhs, Bengalis, Tamils, and Assamese, to name a few. In Southeast Asia the several separate political states each contain numerous minority peoples, such as the Shans and Karens in Burma and Thailand, the so-called Moi of Indochina, the Moros and Negritos of the Philippines, the Minangkabau of Indonesian Sumatra, and the Dyaks of Borneo. It is possible to extend greatly the list of differing peoples in Indonesia if one recognizes the Javanese, Sudanese, Madurese, Balinese, and Buginese, for example, as having distinctive ethnic character. In East Asia, China exhibits wondrous ethnic diversity despite its vast and monolithic culture, especially in its marchlands, where Mongols, Tibetans, Uigurs,

Uzbeks, Thai, Hui, and the aborigines of Taiwan form only a partial list of the minorities. In Korea and Japan ethnic homogeneity is perhaps greater than elsewhere; both represent Sinitic variants, though so differentiated with time that they have come to possess distinctive if related culture patterns of their own.

Religious differences within the Triangle are no less significant than ethnic differences. South Asia includes not merely Muslims and Hindus, but numerous Muslim and Hindu sects, as well as sizable minorities of Christians in the more urbanized areas, animists in the peninsular and Assamese hills, and Mahayana Buddhists in the northern mountain border regions. In Southeast Asia, Theravada Buddhism in Burma and Thailand contrasts with the Catholicism of the Philippines, the predominant Muhammadanism of Indonesia and Malaya, and the Chinese eclecticism of the Annamese; animists hold firm in the sparsely populated uplands or peripheral islands of each country. In East Asia, the Confucian code of ethics historically has dominated much of China, though weakened by the conflict with Communism and the presence of impressive numbers of Muslims and Mahayana Buddhists among the minority peoples of the west and Christians in the coastal areas of the east. In Japan Buddhism resides in peculiar amalgam with state Shintoism, both overlain with Chinese influences and underlain by a still-important animism, whereas in the larger cities Christianity has numerous converts.

Cultural complexity is further evidenced in terms of linguistic differences. The actual variety of languages and dialects in Asian Asia defies brief description, but in general there are differences of such dimensions that mutual incomprehensibility is the rule rather than the exception. South Asia contains Hindi and related dialects in northern India and the Dravidian languages in the south; Southeast Asians speak Burmese, Thai, Annamese, and the Malayan dialects; and Chinese in its various forms, Korean, and Japanese are spoken in East Asia. These represent only a sample of the existing languages and dialects. The interchange of scripts, words, and ideas within languages that further complicates the problem is indicated by the case of Chinese, Korean, Japanese and Annamese. The last-named three are much indebted to Chinese for forms of writing and numerous words and sounds, but all three languages have different linguistic origins, and none of the four in colloquial form is similar to the others.

The number of significantly differing languages and dialects within certain countries has made it necessary to establish, or attempt to establish, so-called "national," or "official," languages. In China, where a common written language is shared by all ethnic Chinese, there are several groups of thirty million persons or more who speak dialects not comprehensible to their ethnic brethren. Thus, there has been established a national language, Kuo-yü, based upon the Peking dialect, sometimes referred to as Mandarin. In the Philippines, where Malaysian languages predominate, Tagalog has been recommended as the national language, although more people speak another Malaysian language, Bisayan, and English is commonly used as a lingua franca. In Indonesia, where Malaysian languages also predominate, dialectical differences have been so great that a national tongue, Bahasa Indonesian, has been established, and Roman script has been officially substituted for the traditional Arabic script that came with Islam into Southeast Asia. In the Federation of Malaya, Malay, again with a romanized script, and English coexist as official languages despite the presence of a very large Chinese minority. In India it is planned to establish Hindi as the national language over the objections of the Dravidian-speaking peoples of the south and despite the use of English as a lingua franca. Similarly, Pakistan may establish Urdu, a Hindi variant, as its national language over the objections of the Bengalis in East Pakistan.

Patterns of Population and Settlement

Along with these cultural differences among and within the realms and the countries that constitute them, there are considerable differences in the distribution of populations, which are 220 million in Southeast Asia, 560 million in South Asia, and 860 million in East Asia. In general, the population pattern of Asian Asia is characterized by heavy densities in the better-watered and more fertile coastal and fluvial lowlands, usually with relatively easy access to the sea. Estimated average densities differ widely, however, from realm to realm: in Southeast Asia, 46 per square kilometer; in South Asia, 107; and in East Asia as a whole, 67.

In South Asia, rural densities range from those of 2,000 per square kilometer in portions of the Indo-Gangetic plain to almost uninhabited regions in Kashmir. In general, the heaviest population densities are in the plain and in the coastal lowlands of peninsular India.

Southeast Asia is characterized by vast areas of sparsely populated land lying between relatively restricted population cores where local densities run as high as those in the north of India but where overall densities are far less. Higher densities are associated with the fluvial plains of the realm, but in Java densities are also high on the uplands nourished by ejecta from still-active volcanoes.

In East Asia the same general pattern holds as in Southeast Asia, but on a much larger scale, with the bulk of the population residing in the coastal and riverine lowlands of China, Japan, and Korea. However, most of western China, Tibet, and Outer Mongolia have average densities of only 3 per square kilometer, whereas portions of the lower Yangtze and Si river plains and the coastal lowlands of Japan and Korea have densities approaching 1,000 per square kilometer. If the sparsely settled regions of interior Asia are subtracted from the rest of East Asia, the remaining 55 percent of the realm possesses an average density of about 100 per square kilometer, comparable with that of South Asia. Even so, areas of sparse and scattered settlement, not only in China but also in Korea and Japan, anomalously account for by far the larger part of even the eastern area of the realm.

Demographic patterns and trends throughout Asian Asia are characterized by very high birth rates, high but declining death rates, and very high infant-mortality rates. In general, the rate of population increase as represented by the differences between crude birth and death rates is relatively low. The age-distribution curves of the various national populations also resemble each other. The people of the Triangle in general are young, and they are young because they usually do not live long enough to become old. To cite an extreme example, in India, of every 100,000 male children born in a given year, only 40 percent can expect to be alive at the age of 40; in the United States the equivalent percentage is over 85 percent. In Thailand, a more nearly average case, 51 percent can expect to be alive at 40. It should be noted, however, that the low life expectancy of most of Asia reflects very high infant mortality; even if this bias is accounted for, the life expectancy of the Indian child of 5 is only 43 years more.

Although the average rate of population increase in Asia is quite low, or about the same as that of the United States, the actual annual increases are enormous owing to the huge populations involved. Thus, if the current rate of increase for India is assumed to be a conservative 1.5 percent, this means an annual increment of nearly 7 million and a decennial increase of about 80 million. In China, similar proportional increases of even greater magnitude are taking place.

An even more serious problem arises from the trend toward declining death rates without concomitant declines in birth rates. In most regions, death rates have been declining steadily though slowly for decades. Thus Java's population has multiplied fivefold since the first half of the nineteenth century, and Japan has increased her population threefold since 1870. Death rates in certain other areas, as in Ceylon, Taiwan, and Malaya, have fallen very sharply since 1930. In the cases of Ceylon and Taiwan at least, however, birth rates have not fallen, and their annual rates of increase are between 3 and 4 percent or more. Elsewhere, even in India and China, death rates have been declining but are still about three times the Western levels. However, birth rates have remained sufficiently high, with the notable exception of Japan, to create an ever-widening gap between births and deaths. Herein is one of the great problems of Asia, an uncoiling spiral of expanding population that cannot help but rapidly increase the pressures on physical resources and means of livelihood.

The traditional Asian society is based upon the village community, and the bulk of Asians in all the countries of the Triangle live in hamlets or villages. Only in the more rugged and less densely populated regions are examples of dispersed settlement found. In almost all countries, urbanism in the Western sense remains foreign to the traditional patterns of settlement, and the number of great multifunctional metropolises is notably few when considered in relation to the populations involved.

There were, of course, great cities in South, East, and even Southeast Asia before European influences made their appearance in force. Yet these cities for the most part performed a specialized function in that they were political centers, most often being the only political centers within their countries. They contained the seats of government, the sites of the royal palaces, the residences of the court nobles, and the homes and shops of countless artisans and other persons engaged in serving the needs of the court and its hangers-on. Essentially this sort of city was parasitic in its functional relations with its hinterland, which in most cases included an entire country. The city performed few services for its hinterland other than administrative ones. In Edo, now called Tokyo, the seat of the Tokugawa shogunate in pre-Meiji Japan, the produce of the nation pouring into the city was largely in the form of tax levies on grain and other tribute for which little was returned to the countryside. The same sort of functions characterized Changan (now Sian), capital of China during the Han dynasty; Hangchow, capital of China during the later Sung; and Peking (now Peiping), capital during the later Ming and Ching reigns. Agra and

Delhi, capitals of the Mogul empire in India, provide additional examples. If these great capitals were situated near tidewater or on navigable rivers, it was in most cases sheer coincidence since they were centers of societies that primarily were internally rather than externally oriented.

Within the past century there has been a rapid growth of cities on more nearly Western lines, especially along seacoasts and at nodal points along the more modern communications routes within individual countries. These cities are experiencing much more rapid growth than are the countries in which they are located, partly as a result of natural increase but largely because of a continuous migration of people from country to city. This migration, perhaps the greatest the world has seen in terms of sheer numbers, is the result of so-called "push" factors in rural areas—famine, underemployment, general insecurity—and the so-called "pull" factors of the city—greater work opportunities, real or assumed; amenities, and relative security. As a result, large urban proletariats have appeared in the Asian world for the first time, and their political potency is high. Urbanization in Asia is of the greatest importance, however, not just in population terms but, more important, in terms of the increasingly significant roles that the cities are playing in the processes of change that dominate the Asian scene.

Pluralism and the Problem of Asia

One of the major features of homogeneity in Asian Asia is a widespread cultural and economic pluralism, which to a high degree contains the kernel of the problem of Asia.

The world of the Asian village, agriculturally based, relatively small, restricted in outlook, inbred, and self-sufficient, contrasts with the world symbolized by the great and modern port cities of the Triangle, externally oriented and in contact with the world of international commerce. This contrast is one aspect of the basic pluralism that appears almost everywhere in Asia. The two worlds, however, are not completely separated. Improved communications, the transition from a barter to a money economy, and some raising of educational levels, have resulted in substantial increases in communication between the traditional village and the essentially foreign city. The consequence has been a gradual if localized decay in the stability and self-sufficiency of the traditional Asian systems of cultural and economic organization and the partial substitution of Western values. Another consequence has been the fostering in Asians of economic expectations that are not clearly accompanied by proportional increases in the opportunities for satisfying those expectations. Thus there has developed what some have termed a "revolt of the clerks," those Asians of some education but little opportunities, and on a broader basis the "revolution of rising expectations," the satisfaction of which is made all the more difficult by rapid population increases, increasing pressures on the land, inadequate transportation facilities, and scarcities of capital and skilled labor forces.

The livelihood and developmental problems of Asia provide one major unifying element in dealing with a part of the world of which the diversity may appear discouragingly great. In Asian Asia the basis for livelihood in every country, with the exception of Japan, is agriculture, often irrigated agriculture. Most of the population is rural and resides in small village occupance units. In almost all areas, agricultural productivity is low, technologies are primitive if often effective, and major seasonal surpluses of labor are everywhere in evidence. The ratio of population to cultivated land is enormously high, absolutely as well as relative to Western standards, and this fact is all the more significant in the light of the relatively few livelihood opportunities other than agriculture. Industrialization has not taken place or is taking place slowly except in Japan and, to a lesser degree, in China. In those places where it is proceeding at all, the problem of acquiring skilled labor in countries where practical literacy is shockingly low provides constant barriers to change and development.

In brief, the Triangle areas are characterized by poverty, overpopulation relative to arable land and current agricultural practices, potential or actual rapid increases in population, folk societies ill-prepared for rapid social and economic change, and burgeoning nationalisms that in their often irrational orientations demand a paradoxical mating of painless industrialization with traditional noneconomic value systems. It is these elements, set upon resource endowments of limited scope and capabilities, that are interacting within the world's rapidly changing political and social climate to create a fundamentally altered geographical pattern for Asia.

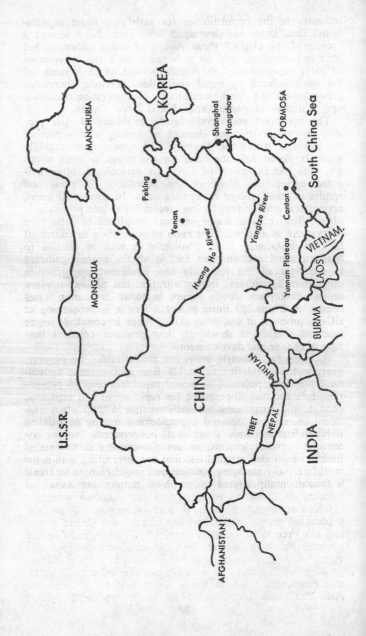

China

CHINA HAS demanded much American attention during the past quarter century. During the 1930's and early 1940's the United States gave moral support and, finally, military support to China's struggle against Japanese domination. Then came a civil war in China, climaxed by the establishment of a Communist regime at Peking in 1949, that provoked serious frustrations and recriminations in American politics. Direct American-Chinese conflict in Korea soon followed. Subsequently, through the 1950's and into the 1960's, the United States has repeatedly had to make important and difficult decisions about China, decisions concerning mutual-defense arrangements with the Nationalist Chinese on Formosa, the diplomatic recognition of Communist China, and the seating of Peking representatives in the United Nations. Because of all these interrelations, a great many Americans living today have had personal experience with the Chinese on the mainland, on Formosa, or in Korea; and news of China is commonplace in American newspapers, magazines, radio, and television. Americans of today, in short, are accustomed to thinking of China as an important part of their world.

China is important to us in part because it has become a potential threat to the very security of the United States and our Free World allies. Since 1949 the mainland Chinese government, with almost fanatical single-mindedness and vigor, has been pursuing policies designed to make itself the greatest power center in Asia. It has created armed forces that outnumber those of India, Japan, and all of Southeast Asia combined. It has used its forces creditably against

Americans and other Westerners in Korea, it has equipped them with increasingly modern arms, and it can be expected before long to have at its disposal nuclear weapons and missiles. It has organized China's people and resources in a concentrated drive to surpass Japan, Germany, and Great Britain in manufactures and thus become one of the world's first-rank industrial giants. By a combination of diplomacy, subversion, and military threats, it seeks to overawe all its neighbors; and in particular it openly denounces the United States as an enemy of world peace and progress and has the announced intention of seeing to it that our political institutions, economic system, and intellectual values crumble and disappear from history.

Such hostility toward the United States is of course prevalent throughout the Communist world, in which since 1949 mainland China has been a junior partner of the Soviet Union. But by the 1960's China had become the most outspoken and belligerent champion of the worldwide Communist revolution and was exerting aggressive influence in such distant places as Africa, Albania, and Cuba, influence that seemed to subvert not only the Free World's interests but also the Soviet Union's. Responsible thinkers were beginning to speculate that Americans and Russians might have to collaborate for defense against China in the not-too-distant future.

This eventuality is by no means inevitable, for no one can be sure that Communist China will persist in its current attitudes or that it will realize its ambition to become a dominant world power, hostile or otherwise. But it does seem inevitable that for the foreseeable future Americans will be watching China with anxious interest and will continue to be called on for important and difficult decisions concerning their relations with China.

Being interested in China is not a phenomenon peculiar to our own time. China has fascinated Americans, and in the longer view, Western man in general for a very long time. In the distant past, Romans clamored for Chinese silk. The thirteenth-century traveler Marco Polo astonished generations of European readers with his awed descriptions of the great cities, the vast population, and the uncountable riches of the Chinese empire. Columbus stumbled on the Americas in 1492 while trying to find a new route to China, and to Henry Hudson in the seventeenth century the lure of China was so strong that North America still seemed just a frustrating obstacle to be got through or around. Meanwhile, reports from China by Jesuits and other Christian missionaries were being read so avidly in Europe that Confucius almost became the patron saint of the eighteenth-century Enlightenment. By the nineteenth century, European and American traders, missionaries, diplomats, sailors, and soldiers had all become entangled inescapably in the turbulent development of modern Chinese history.

Our attitudes toward China have fluctuated between admiration and revulsion, between hope and despair. At times we long to think of the hundreds of millions of Chinese as potential customers and potential converts; at other times we shrink from the Yellow Peril. At times China is symbolized for us by a benign Charlie Chan; at other times, by a malign Fu Manchu. Sometimes we just resign ourselves to being forever unable to make sense out of so strange a country, where the women wear pants and the men wear gowns. But one way or another, China has always fascinated us.

China's importance in the world, therefore, is not related merely to our national defense and to world politics. China is important because it is one of mankind's great storehouses of beauty, wisdom, and experience. Even if China were not a military threat to anyone, men everywhere would still find good reasons for studying its art and literature, its philosophy and religion, its social organization and customs, and its governmental heritage. And most of all, perhaps, the world at large would still be fascinated by the epic drama of modern Chinese history.

What is going on in China is one of the most awesome and fateful chapters of human history. What we are observing is the agonizing, tortuous struggle of a proud and brilliant people to work out a way of living in dignity in a strange, inhospitable modern world that has undermined the values and institutions that formerly made them secure and powerful. The transition from the glorious past to the still undefinable future has been, and continues to be, a very difficult experience indeed for the Chinese.

What are the factors that have shaped this experience?

The Land and the People

China is a vast, diversified land densely populated by a patient, industrious people.

The traditional Chinese heartland, or what might be called China proper, is a rather squared-off area at the eastern end of the Eurasian continent occupying about 1.5 million square miles. It is approximately equal in area to the India-Pakistan subcontinent and about half the size of the continental United States. In recent centuries, however, China's frontiers have been stretched out to include Tibet, Chinese

Turkestan (now called Sinkiang), Inner Mongolia, and Manchuria; so that today the Chinese control a territory of 4.2 million square miles. In this extended definition, China is larger today than any other country except the Soviet Union. It stretches continuously as far as from Maine to Cuba and from Boston to San Francisco.

There is little basic unity in this sprawling land. Tibet, southwest of China proper, is a high plateau ringed round by the most formidable mountain barriers on earth and occupied by a people with a long record of hostility toward their Chinese neighbors. Their language is related only distantly to Chinese, their pastoral way of life is almost the classical opposite of China's sedentary way of life, and their Lamaist religion is completely at odds with the rationalistic modes of thought that have prevailed in China, differing notably even from Chinese Buddhism. Turkestan and Mongolia, west and north of China proper, are low-lying flatlands ranging from unproductive and almost uninhabitable deserts to steppes suitable only for grazing. Their occupants speak various Turkic and Mongolian languages that are no more kin to Chinese than English is. They are in part converts to Islam and in part practitioners of Lamaism mixed with primitive shamanism, and throughout history they have fought the Chinese in the way that nomadic grazers everywhere have always fought farmers. Manchuria, to the northeast, is largely a great plain that is much more suitable to Chinese-style living; but it is separated from China proper by mountains, fluctuates between hot and cold seasons much more drastically than does the Chinese homeland, and has traditionally been occupied by Tungusic-speaking peoples who until recently successfully resisted Chinese migration.

Even China proper itself is naturally divided into diverse regions. Geographers like to call China a checkerboard, and they marvel that its various parts never became distinct nation-states in the European pattern. Even overlooking lesser fragmentations, every observer notes that China proper is divided by the Ching Ling Shan, a mountain range lying west-east across central China, into two major areas that differ from one another in many important ways.

North China is dominated by the valleys of the Yellow River (Hwang Ho) and its tributaries. Its western sector is mountainous and blanketed by thick deposits of a fine-grained, wind-deposited soil called loess. Its eastern sector is the great North China Plain, one of the earth's most extensive and fertile agricultural basins. As a whole, North China is a rather uniformly dry, brown land where the elements are harsh and the people are robust and stolid. Agriculture, disrupted alternately by devastating floods and droughts, is devoted principally to the production of cereals that require little water: wheat, sorghum, and millet. Such foodstuffs as noodles and dumplings are characteristic. Oxen, mules, horses, and even camels are not uncommon, and animal-drawn carts provide the traditional form of transport. Winters are very cold, and dust storms blowing out of the northwestern wastelands are a frequent nuisance.

South China encompasses the basins and valleys of the Yangtze River and, farther south, a broad coastal zone of densely folded hills that rise in the west into the rugged Yunnan Plateau, which separates China from mainland Southeast Asia. In sharp contrast to North China, this entire southern half of the country is uniformly lush and green. Well watered by rivers and summer rainfall, it is one of the most intensively cultivated regions on earth. Rice is the principal crop and the staple food. Almost year-round, it is grown under water in tiny fields linked by endless mazes of irrigation canals, and the flooded fields stretch high up the hillsides, terrace by terrace. Water buffaloes are the only common draft animals, and various kinds of boats—small sampans and large junks—provide the most important transport services. Millions of South Chinese even make their permanent homes aboard the riverboats with which they earn their livings. In general, the South Chinese are slighter in physique and somewhat more emotional in temperament than their North Chinese compatriots. Their lives are by no means easy, but they are less harassed by the elements than the North Chinese.

The geographical diversity of China is offset in some measure by the fact that the inhabitants of the whole territory are a remarkably homogeneous group in terms of race. Modern Chinese governments say the population includes five races: the Han peoples (that is, the traditional Chinese themselves, named in this way after one of their great ancient dynasties), Muslims, Mongols, Manchus, and Tibetans. But these groups, differing from one another in languages, religions, and ways of life to be sure, cannot easily be differentiated on the basis of their physical characteristics, by which races are usually defined. All of them belong in the great racial category that we call Mongoloid, and share its characteristics: a skin color that we Westerners call yellow, straight black hair, eyelids that give what we consider a slant-eyed effect, a small nose, and several others. This racial homogeneity in China contrasts markedly to the racial diversity of some other Asian areas, most notably, India.

But China has no comparable homogeneity in language. Not only do the Tibetans, the Mongols, and some other peoples on China's periphery speak languages entirely their own but also the so-called Han Chinese themselves cannot always understand one another's speech. They all speak the same language with a common grammar and, for the most part, common idioms, but the pronunciation of words differs greatly from region to region. Thus, for example, the personal name of Nationalist China's famous Generalissimo Chiang is pronounced Kai-shek by some and Chieh-shih by others, and still other Chinese pronounce it in still other ways. We in America, as all peoples, have our own dialectal differences, but we manage to understand both the Brooklyn bleacherite and the Georgia belle. The Chinese of one province, however, may find it totally impossible to carry on a conversation with a Chinese from a neighboring province, so great are the dialectal differences. Moreover, the number of mutually unintelligible Chinese dialects is very large. In Fukien province alone, 108 distinct dialects have been identified.

China's dialectal problem should not be exaggerated. It is only in the south coastal provinces that varying dialects abound. In the Yangtze valley and throughout North China, there is a standard, uniform dialect called Kuo-yü or "the national speech" (Westerners call it Mandarin), and in the twentieth century Chinese governments have vigorously promoted the use of Kuo-yü among the traditional speakers of Cantonese and other dialects of South China. Nevertheless, language diversity like geographical diversity has been a liability in China's efforts to develop the strong sense of national unity that is required of modern nations.

The writing system presents another kind of problem. Chinese words as written are not alphabetical representations of sounds, but instead are basically pictorial representations of meanings. We call them ideographs. The ideograph for "man," for example, clearly suggests a human figure, even if in a somewhat simplified and conventionalized way, and there is nothing about it to suggest any particular pronunciation. In other words, it does not "spell out" anything. This means that any literate Chinese can read and understand what any other Chinese writes, despite the fact that they might not be able to converse intelligibly. In just the same way that Englishmen, Frenchmen, Germans, or Spaniards all can read and understand the numerical symbol 3 although they pronounce it differently as *three, trois, drei,* and *tres,* so all Chinese writers use a common symbol for the idea "man" despite their differences in speech. (As a matter of fact, such non-Chinese peoples as the Japanese, the Koreans, and the Vietnamese long ago adopted the Chinese ideographs for writing their own languages, and we Westerners could do the same if we were willing to give up our alphabetical systems.) The nonalphabetical script, therefore, has given the Chinese a common literary heritage and has been a major factor in the persisting cohesion of Chinese civilization. However, because it is much more difficult to learn than an alphabetical script, a relatively small proportion of the Chinese have managed to attain literacy at all times in the past, and China's modern efforts to become a world power have been handicapped by the lack of an informed, educated citizenry at large.

All the problems that confront China because of its size, its geographical diversity, its linguistic disunity, and the difficulty of its writing system are further complicated by the fact that any Chinese government has to be able to manage vast numbers of people. By the time of Christ, China had developed a population of about 60 million, a larger population than can be claimed by modern England, France, or Germany. For some fifteen centuries thereafter, census figures hovered between 60 and 100 million. In the thirteenth century, one great Chinese city alone, Hangchow, near present-day Shanghai, had a resident population of two million within the city walls and another two million suburbanites in the immediate environs, forming a great metropolitan center with a population probably outnumbering that of thirteenth-century France in its entirety. Around 1600 China's population began to grow dramatically, perhaps because of political stability combined with the production of newly introduced food crops such as sweet potatoes, peanuts, and maize. By 1800 census officials were reporting totals around 300 million, and since then growth has continued at a fast pace. In 1960 indications were that there were some 650 million Chinese in mainland China, and what is more, that they were continuing to increase by some fifteen million a year, or some two thousand an hour. Barring large-scale wars, extensive natural calamities, or the adoption of successful birth-control techniques, it appears likely that the Chinese will number one billion in the 1980's.

Not only are the Chinese very numerous. In relation to the land that they occupy, they are very dense. Whereas the population density of the United States is less than sixty per square mile, that of China, including all its vast frontier regions, is about 150. Considering only China proper, the population density of about 400 per square mile is greater than that of New York State. Since only some fifteen percent of China proper's land surface is suitable for agricultural cultivation (a far lesser percentage than in the United States) and little of the remainder provides pasturage for livestock, the problem of just feeding such a vast population takes on colossal proportions. Furthermore, even taking into account modern progress in communications techniques, the task of organizing such a numerous people in a determined nation-wide effort of any sort, either for wartime or for peaceful purposes, must appear forbidding to anyone.

Aside from the land, China does not appear to be richly endowed with natural resources, and even in modern times it has been slow to develop what resources it has. It does have coal and iron, but whether they are abundant enough and of good enough quality ever to support a steel industry comparable to that of the Soviet Union or of the United States is questionable. The supply of petroleum is negligible, unless the far western frontier province, Sinkiang, provides unexpected reservoirs. Hydroelectric power is underdeveloped and may be impossible to develop significantly for want of natural water-storage areas where effective dams might be built, and because of the heavy burden of silt that is carried by many of China's rivers, which threatens to cut short the usefulness of whatever dams might be built.

On the other hand, the Chinese people themselves, however unwieldy may be their numbers, constitute a natural resource that should not be underestimated. Whether wily rogues, scowling bullies, self-effacing plodders, or self-sacrificing zealots, they are among the most wondrously human of human beings, men and women alike. They include scintillating intellectuals, shrewd businessmen, and marvelously skilled craftsmen. Accustomed to work arduously for very little reward, they are in general both physically tough and tough-mindedly realistic; and above all, they are orderly, patient, and persistent. Though naturally tolerant and good-humored, they are capable of becoming intensely dedicated to causes and aroused in righteous indignation. They may not be either as disciplined as the Japanese or as idealistic as the Indians, but they have a long tradition of sober responsibility and have repeatedly responded with vigor to effective leadership. On overall balance, their record of past achievements is possibly unparalleled in human history, and few outsiders who know the Chinese doubt their capacity for continuing creativity and achievement.

Awareness of all these varied characteristics of China's lands and peoples is fundamental for an understanding of modern China's strengths and weaknesses and its causes for mixed hope and despair.

Historical Patterns

China has an incomparably long and glorious history. The great North China Plain, on which Chinese civilization originally emerged, has apparently been occupied for as long and as continuously as any area on earth. Modern archaeologists have discovered in caves near Peking the remains of manlike creatures whom they collectively designate Peking Man *(Sinanthropus pekinensis)* and whom they rank among the very oldest protohumans yet known, heavy-jawed, stooping creatures capable of speech who hunted and built fires in the Yellow River valley some half million years ago. For a long while after Peking Man, the archaeological record is not very full or clear, but it reveals that by the second millennium B.C., when early civilizations were developing in Mesopotamia, Egypt, and the Indus valley of India, the whole of North China had been settled by distinctively Chinese people living in traditional Chinese peasant fashion.

Amidst their Neolithic-stage settlements, at about the middle of the second millennium B.C., there emerged a Bronze Age civilization complete with horse-drawn chariots, the Chinese writing system in its earliest known form, high-quality sculptures and bronze vessels, and a large, unified state governed by hereditary rulers. This was the Shang dynasty, which Chinese tradition says began in 1766 B.C. and ended in 1122 B.C.; and with it Chinese history really begins.

The Shang state had to defend itself regularly against uncivilized peoples who surrounded it, and it was finally overthrown by a group of rebellious chieftains from its western frontier. They established a new ruling dynasty, called Chou (c. 1122–256 B.C.). Parceling out the conquered territory among themselves and their allies, they inaugurated a feudal age in China that had many of the characteristics of medieval Europe's. There was a governmental hierarchy beginning with local barons who were vassals of regional lords, who in turn were vassals of the Chou kings. The kings, lords, barons, and their warrior retainers were hereditary aristocrats, owning all land and monopolizing all wealth and power. They fought among themselves in a knightly fashion, not very viciously; they hunted and practiced archery and charioteering; they worshiped their ancestors in elaborate rituals and cultivated a gentlemanly code of etiquette. The common people, on the other hand, were serfs bound to the land, who produced the agricultural surpluses that supported the aristocracy.

The Chou ruling family lasted longer than any other in Chinese history, but from the eighth century B.C. on, its actual power declined. Great vassal states grew stronger and began wrangling with one another for influence. Wars became common and devastating, with massed forces of commoner infantrymen and cavalrymen thrown against one another as states set out to crush and absorb their neighbors. Along with the collapse of the old political order came erosion of the old religious beliefs, standards of morality, and social stability. Increasing chaos provoked men to reconsider the meaning and purpose of life, and out of this intellectual ferment arose China's great native philosophical traditions, most notably, Confucianism and Taoism. But their prescriptions did not cure China's immediate ills. Interstate warfare became more intense and almost incessant. The Chou dynasty itself was exterminated in 256 B.C., and order was not restored until the northwestern frontier state of Chin crushed all its rivals and forcibly reunified China in 221 B.C.

The victorious Chin ruler, a strong-willed and powerful man who took the title First Emperor (*Shih Huang Ti*), has consistently been condemned by Chinese historians for his ruthless methods. He was so hated in his own time that his dynasty was overthrown almost immediately after his own death. But he provided an important historical function in relation to China's overall development in that he abolished the old feudal relationships, made nationwide a pattern of free peasant ownership of land, and united China under a governmental structure in which all officials down to the local level were appointed agents of the emperor and all authority was centralized in the national capital. In its essential principles, the unitary, bureaucratic form of government that he instituted lasted from his time until 1912, when China's last imperial dynasty was overthrown and succeeded by a republic; and the free peasantry that he created out of feudal serfdom has remained the backbone of China's social order up to the present.

The feudal age in China, therefore, ended centuries before European feudalism began, giving way to a long era that might be called an Imperial Age.

Several significant patterns or themes dominate this long period of traditional China's maturity. From one point of view, the history of this age can be seen as the gradual spread of the Chinese people and their social and political institutions out of the Yellow River valley. In the third century B.C. even the Yangtze River valley was still a somewhat "barbarian" frontier zone. It became an important center of population in the third and fourth centuries A.D. By the seventh and eighth centuries the south coastal regions had been securely incorporated into the Chinese realm, and the North China Plain was beginning to lose its predominant role in Chinese affairs. In the twelfth and thirteenth centuries the balance of population shifted to the south, and China proper as we know it today became fully occupied and cultivated by the Chinese. Subsequently there were alternately advancing and receding migrations on a small scale in and out of the marginal-farming lands of Inner Mongolia, and in the nineteenth and twentieth centuries large numbers of Chinese have moved into Manchuria. Within these territorial limits the Chinese have multiplied enormously in recent centuries, but they have not spread their total way of life beyond them. Although Chinese governments throughout history repeatedly extended their direct political control into Tibet, Central Asia, Outer Mongolia, and Korea, the Chinese people have not substantially established themselves and their social institutions there. On the other hand, in recent centuries there have been substantial migrations of Chinese with their social institutions into the countries of Southeast Asia, so that today they form influential minority groups in Thailand, Malaya, Indonesia, and the Philippines; but Chinese political institutions have not followed them there. In general, these mass movements of the Chinese people, their displacements of other peoples in the process, and the shifts of political and economic power among them from area to area form the fundamental background of China's imperial history.

From another point of view, imperial history can be seen as the successive risings and decayings of ruling families in a recurring dynastic cycle. This theme dominates the traditional Chinese presentation of history: a strong, capable man seizes power and inaugurates a period of stability and prosperity; in time his descendants lose control of affairs because of their own lack of ability or because of overwhelming challenges such as invasions or natural calamities; finally some new strong, capable man wrests power from them, and the cycle begins all over again. Thus dynasty succeeded dynasty, some enduring for very long times, some being very quickly overthrown, and sometimes several regional dynasties existing simultaneously in a temporarily fragmented China. A casual sweep through China's long history can leave the impression that there must have been constant turmoil, so numerous were the civil wars, usurpations, assassinations, and similar disruptions of the political scene.

It is true that imperial China was repeatedly plunged into disunity and chaos, as had been the case in the latter centuries of the ancient Chou dynasty. At times China seemed to be slipping back into a pattern of feudal regionalism. But the ideal of a centrally controlled, bureaucratically administered empire persisted. And, remarkably, the ideal was realized for very long periods between the chaotic interludes, when stable dynasties endured for centuries in succession and China under their rule prospered, expanded, produced flourishing literature and arts, and completely overawed the rest of East Asia. We Americans in particular should keep in mind that each of the great Chinese dynasties lasted longer than the United States has yet endured.

One of the greatest was the Han dynasty (206 B.C.–A.D. 220), which succeeded the short-lived, tyrannical Chin dynasty and brought China to an early peak in its political and cultural development. Over the same long span of time when Rome's domination of the Mediterranean world waxed and waned, Han China was the great governor and civilizer of the eastern end of Eurasia. Because of its awesome military, administrative, and cultural achievements, the Chinese still proudly call themselves men of Han.

Another great age was that of the Tang (A.D. 618–906) and Sung (A.D. 960–1279) dynasties, especially noted for achievements in literature and art, but rivaling or surpassing Han China in military and political achievements as well. In their time, when European civilization was at a relatively low ebb, China was unquestionably the most powerful, cultured, and sophisticated nation on earth. The Ming dynasty (1368–1644) brought China once more to a peak of military power, administrative excellence, and achievement in literature and art, just when Europe was falteringly organizing itself in modern nation-states and the great era of European exploration and colonization was beginning.

Thus, as dynasties appeared and disappeared, the Chinese repeatedly struggled out of chaos into great ages that have had few parallels in human history. Concurrently, without much direct relevance to the rise and fall of dynasties, all the varied facets of Chinese civilization—philosophy, literature, art, political institutions, social customs, and so on—steadily evolved and changed in patterns and rhythms of their own.

From yet another point of view, the history of imperial China can be understood as a continuing struggle of the Chinese people for the survival of their way of life against the pastoral, nomadic peoples who challenged them from the north and west. The successive emergence of these peoples on the steppes of Mongolia, their batterings at the rich Chinese empire, their wanderings across Central Asia, and their eventual impacts on the civilizations of India, the Near East, Russia, and southern and eastern Europe form one of the great basic themes in the history of Eurasia as a whole. With specific reference to China, their assaults can be correlated in enlightening ways with the rhythmic expansion and contraction of China's national power and with the migrations of the Chinese people southward. The Great Wall of China across the northern frontier, originally consolidated by the First Emperor of Chin in the third century B.C., stands today as a monumental reminder of the nomads' role in Chinese history; and the constant threat from the steppes accounts for the fact that China kept its national capital in the north even after the center of population and wealth had shifted to the south.

The first great nomadic confederation was that of the Hsiung-nu. During the entire Han era the Hsiung-nu pressed against China's frontiers. Eventually some moved off westward and became known to Europe as the Huns, but others infiltrated North China as the Han dynasty declined. Through a long period of disunity in China in the fourth, fifth, and sixth centuries, the Hsiung-nu and related Turkic-speaking invaders ruled North China, gradually assimilating the Chinese way of life but modifying it greatly at the same time.

The Tang dynasty, ruling a reunited China in the seventh, eighth, and ninth centuries, was harassed by a new nomad empire in Mongolia, that of the Tu-chüeh (Turks). The Tu-chüeh were never able to break down China's defenses, but eventually created the great Turkish empires of Near Eastern history. They also spawned such peoples as the Kirghiz, the Uigurs, and the Kazakhs (Cossacks), who have played important roles in the history of Central Asia and the Soviet Union.

China's long struggles with the northern nomads reached a climax in the thirteenth century with the appearance of the Mongols under the leadership of Genghis Khan. The Mongols conquered North China and then swarmed westward to establish great branch empires in Central Asia, the Near East, and Russia, creating world history's most extensive continental realm. They defeated and terrified Europeans in Poland and Hungary and drove across Austria almost to the Adriatic coast before withdrawing undefeated. Only later, under Genghis' great grandson Kublai Khan, did they painfully overcome Chinese resistance in South China, exterminating the Sung dynasty in 1279 and thus becoming the first foreigners ever to subjugate all China. They ruled the Chinese harshly for a century, adopting China's dynastic form of government but never becoming assimilated into Chinese civilization. In 1368 nationalistic Chinese rebels drove them back into Mongolia and restored native rule with the Ming dynasty.

China's last imperial dynasty, called Ching (1644–1912), was also a conquest dynasty—that of the Tungusic-speaking Manchus, who originated in the northeastern frontier region that Westerners now call Manchuria. Even before they superseded the Ming rulers in 1644, the Manchus had become thoroughly "Chinesified," and their takeover in China was the least disruptive of all the foreign assaults of Chinese history. The Manchus even produced two of the greatest emperors of the Chinese tradition: the Kang-hsi emperor (1662–1722) and the Chien Lung emperor (1736–1796), who were grand monarchs in the fashion of Louis XIV and must rank among the most able rulers of modern world history. Under Manchu rule, Chinese civilization attained its last great peak of the imperial age, only to collapse into chaos at the beginning of the twentieth century as a result of accumulating domestic problems and the impact of the modern Western world.

Throughout this long history, the Chinese grew accustomed to being the leaders and the civilization-givers of the world as they knew it, the defenders of civilization against barbarism. At times, "barbarians" overwhelmed native governments by force, but until the nineteenth and twentieth centuries the Chinese never had occasion to question the inherent superiority of their civilization, which had withstood every onslaught. Moreover, they have accumulated abundant historical records and have been avid students of them. Knowledge of and pride in the past, therefore, weigh heavily on the modern Chinese. They have not been able to reconcile themselves to playing a subordinate role in world affairs.

Thought, Literature, and Art

China's intellectual and aesthetic achievements reflect a strikingly creative national character and a value system that is uniquely Chinese.

The traditional Chinese way of thinking about life, man, and the universe has two fundamental characteristics. For one thing, the Chinese seem always to have taken for granted that in addition to the living creatures that we all see and know in everyday life, the universe is peopled with many kinds and almost infinite numbers of spirits or demons (or, in more sophisticated terms, spiritual forces), which account for all happenings that are not obviously man-made and cannot be explained in ordinary ways. Earth itself was considered such a force. So was the famous Chinese dragon, which was thought to control the regular, cyclical sequence of the seasons. There were the souls of the countless dead and particularized "gods" of all sorts: harvest gods, river gods, town gods, gods of the various diseases, gods of literature, gods of war, and so on. The chief spiritual force was heaven, which had some of the aspects of our concept nature and some of the aspects of our concept fate. But there was no belief in a single, all-powerful Supreme Being.

In short, the Chinese have traditionally been polytheistic rather than monotheistic.

On the other hand, the Chinese have not divided the universe into a worldly realm and a spiritual realm, but have considered it a great integrated unity. All that exists, they thought, is a vast natural reality, in which men and spirits share the same plane of existence, without either one being "better" in any sense than the other. The Chinese, consequently, have not concerned themselves with distinctions between existence and nonexistence, between what is real and what is ideal, between the natural and the unnatural, or between the sacred and the profane. They have seen nothing either in their many "gods" or in themselves that corresponds to the Westerner's notion of awesome divinity.

What all this adds up to is that the Chinese have not been what we would call a religious people. They traditionally rendered homage to the spiritual forces, chiefly by making sacrificial offerings to them so as to fend off their wrath and win their favor; they utilized divination, exorcism, prognostication, and other techniques that might smooth their relations with the spirits; and they sometimes engaged in fasts and meditations that might clarify and purify their own powers of understanding. Especially in the practice of ancestor worship, their attitudes might be profoundly sincere. But on the whole, the relations between a traditional Chinese and the spirits were rather businesslike arrangements between equals, calculated to achieve a state of harmonious and mutually beneficial coexistence. As circumstances suggested, the Chinese might be respectful or denunciatory, awed or contemptuous, grateful or resentful. The consolations of faith, the joyous exultation in divine grace, the exquisitely private communion between oneself and God in prayer, the guilt-ridden consciousness of having sinned against God's will—all these familiar aspects of monotheistic religions were quite foreign to him. His harmonizing with the universe was a different thing entirely, for example, from the Christian's ecstatic surrendering of himself to God.

But China did produce many great thinkers. The chief intellectual currents or focuses of the native tradition are Confucianism and Taoism. Both originated in the turbulent ancient age when the Chou feudal order was collapsing, and they are responses, though of different sorts, to the principal challenge of that time: how to define and achieve a way of life that might make men as individuals happy, in harmony with their society and with the universe at large.

Confucianism emphasizes man's relations within human society. Confucius (c. 551–479 B.C.) and the chief early developers of his views, Mencius (c. 371–289 B.C.) and Hsün

Tzǔ (c. 300–235 B.C.), defined goodness and propriety largely in terms of father-son, ruler-subject, husband-wife, elder brother-younger brother, and friend-friend relationships. They laid special stress on filial piety, from which they thought all other virtues derived. They also dwelt at length on what government ought to be, denouncing tyranny and injustice, advocating state responsibility for popular welfare, and especially urging that government should be entrusted to learned men of proved moral character who might serve as exemplars of proper thought and conduct for the common people. To be a Confucian is not easy. It requires assimilation of the experience and wisdom of the past, unwavering dedication to a life of ceremonious and gentlemanly conduct, and sober acceptance of a heavy burden of social and political responsibilities. Above all, it requires constant, earnest efforts to decide what is the right thing to do in any given circumstance, for Confucius did not presume to prescribe absolute standards. Confucianism, then, is a rational, humanistic approach to the problems of life and society.

Taoism is different. Its founders were two legendary sages called Lao-tzu and Chuang-tzu, of whose lives little is known but who seem to have been contemporaries of the early Confucians. Their thinking was somewhat mystical and intuitive, and it emphasized man's relations with the great natural forces of the universe rather than his relations with society. As a matter of fact, the Taoists viewed social institutions— and the obligations and responsibilities that Confucians emphasized—as fetters that prevent man's self-fulfillment. In their conception, what is good and proper is whatever is natural, spontaneous, and real (that is, not artificial). The Taoists thus reject all the standards and inhibitions that living in society necessarily imposes; their urge is to escape from society as hermits, to be free and individualistic. But they have no wish to flee from reality as dreamers do. They want to live life to the full, without self-consciousness and without inhibitions. By so doing, they believe they can "get in tune," so to speak, with the natural rhythms of the spontaneous, unguided, aimless universal mechanism (the Tao). They sometimes suggest that harmonizing with the universe in this way will enable one to soar through the sky, to rule the world effortlessly, and to live forever; but the Taoist is not really concerned with the consequences of his self-fulfillment. He lives in accordance with the Tao because the Tao is just the way things are; whether things "ought" to be so and whether he gains or loses anything by living so are irrelevant questions. If he successfully maintains the Taoist point of view, nevertheless, he does gain release from emotional tensions and an unruffled peace of mind that are enviable indeed.

These two basic attitudes, earnest Confucianism and escapist Taoism, are not so much contradictory as they are complementary. They reflect one of the most intriguing facets of the Chinese national character: the Chinese can be a cooperative and responsible member of society and at the same time be an individualistic noncomformist. Thus every Chinese tends to be a Confucian in public but a Taoist in private.

Because of its very nature, Taoism could not easily be perpetuated as an organized school of philosophy having practical influence on public affairs. Before the Tang era it had lost much of its intellectual force. Subsequently, Taoist practitioners have devoted themselves to divination, exorcism, and other aspects of the folk religion. Confucianism, on the other hand, became the state-supported official philosophy in Han times, and the bureaucrats who administered China's government throughout the imperial age were committed to the Confucian point of view. Its doctrines grew and changed over the centuries, absorbing elements from Taoism and from some other ancient rivals of Confucianism. In the Sung dynasty the doctrines were significantly revitalized, with many new emphases, by a group of brilliant thinkers including Chu Hsi (1130–1200). Their Neo-Confucianism, as it is called in the West, buttressed the old Confucian moral values with brilliant new cosmological theories and tended to emphasize the authority of ancient texts and precedents rather than individual judgment as regards moral issues. Their influence thus lent a conservative, authoritarian cast to the Confucians of recent centuries.

Sung Neo-Confucianism was a direct and successful response to the only serious challenge ever faced by the native philosophical tradition up to the nineteenth century. This was the introduction of Buddhism into China from India. Buddhism appeared in China in Han times, and during the centuries of disunity that followed the collapse of the Han empire in A.D. 220, it provided the most vigorous intellectual leadership in China. By the Tang era it was universally influential. Then, because its monastic system was severely disrupting the traditional Chinese social order and the state's economic stability, some Tang rulers tried to suppress it. Sung philosophers attacked it on other grounds, and by adapting some Buddhist elements into Neo-Confucianism, stole away its intellectual attractions. Thereafter Chinese Buddhism deteriorated to the level of a folk religion, competing with low-fallen Taoism for popular patronage. In recent centuries it has not been a major intellectual force in China, but it has yet left its mark on Chinese character.

Buddhism introduced into China a number of glittering Indian conceptions that had no counterparts in Confucianism or Taoism—the idea that life is perpetuated indefinitely through a series of rebirths, the idea that one's past conduct determines what his future lives will be like, the idea that one can attain personal salvation and escape the cycle of rebirths, the idea of congregational worship and of monastic life, the idea of heavens and hells, and others. It satisfied yearnings and questionings for which neither austere, rational Confucianism nor seemingly irresponsible Taoism provided. At the same time, however, it reinforced Confucianism's emphasis on the moral life as well as Taoism's rather fatalistic detachment from the concerns of everyday living. The Chinese, consequently, have not found it impossible to consider themselves, all at once, Confucians, Taoists, and Buddhists too.

The Buddhism that flourished in medieval China was of the Mahayana variety rather than the Hinayana, or Theravada, variety, which came to dominate Southeast Asia. Whereas Hinayanists lay great stress on monastic life as a prerequisite to salvation, Mahayanists are much more concerned about lay believers. Chinese Buddhism produced many popularized sects with great mass appeal, centering upon the worship of Bodhisattvas, or saints who offer themselves as personal saviors and demand little more than faith and sincerity. But China also produced some remarkable meditative sects, most notably an intensely intellectual Chan sect, which is best known in the West by its Japanese name, Zen. Chan Buddhism is an amalgam of Buddhist and Taoist ideas. It teaches that Buddhahood, or ultimate reality, is the reality that surrounds every man here and now and that "salvation" is nothing more than an attitude of mind that is obtained in a sudden, intuitive enlightenment. Chan is the most impressive intellectual achievement of Chinese Buddhism, and through its development in Japan it is attracting increasing attention in the modern Western world.

All these varied Chinese contributions to the world's store of philosophical insights are more than matched by China's contributions in the realm of literature and art. For more than the last thousand years, every educated Chinese has been an active litterateur and has at least dabbled, if nothing more, at calligraphy and painting. Moreover, such has been China's reverence for beautiful things that a substantial proportion of what was produced has been preserved. In quantity, therefore, the corpus of traditional Chinese literature and art dwarfs that of any other nation. And there is much in it of excellent quality.

There are two literary traditions. One is the tradition of

the educated elite, which produced elegant literature in a highly formalized classical style quite unrelated to the patterns of spoken Chinese. Early monuments of this classical-style literature are the so-called Chinese Classics, a group of works produced in the ancient Chou period, including histories, a poetry anthology, treatises on morality and propriety, and philosophical texts. In the imperial age the educated class (the literati) was profusely productive in essay forms, epistolary forms, historiographic forms, short-story forms, and poetry forms. Because the literati were the upholders of the prevailing political and social order, their literature in all forms was generally rather sober and didactic, both reflecting and reinforcing the orthodox value system; but it was not lacking in wit, humor, and human warmth.

In keeping with their Confucian-oriented outlook, the literati were devoted students of history, and history writing came to be one of the glories of the literary tradition. The great master was Ssŭ-ma Chien (145–c. 87 B.C.), who created a historiographic pattern that was subsequently accepted as a model throughout East Asia. In this pattern, Chinese histories characteristically do not stop with chronological accounts of important events, but also include chronological tables that correlate diverse kinds of events for easy reference (e.g., appointments to major offices), topical treatises discussing institutional developments (organization of government, law, costume, etc.), and biographies of all important and many interesting though unimportant people. Eventually government-sponsored historiographic commissions produced such histories for dynasty after dynasty, with the result that China has the most complete and detailed record of the past to be found among existing nations.

But poetry is generally considered China's greatest achievement in the classical-language tradition. The Chinese literati wrote poems in the same spirit in which some Westerners have kept diaries, or in which camera manufacturers would like us all to take pictures. That is, they wrote poems to capture and commemorate fleeting thoughts or moods or observations. Very few Chinese poems, consequently, are comparable to the long, sustained poetic creations of the Western tradition. There are no Chinese epics. For the most part, Chinese poems are compact and cryptic, with a gemlike precision of statement, and highly impressionistic. The Chinese does not wail and groan in a fine poetic frenzy; he does not set forth his thoughts and feelings torrentially like a Shelley or a Tennyson or a Milton. Rather, he states what he has seen or done, calmly and succinctly, in such a subtle way as to suggest a train of thought or feeling to the reader, and he leaves it at that. His products seem gentle rather than bombastic, understated rather than overwhelming, delicate rather than majestic.

Chinese poetry has rhyme and meter. It also has many carefully prescribed forms, some of which are far more complex than our sonnets and triolets. It includes narrative poems and lyric poems, satirical poems and poems of praise, gay poems and melancholy poems—just about the whole range of themes and moods that characterize our own poetic tradition. In subject matter, however, there are some noteworthy differences, for the Chinese have seldom written poems about romantic love, patriotic poems, or what we would consider religious poems. To a greater extent than ourselves, on the other hand, they have written poems about nature, and they have been especially fond of making metaphorical use of natural phenomena, the silver moon, falling leaves, and so on, to suggest their own unexpressed emotions.

Every dynasty had celebrated poets, but the Tang dynasty has generally been considered the golden age of Chinese poetry. Of the many great Tang poets, two stand out as being preeminent. These are Li Po and Tu Fu, who were contemporaries and friends in the eighth century, though almost opposites as personalities and technicians. Li Po was a Taoist-inspired free soul who was irresistibly drawn to wine, women, and song and tossed off happy and sad songs alike with an effortlessness that gained him recognition as an immortal in his own time. Tu Fu, a Confucian bureaucrat, was a more sober and painstaking craftsman. His reputation grew more slowly than Li's, but it is solidly based on the recognition that no one has been a more poignantly compassionate observer of the tribulations of human life.

The other great literary tradition in China is a colloquial tradition, especially associated in its early development with itinerant professional storytellers who entertained the masses on market days. From their half-narrative, half-dramatic efforts eventually evolved both dramatic operas and written fiction in long and short forms. Since such works utilized the language as it was spoken rather than the elegant classical style, and since they did not always reflect the orthodox standards of morality, the educated class did not consider them proper literature. But they have gained great popularity in recent centuries, and twentieth-century Chinese consider them to rank among traditional China's greatest masterpieces.

Chinese drama, which was first developed in the thirteenth century, consists of arias, dialogue, and action in about the same mixture as our musical comedies. It is performed with a minimum of stage sets and props but with elaborate costumes and facial makeup, which readily identify the rather stereotyped characters for the spectators. Both singing and acting are done in highly conventionalized styles rather than a natural style. The performances are interminably long by Western standards. Plots are usually well developed and melodramatic, and the action on stage often becomes boisterously acrobatic. A long day's visit in the Chinese theater exposes one to a thrilling mélange of comic and tragic episodes, and especially to the virtuoso wizardry of some of the world's most skillful stage performers.

Colloquial fiction, which began to appear significantly in the fifteenth century, is notable chiefly for a succession of long, episodic novels. They represent a variety of genres, or types. Among historical novels, the acknowledged masterpiece in *Romance of the Three Kingdoms,* dealing with the chaotic political events of the third century, beginning with the decline of the Han dynasty. *Water Margin* (also known in translation as *All Men Are Brothers*) is a rambling, semihistorical adventure tale, recounting the struggles of Robin Hood-like outlaws and rogues against a cruel, corrupt officialdom. *Monkey,* an allegorical tale of the supernatural, is based on the journey of a seventh-century Chinese Buddhist to India, and has sometimes been called a kind of Buddhist *Pilgrim's Progress. The Scholars* is a satirical novel lampooning the Confucian bureaucracy. *Chin Ping Mei* (also known in translation as *The Golden Lotus*) is a rather comic, sometimes pornographic, but in the end moralistic story of domestic life—in a household with six wives. *Dream of the Red Chamber* is a melancholy love story set in the framework of a great family's slow decay. These by no means exhaust the list of traditional China's great novels, but they are the masterpieces. Among them, *Dream of the Red Chamber* is most admired by the Chinese, who often say that one cannot understand the Chinese spirit without reading it.

In art the Chinese have been equally productive, and in equal variety. The cultured Chinese has a strong sense of style and proportion that supplements his sophisticated intellectual outlook, and the arts of which he has been a patron, connoisseur, and sometimes producer are characterized by a remarkably consistent good taste.

Among China's most admired art productions are sacrificial vessels in bronze cast in the ancient Shang and Chou periods, which are bold and ornate in design, strikingly symmetrical in form, and exquisite in decorative detail. China's ceramics are also impressive, especially the lustrous monochrome porcelain wares of the Sung dynasty and the blue-and-white and other polychrome porcelain wares of the Ming and Ching dynasties, which are beautiful in shape as well as decor. There is a great tradition in sculpture, ranging from small-scale jade carvings to massive and yet soft-seeming Buddha statues. Chinese architecture and landscape gardening are also notable achievements, and perhaps more clearly than any other art forms, reflect the Chinese urge to conform to nature.

As poetry is the most esteemed form of Chinese literature, so painting is the most esteemed form of Chinese art, and there is a close relationship between poetry and painting in the Chinese tradition. Many poems have been written to accompany paintings, and many paintings have been intended to illustrate poems. The Chinese have liked to think that a good poem is a kind of "oral picture," whereas a good painting is a kind of "visual poem."

A substantial tradition of painting had developed by the Tang age, and the Sung, Yuan, Ming, and Ching dynasties all produced numerous painters of note. They painted murals and painted on screens and fans, but most of all they painted on paper or silk to be mounted either on vertical scrolls for hanging or on horizontal hand-scrolls for unrolling bit by bit at one's desk. They did not use oils but painted with water colors and with monochrome lampblack ink. In style, their productions range from the most naturalistic (portraits, landscapes, animals, flowers, birds, insects) to near-abstractions (calligraphy, bamboo shoots).

The most famed Chinese paintings are impressionistic black-and-white landscapes originated by a group of Sung masters who were assiduously imitated in later times but never surpassed. Like China's most famous poets, these masters (Ma Yuan, Hsia Kuei, and others) tried to capture moods or trains of thought in a simple, understated, unembellished approach. Their works are not detailed, realistic representations of particular scenes but are efforts to manifest the refined essence of the natural forces that motivate the universe. There are jagged, towering mountains losing themselves in swirling mists, and in the foreground there is often a human figure—perhaps a scholar sitting in an open-air pavilion—that is dwarfed by the immensity of nature surrounding it. The viewer's eye is led irresistibly back into the landscape and ultimately into the distant mists that symbolize nature itself, the Tao of the Taoist tradition. Such landscapes are not just to be looked at; to the Chinese mind, they are to be experienced and "lived in," for the sake of a sense of contentment and well-being such as we sometimes find during quiet walks in autumn woods. They put one "in tune with the universe."

China's intellectual and aesthetic traditions are so varied and contradictory that any capsule definition of the Chinese national character is bound to be inadequate and misleading. But, clearly, China's traditional values differ notably from those of traditional Western civilization, and these differences have complicated China's adjustment to the modern world. It is not just that the Chinese have proudly clung to the traditions of their past, though doing so would hardly be inexcusable. Their way of looking at man, society, and the universe is fundamentally different from our own, and they have found it impossible to see things with our eyes, whether or not they might think this desirable. We would be deluding ourselves to think they would gladly or easily transform themselves into Americans.

One difference, unquestionably related to China's polytheism, is that the Chinese have traditionally been more tolerant and reasonable about other men's beliefs than have Westerners; they have no history of religious wars. From another point of view, not having puritanical feelings about sin, they have tended to take a rational, "reasonable" approach to questions of right and wrong. Also, not having a conception of the divine soul, the Chinese as individuals have found satisfaction in accommodating themselves to society (Confucianism) or to the natural universe at large (Taoism, Buddhism). Finally, being somewhat fatalistic, they have thought it unpromising and in fact improper to attempt to bend either society or nature to their individual wills. Such attitudes have made China relatively unfertile ground for planting nationalism and science in the modern Western style.

Social Patterns

China has had an agrarian, family-oriented society that by the nineteenth century was losing its traditional stability.

We are accustomed to think of China as a sadly underdeveloped country economically. This is a modern phenomenon. Up into the eighteenth century, China seems to have been one of the richest, most prosperous countries on earth, and through much of its history it was unquestionably more advanced than Europe: in the extent of its trade, domestic and foreign; in its accumulations of capital and its luxuries; in its development of great urban concentrations of population; and in the productivity of its crafts and small-scale industries. If it could be measured satisfactorily, per-capita income might well prove to have been higher in medieval China than in any medieval European country. But China, although experiencing a dramatic growth in population from the sixteenth century on, did not experience an industrial revolution of the sort that transformed and revitalized Europe in the eighteenth and nineteenth centuries.

In other words, China remained a predominantly agrarian nation, with more than eighty percent of its population engaged directly in agricultural pursuits and with agricultural production accounting for the overwhelming majority of the nation's economic wealth. And just in the period when per-capita income and capital accumulations were rapidly rising in the Western world, China's population was growing at a far faster rate than its economic production, so that per-capita income was declining and capital accumulations were being dissipated. Thus China has found itself at a severe economic disadvantage in facing the challenge of the expanding West in the nineteenth and twentieth centuries.

China's disadvantage in this regard is increased by traditional Confucianism's contempt for the profit motive, which was thought to distract people from their proper moral concerns. Persons who devoted themselves to mercantile careers, though it was recognized they served a necessary function, were considered to be at the very margin of respectability at best, little better than entertainers, nonagricultural laborers, homeless wanderers, and soldiers, who were almost totally unrespectable in theory and not even as esteemed as common artisans, who at least were actively productive. In the interests of the general welfare, the state saw to it that any "exploitive" and "corruptive" inclinations of the mercantile class were kept in check by (a) producing in state-owned factories most of the nonagricultural goods that the government itself required, (b) establishing state monopolies of both the production and distribution of essential consumer commodities such as salt and iron, and (c) keeping the mercantile class under the careful scrutiny of, and its wealth largely at the mercy of, the officialdom by licensing and taxing practices. Businessmen, then, did not have either the power or the prestige that so characterize their role in modern Western society; they had little chance to become leaders in social change.

The unchallenged leaders of traditional Chinese society were the educated elite, who staffed the state administration. Because of their governmental status as bureaucrats, they were the only legitimate wielders of public authority. Because they were recognized as being morally superior persons, they had great prestige in the eyes of the common people. By means of the wealth they acquired in both public and private service, they became large landowners and moneylenders and thus increasingly wealthy and influential. Westerners often refer to this class as "the gentry." It was not a hereditary, self-perpetuating class such as a feudal aristocracy. The literati attained their status through their individual educational achievements as measured in state-sponsored examinations. Since one could not hope for success in the examinations without having leisure to study, however, men of well-to-do families gained literati status more easily than men of poor families. Thus, in some degree, the educated elite did tend to perpetuate itself hereditarily. Moreover, since they were devoted students of the prevailing ideology, it was natural for the literati to be champions of the existing social and political order. Like China's traditional merchants, they were not inclined to strive for social change.

Social stability was further assured by China's traditional family organization. The family was the basic social unit, and relations within the family were the principal focus of the Confucian emphasis on social harmony. The individual was expected to subordinate his personal needs and goals to those of the family. He had almost no identity except as a member of his family, and when he wanted to accomplish anything, he thought of doing so in the family, not by himself. The individual Chinese had a much stronger sense of "belonging," or "togetherness," than has been common in the West, and Western-style individualism was positively frowned on.

The woman's role was a particularly subordinate one. The family was held together principally by ancestor worship, which involved the concept that the family was something like an indefinitely perpetuated corporation of which the living members were but temporary trustees. Since the family was perpetuated only in the male line, and since women became members of their husbands' families upon marriage, daughters were ordinarily not wished for. As soon as possible they were married off, the marriage arrangements being made entirely by the elders of the families concerned. As wives and daughters-in-law, they were relatively unimportant members of their new families and gained esteem only to the extent that they bore sons for their husbands. If a wife was not pleasing or did not bear sons, she could be sent away in disgrace, or her husband could freely take secondary wives so long as he had the means.

Sons were subordinate in other ways. The father controlled the family's property, and there was ordinarily little opportunity for a son to make a living except by working with his father on the land and receiving a share of his father's income. The ideal was that the family should be one great household incorporating all the sons, grandsons, and if possible great-grandsons of the oldest living male, and this ideal was realized in practice by many well-to-do families. When the father died, his property was divided equally among all his sons; and only then, when in middle age or perhaps already growing old, were the sons able to set up separate establishments and begin creating their own great households.

However, since there was no tradition of primogeniture or entailment, it was very difficult for any one family to remain wealthy and powerful for more than a few generations. The dynastic cycle in government was thus mirrored in the rise and fall of particular families in the social scale. Even the poorest peasant could dream that with intelligence, hard work, and good luck he could become a great landowner and his sons might join the educated, bureaucratic elite; and even the wealthiest and most powerful landowner-bureaucrat could foresee that his wealth and power would easily be fragmented among his descendants until most if not all were poor peasants. Social mobility in traditional China, both up and down the scale, was markedly greater than in either caste-bound India or semi-feudal Japan. Though China's society was highly stable in the overall view, it was not immobile in the view of any particular Chinese.

Family "togetherness" was extended into other social relationships. Families were associated with related families in clans, the elders of which settled intraclan disputes, looked after clan ancestral temples, perhaps supported clan schools, and in general assumed responsibility for the welfare and good conduct of all clan members. The elders of various clans also associated with one another in informal governing councils for local communities, which settled interclan disputes and in other ways looked after common interests. For other purposes, the Chinese regularly organized themselves into mercantile guilds, scholarly associations, secret societies, mutual-aid charitable groups, and so on. Such "contacts" were all-important. One was never just himself, in his own thinking or in the thinking of others; he was so-and-so's son, of such-and-such clan, of a particular county and province, a member of such-and-such groups, and a friend of particular influential people. Whereas we are normally satisfied to label people according to their achievements (Brown the industrialist, Smith the politician, Jones the publisher, Johnson the musician, and so on), the Chinese have traditionally labeled and dealt with people in accordance with their "contacts" of the sorts mentioned. Chinese society, consequently, was dominated by family loyalties and local patriotisms, to the detriment of a sense of nationalism; and as noted previously, it was anti-individualistic.

The subordination of the individual Chinese to the family and to the other groups into which he was organized, however, was not as oppressive as it might at first glance seem to modern Westerners. Anti-individualism was greatly modified by an insistence on respect for the individual personality, and this accounts for the traditional Chinese politeness or ceremoniousness that has always impressed outsiders. Problems in social relations could not properly be resolved except by solutions that "saved face" for all concerned. Not obsessed by any abstract concepts of rightness, the Chinese aimed at moderation and reasonableness in human relations as in all other things. A son had to expect that his father would be tyrannical at times, and a father had to expect that his son would be impudent and disobedient at times. To demand otherwise would be to guarantee that someone must "lose face." In Chinese eyes, tolerance and a willingness to compromise were admirable qualities, so that for all its well-organized subordination of individuals to groups, Chinese society has produced and tolerated a remarkable variation of behavioral types.

Such forces as modern nationalism and Western-style individualism were destined, obviously, to have great impact on these traditional patterns of social organization in China. But forces within China itself were already at work undermining the old social order well before the nineteenth century. A social order can survive only as long as it provides satisfying roles for most of its members, and by the nineteenth century this was clearly no longer the case in China, regardless of the coming challenge from the West. China's population was growing at such a rate and its economy was lagging in growth to such an extent that by 1800 there had come into being a large class of people who were permanently dispossessed. They had no land and had little hope, as a group, of ever acquiring any. They had no regular jobs, and the existing society could not expect to provide jobs for them. They had no status and not even marginal security. Naturally, they felt little loyalty for a regime that offered them so little, especially since the regime was dominated by foreign rulers, the Manchus. The dispossessed were a highly explosive element in a society that still seemed stable on the surface, and China was ripening for a traditional-style dynastic upheaval or something even more disruptive.

Governmental Patterns

China has a tradition of centralized and bureaucratic, authoritarian but paternalistic government.

Government has played a more important role in Chinese life than was the case in the Western world until very modern times. At least after the destruction of the ancient feudal system in the third century B.C., the Chinese state was totalitarian in the sense that the government's octopus-like tentacles controlled all the varied aspects of Chinese life. No group in Chinese society competed with the government for influence as big business, the churches, the communications media, and other power centers can and do compete with government for influence in modern democratic societies.

The Chinese rationalized this concentration of all power in the government in terms of family relationships. The state was a macrocosmic family. The emperor was known as "the father and mother of the people," and local officials were commonly called "father-and-mother officials." The emperor or his agents were considered to have total authority over all the activities of the Chinese people in just the same way that a conscientious father accepts total responsibility for the well-being of his children.

This is not only how things were; this was how things ought to be, in the Chinese view. There was no conception of popular sovereignty, no such thing as a popular election, no doctrine of states' rights, no constitutional guarantees of individual liberties, and no system of checks and balances or separation of governmental powers. The whole of China was organized under a single monolithic pyramid with the emperor on top, the vast populace beneath, and in between an elaborate and well-articulated hierarchy of civil and military officials in the emperor's service—in a multitude of ministries and bureaus in the central government at the national capital, in provincial administrations, in prefectural and subprefectural administrations, and in most direct contact with the people at large, in county magistracies. And governmental "thrust," so to speak, was from the top down rather than from the bottom up, as we like to think is the case among ourselves.

Not only was the state unitary and centralized, it was universalist in conception. In the Chinese view there were only two kinds of people in the world: on one hand were civilized people who practiced the Chinese way of life and enjoyed the benefits of Chinese government; on the other hand were barbarians who, for whatever reasons, had not yet had the good fortune to become "Chinesified" and thus deserved to be tolerated pityingly, aided and educated, and when necessary, disciplined by civilized men. Barbarian chiefs, whether they realized it or not, obviously ruled by grace of the Chinese emperor and owed him tribute and obeisance. Even as late as 1793, after China had been in contact with the modern West for 250 years, an emperor could address King George III of England in the most condescending manner as a wayward, presumptuous vassal who had better mend his ways. The Chinese assumed that their civilization was superior to all others and that their interests would dominate all international relations.

Since all authority emanated from them, traditional Chinese emperors might be considered despots. But it was not expected that they would be tyrants. True, they were "fathers and mothers of the people." In turn, however, they were sons of heaven, and this imposed heavy obligations on them, both in Confucian theory and in consideration of practical realities. Ruling by the mandate of heaven was not the same thing as ruling by divine right in the traditional West. Since heaven was understood, from ancient times on, to will that the people be happy and prosperous, any son of heaven in the Confucian system was expected to rule paternalistically for the popular welfare. And it was considered proper for good men to help overthrow a ruling dynasty if it failed to do so. The threat of disaffection and rebellion, then, was constantly in the minds of emperors.

Imperial despotism was further alleviated by the fact that emperors entrusted the administration of their vast empire to Confucian-indoctrinated officials.

Much was required of the traditional officials, whom we in the West commonly call mandarins. At the lowest level of governmental service, the mandarin had to be the all-round local representative of the whole state apparatus, in a community that might range from fifty thousand to a million in population. He appointed and supervised a staff of clerical subordinates. He assessed and collected taxes. He controlled and on occasion actively commanded a local garrison of military forces, and he organized, trained, and led supplementary militiamen when necessary. He ran a police organization, a fire-fighting organization, and all local schools. He performed ceremonial rituals ranging from celebrations of Confucius' birthday to elaborate public prayers for rain. He organized and supervised public-welfare enterprises, including charity granaries and old-folks' homes. He looked after widows and orphans. He controlled local commerce by licensing various traders, regulating local market prices, and checking on the quality standards of local mercantile and craft guilds. He organized and directed local public works of all kinds, including the construction and maintenance of roads, canals, parks, irrigation systems, temples, schools, and so on. He provided justice, serving all at once as police investigator, prosecutor, defender, judge, and jury. He patronized literature and the arts. He sought out worthy citizens of many categories (specially filial sons and specially chaste widows, for example), encouraged and rewarded them, and recommended them to the central government for further honors. He sent reports and suggestions regularly to his superiors in higher echelons of government and, through them, to the central government and the throne; and all these superiors held him totally accountable for everything that happened in his jurisdiction. Above all, they expected the local mandarin to set a proper moral example for the people of his county. This is a simplified schedule of the responsibilities of a typical "father-and-mother official" in the lowest governmental echelon. At higher levels, the responsibilities naturally grew broader and heavier.

To fill these positions effectively, the state needed broad-gauged men who were conscientious, dedicated, public-spirited exemplars of the highly moralistic value system that the state espoused. It obtained them through a recruitment system based on public, competitive written examinations, the model from which have evolved the civil-service examination systems that are so much a part of government throughout the civilized world today. It comes as something of a shock to us to realize that just a century ago when England adopted the civil-service system that has come almost to symbolize the greatness of British administration, it was derided and denounced as a foolish, subversive effort to "Chincsify" England.

Civil-service recruitment through examinations originated in China in the second century B.C. In the seventh century the system was restructured so as to play a more important part in government than before; and from the tenth century to 1905 it provided a civil-service bureaucracy that almost entirely managed the state administration and constituted "the Establishment" that dominated the whole of Chinese society.

The examinations were given at successive levels—annually in local areas, then triennially at all provincial capitals and, at the highest level, at the national capital. The passers, who were very few in relation to the number of candidates, were awarded titles that are sometimes compared with the bachelor's, master's, and doctor's degrees in our academic life. They were given tax exemptions and various official immunities and privileges. They were hailed as local, provincial, and finally national heroes; they were sought after as educators of the next generation; and their judgments on public and private affairs were given great weight.

To hope for success in the examinations, one had to master the classical Confucian literature, a body of writings more substantial than our Bible. One had to know this literature by heart so that he could reproduce any part of it verbatim on demand. More than that, he had to be able to marshal precepts and precedents out of this bulk of literature into acceptable and convincing arguments about timeless philosophical problems, historical problems, or current policy problems—and present them in beautifully proportioned, highly stylized, rigidly disciplined essays. Also, he had to be able on demand to compose a poem in a prescribed rhyme scheme, in a prescribed metrical pattern, on a prescribed theme, an immeasurably more difficult task in Chinese than in English. Anyone who passed, especially at the doctoral level, thus had to be a philosopher and moralist, a philologist, a historian, a political theorist, a poet and prose stylist: in general, a highly polished and thoroughly rounded litterateur. In addition, he was ordinarily a calligrapher, painter, and connoisseur of the arts, though this aspect of his achievements was not tested in the examinations. The only even fairly near equivalent to him in the modern West is the educated gentleman of the English tradition. Having had to spend the first twenty-five or thirty years of his life in the most intense book work, he always remained a man of genteel and scholarly inclinations.

Such were the men called upon to govern China's cities and to defend China from its enemies, for the degree holders, or literati, constituted a personnel pool from which the government drew its bureaucratic appointees. Not all degree holders got bureaucratic appointments. Those who did had to endure the constant surveillance of their peers. They received regular efficiency ratings from their administrative superiors, and they were constantly liable to impeachment by special investigating officials called censors. If one's deportment were questionable or his performance of duty unsatisfactory, he could be demoted, dismissed, or punished even more severely. If he were adequate, he would gradually creep up the bureaucratic ladder of ranks until, in the twilight of his career, he might emerge into the upper plateau of distinguished advisers to the emperor, wise with experience and loaded with honors, a man sufficient to overawe and manipulate all but the most strong-willed hereditary rulers.

In sum, then, one might say that the Confucian state system of traditional China provided government *for* the people, *of* despots, *by* an aristocracy of merit, the bureaucrat's merit being tested in competitive examinations, proved competitively in service, and defined largely in moralistic terms. And it was largely the Confucian bureaucrat who contributed stability, cohesion, and continuity to the Chinese way of life throughout the last millennium of China's imperial history, despite dynastic changes, foreign invasions, and domestic upheavals. But a state so governed was bound to have many difficulties in adjusting to the world of the nineteenth and twentieth centuries.

From Empire to Republic

This vast, old country with these traditions of achievement in intellectual, social, and political realms found its civilization challenged both from within and from without before the nineteenth century was far along. No nation in China's circumstances could have been expected to adapt easily to drastically changing conditions; the very factors that made China great and proud seem to have made change difficult. But China was specially handicapped just at this period of its history. For one thing, as has been noted above, since 1644 the Chinese had been governed by Manchu conquerors. There was a natural antipathy between the rulers and the ruled, which made it particularly unlikely that nineteenth-century China might arouse itself in an intense, nationalistic effort to respond effectively to its challenges, as Japan proved capable of doing. On the other hand, popular respect for the natural elite of the Chinese tradition, the literati, was at a relatively low ebb because of their willing association with alien masters. Moreover, the natural conservatism of the literati had been strengthened by their increasing concern, under Manchu encouragement, for literary and scholarly rather than political matters, so that the literati were less likely than ever before to provide dynamic, progressive leadership in a time of national crisis. With all these handicaps, it is perhaps surprising that the old regime survived as long as it did.

The impact of the modern West broke upon China in 1839, and the Chinese were totally unprepared for it. Since 1514, when the first Portuguese squadron appeared at Canton, the Chinese had grown accustomed to dealing with Western traders, but they dealt with them haughtily. For more than two centuries the Westerners had been given no opportunity to trade except in the Canton area, and they had been in the unfavorable position of wanting much from China (principally tea, silks, and art objects) while offering little that the Chinese had any interest in. The trade was badly unbalanced; Western silver poured into China, and Chinese goods poured into Europe and America, where things Chinese (chinoiserie) became a great rage in the eighteenth century. The Western missionary effort had been no less frustrating. In 1582 a great Jesuit leader, Matteo Ricci, had been allowed to enter China; and during the seventeenth century there had been influential Jesuit establishments at the national capital and in some other inland cities. But a "rites controversy" soon developed within Catholicism over whether or not Chinese converts should be permitted to continue their ancestor-worship practices, and the Chinese government had become alarmed about papal interference with Chinese beliefs. The eighteenth century brought increasing restrictions on Catholic activities. In 1807 the first Protestant missionary to China, the Englishman Robert Morrison, began work at Canton. But by this time missionaries endured the same frustrations and harassments that so irritated the Western traders. China was aloof and condescending toward them all. Even in 1839, when England declared war on China, the Chinese government was not overawed.

What prompted this explosive change in the relations between China and the West was trade in opium. Western traders had at last found a way to balance the trade, and eventually to unbalance it in their own favor. They found that the Chinese people would buy opium, though such trade was unlawful; and during the 1830's they dumped shipload after shipload of opium chests onto the Canton market. In 1839 the Chinese government seized and destroyed the British stocks of opium at Canton, and the British retaliated with war.

The so-called Opium War was not fought with much vigor on either side. The Chinese, at last recognizing that their troops and weapons were no match for those of the British, capitulated in 1842.

The treaties that the Chinese government negotiated with England and other countries at the end of the Opium War —and modified after a similarly small-scale though drawnout war with the British and the French in 1856–1860— opened China to a flood of Western influences. They inaugurated the Treaty Port system, which permitted foreigners to reside at many key points throughout China, to develop foreigner-governed cities such as Shanghai, and to introduce Western manufactures and Western ideas into China almost without hindrance. Western influence permeated China slowly, but it was inexorably eroding away the foundations of the traditional Chinese way of life. As the nineteenth century wore on, China's economy lost its old self-sufficiency and China's intellectuals lost their old self-confidence.

A far more dramatic shock to China at the time was the eruption of domestic discontent, concurrently with these

Western assaults from outside. Beginning with the last decade of the eighteenth century, the Manchu government had to contend almost annually with uprisings fomented by secret societies, which reflected steadily worsening economic conditions among the peasantry. The humiliation of defeat in the Opium War aggravated antigovernment feelings so that during the 1840's there were vast numbers of malcontents in China just waiting for inspired leadership. When such leadership did emerge, they exploded in one of the most devastating upheavals of all human history, the Taiping rebellion, which racked China from 1850 to 1865 and cost perhaps 30,000,000 lives.

The catalyst in this explosion was a fanatical two-time failure in the civil-service examinations, Hung Hsiu-chüan. Hung studied for a time under a Baptist missionary at Canton and formed a Society of God-Worshipers in nearby Kwangsi province. Inspired by visions in which he claimed God instructed him to destroy all demons (Manchus and other foreigners), he led his followers to revolt in 1850 and soon gained control of the Yangtze valley. He proclaimed a Heavenly Kingdom of Great Peace (*Tai-ping Tien-kuo*) and established a new dynastic capital at Nanking. He adopted a curiously distorted Christianity as his state's official ideology, organized his followers in an egalitarian communelike style, and introduced land reforms, equality of the sexes, and many other things that seem to have anticipated twentieth-century developments. Until 1860 Taiping armies raided freely into North China and even threatened Peking, the Manchu capital, on several occasions. Thereafter, however, the force of the rebellion gradually declined, and it was finally extinguished in 1865 by loyalist armies with help from a Western-organized Shanghai defense force called the Ever-Victorious Army, led chiefly by an Englishman who later became world-renowned, Charles George Gordon. Two other uprisings that overlapped with the Taiping rebellion were also finally put down: a so-called Nien rebellion in North China (1853–1868), a long series of plundering raids by terrorist bandits; and a rebellion of Chinese Muslims in the southwestern and far western provinces (1858–1873).

The Manchu government miraculously recovered from these multiple blows, foreign and domestic, and from the 1860's into the 1890's seemed to be embarked on a new and progressive course. Part of the credit for the recovery must go to the Empress Dowager Tzŭ Hsi, a strong-willed Manchu woman who dominated the imperial court from 1861 until her death in 1908. Credit also belongs to a group of strong Chinese leaders who, alarmed both by the anti-traditional program of the Taiping rebels and by the Western threat to Chinese civilization, effectively rallied support for the Manchu dynasty in the 1860's and thereafter led China's efforts to modernize its armed forces, establish Western-style industries, and adapt Western ideas to Chinese use. Chief among these were Tsêng Kuo-fan, who was principally responsible for the defeat of the Taiping rebels, and his lieutenants Tso Tsung-tang and Li Hung-chang. Under such leaders China repaired its rebellion-shattered economy and patched up its relations with the Western world. By the early 1890's China was enjoying a deceptive tranquillity, convinced that it could make selective use of Western technology without disrupting the age-old patterns and values of the traditional Chinese way of life.

Concurrently, Japan had been making a much more eager effort to adopt Western technology and institutions, driven by an ultranationalistic determination to gain international stature; and Chinese-Japanese relations were rapidly deteriorating. Finally, in 1894–1895, Japan fought China for influence over Korea, and China's humiliating defeat in this war revealed to the world that the imposing Chinese empire, which Westerners still viewed with considerable awe, was now but a hollow shell of its former greatness. The European powers rushed in, as the Chinese said, to "carve it up like a melon." Only rivalries among the European powers themselves prevented China from being divided up into colonies. The Manchu government then made frantic though still half-hearted efforts to reform, but it was too late. The final humiliation was the Boxer Rebellion of 1900, an antiforeign outbreak led by a fanatical religious group that was encouraged by the Manchus in a last desperate effort to stave off the future. It was put down ignominiously by Western and Japanese expeditionary forces. From that time on the imperial government was held in contempt by both Westerners and Chinese. When it at last crumbled in 1912, all the institutions and values that had characterized China for two thousand years went tumbling after it.

The collapse of the old regime ushered in a new era of disunity and disruption. The overthrow of the Manchus was achieved by a group of nationalistic revolutionaries led by Dr. Sun Yat-sen, who intended to establish a Western-style parliamentary republic on the ruins of the empire. But the Chinese people were unprepared for democratic politics, and it turned out that real power was in the hands of regional military commanders, who refused to be dislodged. The parliamentary system quickly foundered, the idealistic revolutionaries were dispersed, and autocratic provincial warlords began ruling the various parts of China as they pleased. The Peking republic, which they maintained as a facade, offered little resistance to continuing demands of the Western powers and Japan for privileges and concessions. During the 1920's, consequently, the government's international prestige and power reached the lowest point of all Chinese history, and it was clearly leading China nowhere.

Meanwhile, however, social and intellectual ferment was intense. It manifested itself most dramatically in the May Fourth Movement of 1919, in which vast numbers of Chinese in Peking, and subsequently throughout the country, arose in a genuinely nationalistic denunciation of the failure of the Western powers to disown Japan's imperialistic claims on Shantung province in the Treaty of Versailles. Thereafter, throughout the 1920's, the Chinese repeatedly organized popular boycotts against foreign goods, especially from Japan and Britain. A New Literature movement also arose, championing writing in the colloquial style in contrast to the old, artificial literary style and provoking revolutionary reinterpretations of Chinese history. Education was reorganized in Western fashion, and Western influences were being felt in all realms of Chinese life. A new intellectual leadership was being created, with a strong Western orientation.

A new political leadership was also developing during the 1920's. After the failure of his original revolutionary efforts, Dr. Sun Yat-sen had been further disillusioned with parliamentary institutions by the grand debacle of the Western world in World War I. The postwar Russian Revolution suggested a new model for revitalizing a humiliated, underdeveloped nation. During the early 1920's, with the help of Russian advisers, he reorganized his political party, the Kuomintang (National People's Party), as a militant revolutionary force after the pattern of a Communist party. Though not agreeing with Communist theory, he set up a new revolutionary government at Canton in collaboration with Chinese Communists, who had organized a party of their own in 1921. He also set a young devotee, Chiang Kai-shek, to building up a Kuomintang revolutionary army that might crush the warlords and support a genuinely progressive national government dominated by the party.

Chiang Kai-shek emerged as the preeminent Kuomintang leader after Dr. Sun's death in 1925, and in 1926 he began a march to the north from Canton. By 1928 the Kuomintang troops had crushed the warlord-supported Peking republic. They then established a new Republic of China with its capital at Nanking, dedicated to restoring China's national dignity and leading the Chinese people into a new way of life suitable to the twentieth-century world. This is the government that ruled the Chinese mainland until 1949 and is today in retreat on Taiwan (Formosa), hoping to regain control of the mainland. Throughout its history, it has been dominated by Chiang Kai-shek.

The failure of the Kuomintang to achieve its goals is the predominant fact of recent Chinese history. Its leaders have been severely criticized for their shortcomings. But they had less than a decade, actually, in which to concentrate on modernizing China. Considering the circumstances, they made some remarkable achievements. They unified China for the first time in twenty years, and they created a stable, effective governmental structure. They fostered the drafting of a constitution that promised to inaugurate full-scale democratic government as soon as proper preparations had been made for it. They reorganized and strengthened China's military forces. They negotiated treaties with the Western powers that gave hope of relieving the Chinese of the humiliations imposed by the century-old "unequal treaties," and they regained much international prestige for China. They drafted and promulgated modern law codes, instituted a modern system of money and banking, greatly improved communications and transportation, extended modern education and research, and encouraged the growth of mechanized industries. Progress was slow and uneven, but during the 1930's there was a notable sense of accomplishment and determination in China.

Two things prevented the Kuomintang from achieving its goals more fully and finally caused it to be driven from the mainland in defeat and disgrace. One was Japanese imperialism. The other was Communist insurrection.

Japan was determined that a strong, modern, independent government could not be permitted to arise in China. Since the 1890's the Japanese had developed extensive financial and industrial interests in Manchuria. When the Nationalist government at Nanking extended its authority into this Japanese sphere, the Japanese attacked, on September 18, 1931. The Nationalists were unable to resist adequately, and the League of Nations was unable to do more than denounce Japan's aggression. The Japanese, undeterred, set up a puppet state called Manchukuo and began extending their influence into the North China Plain. The Nationalists "bought time with land," avoiding open war with Japan while building up strength for future resistance. Finally, in 1937, Japan provoked a fresh conflict on the outskirts of Peking and thus inaugurated the full-scale Sino-Japanese War that lasted until 1945. After Japan's attacks on Pearl Harbor and the Philippines in 1941, China became merely one front in World War II.

The war seriously sapped the strength of the Nationalist government. It was driven into an inland bastion in the upper Yangtze valley (Szechwan province), it was deprived of its main tax revenues, it could not control mounting inflation and consequent bureaucratic corruption, and its heavy battle losses caused a steady lowering of morale among its troops and the Chinese people generally. By the time of the eventual Allied victory over Japan in 1945, the Chinese government was exhausted, bankrupt, disorganized, and hopeful only of having some respite for recovering its strength and resuming the development programs it had initiated a decade before.

The Nationalists got no such respite, because their authority was now vigorously challenged by the Chinese Communists. Chiang Kai-shek had abruptly terminated Dr. Sun's old Kuomintang-Communist alliance in 1927. From that time on, the Communists were insurrectionists against the Nationalist government, just at the time when Chiang was trying to build up China's ability to resist the Japanese. A Communist state emerged within the Nationalist state. Kuomintang troops campaigned against it again and again and drove it from its original territory in southeastern China all the way across to remote northwestern China. There the badly mauled Communists were holed up at Yenan when the all-out Sino-Japanese War began in 1937.

During the long war with Japan, the Red Army and the Nationalist armies were nominally allied in a united front, but both sides constantly maneuvered for positions of advantage against one another. The Nationalists had by far the heavier war burden and far heavier losses. Unlike the Nationalists, the Communists made no pretense of standing up to the Japanese. Rather, they infiltrated behind enemy lines and organized the enthusiastic peasantry for guerrilla-style sabotage and harassment of the invaders. As Nationalist morale declined, Communist morale rose. By the end of the war the Communists had gained a large following of peasants throughout North China, and they had a large, well-disciplined army equipped in part with surrendered Japanese weapons. They claimed the right to share in China's future development.

Civil war consequently broke out almost as soon as hostilities with Japan ended. American intervention achieved a short-lived truce in 1946, while General George C. Marshall tried to get the Nationalists and the Communists to agree on some form of coalition so as to avoid continued turmoil. Neither side was willing to yield its hope for total domination, however, and the civil war was resumed in 1947. In 1948 the tide of war turned in favor of the Communists, and on October 1, 1949, a new, Communist-dominated People's Republic of China was proclaimed at Peking.

By this time the completely demoralized Nationalist government of Chiang Kai-shek had taken refuge in Taiwan. During the 1950's and into the 1960's it remained there, restoring its morale and efficiency, rebuilding its shattered armed forces, and carrying out agrarian reforms of sorts it had never attempted on the mainland to improve the economic lot of the Chinese peasant. It received American aid and advice in both economic and military spheres and had assurances of American support in the event of any Communist attempt at invasion. The United States continued to recognize the Nationalist government as the only rightful government of China, though not all other nations did so even in the non-Communist world; and Nationalists continued to represent the Chinese people in the United Nations.

Communism in China

The Kuomintang's loss of the mainland has caused much soul-searching in American politics. Could China have been saved from Communism if the United States had poured more money and weapons into Nationalist hands after 1945? Or was the Nationalist cause already doomed, so that any amount of American aid would have been futile? We shall never be sure. But it does seem clear that during the 1940's the Nationalist government did not make effective use of the American aid that was given it and that it made few efforts to cleanse itself of corruption and inefficiency. Moreover, it alienated many intellectuals by suppressing criticism and distrusting democratic processes, it alienated many businessmen by its fiscal ineptness and its fostering of state-owned enterprises that stifled competition, and it showed little sympathy for the landless or almost landless peasants who constituted the bulk of the population. After World War II the Kuomintang concentrated on one basic program: to preserve China from the Communist menace at any cost. Perhaps this was the only proper course for farsighted, responsible leaders to take. Unfortunately for the Kuomintang, the Chinese people at large were not so distrustful of the Communists as Chiang Kai-shek was. At least the Communists were efficient, disciplined, and incorrupt; and they showed great concern for the peasants' well-being. Whereas the Nationalists seemed to be clinging fearfully to the past, the Communists dynamically urged marching on into a better future. The evidence suggests that when Communist rule replaced Nationalist rule in 1949, most of the Chinese people had few regrets.

Since 1949 the People's Republic of China on the mainland has been zealously reorganizing China's society and economy with the aim of making the nation once again strong, self-reliant, and the dominant power at least in East Asia. It has had technical advice and material aid from the Soviet Union, and it is committed to the Marxist-Leninist interpretation of history, which postulates that the capitalistic powers are destined to be inundated by a worldwide upsurge of the common people against their exploiters. As the Chinese put it, "the east wind prevails over the west wind." That is, they believe that the irresistible forces of history are on their side and that our way of life cannot possibly survive. They have consequently shown arrogant contempt for the great non-Communist powers, even those that have tried to establish normal relations with the Peking regime such as Great Britain; and the Communist leaders have especially aroused the Chinese people to hate and despise the United States with increasing intensity.

The top leaders of the Peking government are intelligent, capable, dedicated men who have been active in the Communist movement since the time of the Kuomintang-Communist alliance in the 1920's. They experienced the establishment of Chinese soviets in the southeastern hinterlands in the early 1930's, the extermination campaigns mounted against them by the Nationalist government, the subsequent Long March in defeat across South and West China to Yenan in 1934–1936, guerrilla warfare against the Japanese during World War II, and the civil war of the late 1940's. They survived and came to power because they are tough-minded, persistent, and confidence-inspiring leaders, and they have a consistent record of responding flexibly to the changing situations that have confronted them. Mao Tse-tung, chief of state in the Peking government until 1959 and still chairman of the Chinese Communist Party (CCP), is particularly glorified, almost as a father figure, though power seems more diffused among the party leaders than was the case in Stalinist Russia.

The government, under a constitution adopted in 1954, is organized in accordance with the Communist principle of "democratic centralism." Although there are popular elections to people's congresses at the local levels and these representatives in turn elect congresses for higher echelons (hence the system is "democratic"), the state structure is as much a unitary pyramid as in traditional times, and power again emanates from the top of the pyramid (hence "centralism"). Non-Communist parties are recognized and are represented in the various people's congresses as well as in appointive offices, but the CCP dominates all levels of government and establishes in its own councils all major national policies.

This party-dominated government controls Chinese life more pervasively than any Chinese government has ever done before. As in traditional times, there is no other power center in Chinese society that can compete with it. Moreover, the government has not tolerated the family loyalties and local patriotisms that so fragmented Chinese society in the past. It has particularly attacked the traditional family system by giving women a new independence as equal marriage partners and equal wage earners and by drawing family members into a multitude of new nationwide organizations such as youth corps, women's organizations, and so on. Religious organizations have been permitted to exist only as semigovernmental instruments of party-dictated national policy. The individual Chinese thus still subordinates himself to groups. But the family is no longer the predominant focus of his sense of "belonging," and the groups with which he associates in pursuit of identity and satisfactions are now tightly controlled by the party and the central leadership. Also, the old notions of "face," which prevented the "togetherness" of traditional times from becoming oppressive, have been denounced and ridiculed. The Communists, in other words, are trying to forge a new national character in China in which disciplined subordination to national interests is the foremost characteristic. "Hate America" campaigns have undoubtedly been useful for the development of such nationalistic feelings.

The Peking government has determinedly tried to reassert political control, not only within China proper but also in all peripheral areas that were traditionally under Chinese influence. The Central Asian province of Sinkiang, which had known considerable autonomy in the Nationalist era, has been brought under Chinese control as never before. In Outer Mongolia, which is recognized as an independent Communist state, the Chinese have been competing for influence with the Soviet Union. In further competition with the Soviet Union, Peking has tried to make North Korea and North Vietnam its own satellites. The Chinese have quarreled with Burma and India about mutual borders, and during the late 1950's they forcefully subjugated Tibet, which, though considered a part of China since the eighteenth century, had enjoyed almost complete political and cultural autonomy. The fact that Taiwan remains separate from their domain is a source of intense irritation and frustration for the mainland leaders, who insistently threaten to conquer it by force and thus complete the reunification of the historic Chinese realm.

Communist China's determination to assert its influence in these ways and, on the other hand, its fears that it might be challenged from outside have combined to keep the Peking leaders in a militaristic frame of mind. The so-called People's Liberation Army that won the mainland in 1949 was not disbanded. It was strengthened until in 1962 the People's Republic had regular armed forces of approximately 2.5 million men equipped with modern weapons, jet aircraft, and submarines and supported by millions more trained or semitrained fighting men in active reserve or militia units. From the first, the Peking government has apparently expected that the United States would one day try to destroy it. This expectation seemed confirmed in 1950, when during the course of the Korean War American forces under General Douglas MacArthur approached the Chinese-Korean border. The Chinese promptly sent well-organized "volunteers" into Korea. Though ill-equipped then by Western standards, the Chinese forces fought aggressively and skillfully in Korea. At least in their own eyes, they won a great victory over American and other Western forces and imposed a humiliating truce upon the United States in 1953. The Chinese learned many useful lessons in the Korean fighting and have subsequently made many sacrifices to build up their armed strength so that they will never be equally ill-prepared again. Considering Communist dogma about the imperialistic nature of the capitalistic nations, China's past century of humiliations imposed by foreign powers, and the Nationalists' avowed aim to return to the mainland, it appears that the Peking government's fears about outside threats are genuine ones.

The CCP has tried to alert the Chinese people to these dangers and in general evoke a nationwide dedication to all the ideals of the new regime by various tactics. Soon after the inauguration of the People's Republic in 1949, it instituted a great campaign to weed out all those who were considered "enemies of the people" or "counterrevolutionaries." Mao Tse-tung had said that "revolution is not a garden party," and during the first few years of the new regime millions of Chinese were made to suffer grievously in this campaign, especially former landlords, against whom the peasantry had accumulated many resentments. Some were sentenced to death by enraged "people's courts"; others were herded off into labor camps where it was hoped they might reform and redeem themselves. Soon business classes became the target of new nationwide reformist campaigns, so that their wealth was drained off by fines and forced purchases of state bonds, and private businesses became semigovernmental enterprises. Concurrently, intellectuals were organized into study groups in which brainwashing techniques were used to substitute Communist indoctrination for former "liberal," Western-oriented ideas. There were book burnings to get rid of "subversive" literature. Education was reorganized to produce scientists and technicians dedicated to the Marxist-Leninist point of view. Literacy was increased by the spread of part-time schools, night schools, and classes conducted during rest breaks in factories and fields; and the content of this training was all Communist-dictated. Literature, the arts, and theatrical entertainments were encouraged and subsidized by the state, and equally reflected the values and goals of the new government. Great national campaigns were staged in rapid succession, keeping the people under great social pressure to do extra, volunteer work to aid the Chinese forces in Korea, to exterminate flies, to produce steel in homemade blast furnaces, and so on. In all these and many other ways, sources of potential opposition were destroyed or neutralized, and the entire nation was being organized to give positive, enthusiastic support in the government's drive to make China once more great and powerful.

Obviously, economic development is the real key to China's future. To become a great modern nation—to be self-reliant and strong in today's world—China must industrialize. All other efforts of the Communist government, consequently, have been geared and subordinated to the need for industrialization, and in this realm the People's Republic has made its most dramatic progress. China is slowly changing from an agrarian nation into an industrial one. Prior to 1949 the whole of China (even including Japanese industries in Manchuria) had never produced more than one million tons of steel in any year, but by the early 1960's it was producing well over ten million tons annually. Production of coal, iron, cement, chemicals, and electric power had also risen markedly. China was manufacturing things it had never manufactured before, including automobiles, tractors, railroad engines, and aircraft. It was also exporting manufactured goods to Southeast Asia and to Communist-bloc nations in Europe. Especially in the first years of the new regime, the Soviet Union helped China by giving factories, machine tools, and technical advisers. But most of China's industrial progress has been achieved by its own efforts in a series of Five-Year Development Plans beginning in 1953. The production of consumer goods has not been emphasized. Rather, the major effort has been to produce steel, cement, machine tools, and other capital goods that can be reinvested in further productive enterprises or to produce goods that can be sold outside China to pay for petroleum products and other industrial necessities that China cannot yet produce, or at least cannot produce in sufficient quantity. Investments in scientific work have also been large in proportion to the national income, and by 1962, reportedly, China had four nuclear reactors in operation.

This progress in industrialization has principally been paid for by China's peasants. Despite its rapid development of manufacturing industries, China still—and for decades to come—must export agricultural produce (grain, tea, soybeans, and so on) to pay for its foreign-trade needs. Since China in modern times has been a food-deficiency area unable to supply its own consumer wants, and since its population is growing at an astonishing rate, the problem of agricultural production has been a monumental challenge to the People's Republic. The government has had to expect the peasants to make immense sacrifices, to produce more and consume less, in order that the nation as a whole might attain its goals in what, to the peasants, must seem a very distant future. For the sake of their grandchildren, they are asked to bear with a very low standard of living now. In the last analysis, China's hope for progress depends on the peasants' indefinite willingness to play this self-sacrificing role.

To increase agricultural productivity, the government has subjected the peasantry to increasing collectivization and regimentation. At the outset, the Communists won peasant support by land reforms that abolished landlordism and divided the land more or less equally among free peasant owners. Then, during the Korean fighting, the peasants were organized into mutual-aid teams in which, although retaining ownership and management of their own lands, they pooled their skills, their tools, their animals, and their labor in small neighborhood groups for mutual advantage. Meanwhile, the virtues of collectivism were constantly preached, and some state-owned collective farms were created to show the peasants what could be accomplished by large-scale planning and management. From 1954 to 1956 there was a drive to organize peasants into agricultural-producer cooperatives, in which the free owner for the first time yielded his land to the group for management and became a profit-sharing employee of the cooperative. Finally, in 1958, the cooperatives and collectives were merged into thousands of giant communes, in what the Chinese called a "great leap forward."

The commune was a more drastic effort to evoke full peasant productivity than had ever been tried in the Soviet Union. It was an amalgamation of all land and people of a large natural area, on average involving five to ten thousand households, into a unitary living and producing unit. It established communal mess halls and communal nurseries so as to release women from their housewifely chores, and it marshaled all men and women into military-style work brigades and teams. These were assigned, as circumstances warranted, to planting and harvesting duties in the fields, to regular maintenance work in the kitchens, nurseries, sewing centers, and so on, and in agricultural off-seasons to fertilizer collection, reforestation, irrigation construction work, and opening of new lands to cultivation. Attempts were made to resettle peasants in highly concentrated housing centers and to move graves into nonproductive land so as to make available for agricultural cultivation all possible land in the area. In what time could be spared from productive work, the commune teams were assigned to study and indoctrination sessions, to militia training, and to such recreations as organized calisthenics.

But the commune was more than an agricultural combine. The commune management controlled all purchasing of supplies and marketing of produce; it established its own educational, medical, and research agencies, including hospitals, night schools, agricultural colleges, agricultural experiment stations, and even communal universities; and it ran its own entertainment and recreation programs. Gradually it became the new basic unit of political organization as well. Most dramatically, it also undertook industrial development, assigning work teams to various manufacturing tasks in small-scale factories. Peasants were turned almost overnight into semiskilled industrial workers, producing electric power, chemicals, ball bearings, and a multitude of other products for local needs or for the great industrial complexes that were appearing in China's cities. In 1959 and 1960 city dwellers themselves began to be organized commune-style, principally so that more women might be brought into productive work as small subcontractors for large factories.

The Communist leaders hailed the commune development as a mighty step toward ideal communism in China, and exaggerated claims were made for production achievements both in agriculture and in industry. It is clear that in the "great leap forward" China experienced as drastic and as sudden a social reorganization as any nation has ever experienced. But the early optimism soon had to be modified. Production increases did not, after all, fulfill expectations, and there arose widespread discontent about overregimentation and overwork. Moreover, in 1959 China entered a long period of unfavorable weather conditions, so that by 1961 it was having to buy great quantities of grain on the world market just to maintain a minimal diet and stave off famine. The commune experiment was by no means abandoned, but the commune structure was changed so that the peasant might again have some private possessions and might have greater incentive to produce than the original commune system offered him.

In the early 1960's, then, the People's Republic was committed to retrenchment and consolidation, following the hectic upheavals of the 1950's. The China that had emerged after a decade of Communist rule was a remarkably new and different China in many ways. As in great eras of the past, it was politically unified and militarily strong, but now it radiated intense nationalism. It had vigorous and unchallenged leadership. It had made great gains in industrial development, and its agriculture had been completely reorganized. It had not conquered its basic economic problems, but it was struggling with them mightily and imaginatively. The transformation of China was by no means finished.

Meanwhile, Communist China's relations with the Soviet Union had changed perceptibly, especially after the "great leap forward." Chairman Khrushchev in Moscow and Chairman Mao in Peking plainly did not see eye-to-eye on many issues, and China seemed determined to pursue an independent course of development and have an independent voice in the councils of the Communist bloc. While Moscow seemed more and more inclined toward peaceable relations with the non-Communist world, Peking seemed stubbornly rooted in an uncompromising, belligerent stance. In 1961 smoldering differences flared up in an open dispute between the Soviet Union and China over relations with the Stalinist government of Communist Albania, which the Russians denounced and the Chinese befriended. The 1960's would obviously be a decisive era in the history of Sino-Soviet relations. But whether changes in this relationship might prove advantageous or disadvantageous for the non-Communist world was not at all clear.

Whatever may happen in this regard, it is clear that China today is more than ever a vital force in human history. What the Chinese think and do in the remainder of the twentieth century will unquestionably have a large part in shaping what the world will be like in the twenty-first century. There is no good reason for us to resign ourselves to a Chinese world of the future, but the Chinese do not expect it to be an American world either.

Japan

Land and Culture

THE FOUR major islands of Japan, together with their
adjacent smaller islands amounting to nearly 3,000 in all,
cover an area of approximately 143,000 square miles. This
makes Japan rather larger than Italy, slightly smaller than
France; the whole could be fitted into the state of California. A relatively small part of the island, under twenty
percent, is fit for cultivation because most of Japan is mountainous and forested.

For more than two thousand years these islands have
been inhabited by a race whose ancestors probably crossed
over by sea from Korea and China. It may be that some of
them in the distant past came north from the Malay Archipelago. But of such migrations there are no historical records.
All that is known is that an aboriginal people, the Ainu, were
gradually supplanted by invaders and that these invaders are
the remote forebears of the present Japanese population.

The Japanese have always been both vigorous and artistic.
We shall be considering the effects of their vigor when we
look at their history, especially the bitter history of their
actions in China and the Pacific during the first half of this
century.

The energy that has gone into Japanese art and culture,
however, deserves equal attention. For wars, until this nuclear age at any rate, come and go, but traditions of art and
culture abide.

A great part of traditional Japanese culture, like the culture of many other countries, is derivative. That is to say, its

origins are foreign, specifically, Chinese. Yet over the course of centuries, what was imported from China became transmuted into a decidedly Japanese product. Thus Japanese art is not the same as Chinese art, and Japanese verse is to be distinguished from Chinese poetry; between the Noh drama of Japan and the classical theater of China there is the minimum of resemblance. Traditional Japanese painting, architecture, sculpture, music, and landscape gardening all owe something to Chinese influence, but they are distinctively Japanese all the same. It is in matters of religion and philosophy that we find Chinese models least changed after adaptation by the Japanese. Buddhism, including the school of Zen, was certainly modified through the centuries after being introduced into Japan. Its Indian-Chinese essence, nevertheless, remained unaltered. Similarly, Confucianism preserved in Japan its basic principles, molding the outlook and behavior of generation upon generation of the Japanese.

Later we shall speak of Japan's Heian Age (A.D. 794–1185), rich in painting, sculpture, architecture, and literature. This was the period of a style of painting known as Yamato-e, in which, to show the inside of a room, the artist leaves out the ceiling but shows all four walls, tilting the angle of view so that one looks down obliquely into the interior of some elegant court scene. Such paintings were often done in the form of a continuous series of pictures on a long scroll. Some of the best examples of these Heian scroll paintings are to be found in the Boston Museum of Fine Arts. A number of them are illustrations to the famous *Genji Monogatari* (*The Tale of Genji*), written by Murasaki Shikibu in the first quarter of the eleventh century.

Another notable period of artistic efflorescence occurred during the fourteenth and fifteenth centuries when, as it happened, the country was rent by destructive civil wars. But as G. B. Sansom remarked in *Japan: A Short Cultural History,* "the Japanese, whether by instinct or tradition, have always had a thirst for beauty of colour and form, a taste which even great disaster could not suppress."

At this time Chinese influence was once more very important. Its effect, however, was to produce within a few decades no mere imitation but a genuine adaptation along strictly Japanese lines. For example, the ceremonial preparation and drinking of tea, introduced from China, developed into a form of art still widely practiced in Japan. The tea ceremony is in fact an aesthetic ritual with a spiritual purpose: to induce in the participants a sense of deep tranquillity. Hence the rite is performed in a quiet, bare room amid surroundings of great simplicity.

Simplicity and restraint—these are the two enduring

SEA OF JAPAN

JAPAN

HOKKAIDO
● Sapporo

HONSHU

Tokyo
Yokohama ●

Hiroshima   Kyoto

SHIKOKU

Nagasaki

PACIFIC OCEAN

KYUSHU

canons or, better, ideals of Japanese good taste. With its plain, matted floor, its lack of furniture, its decoration confined to a scroll hanging above a vase containing perhaps a single flower in season, the traditional Japanese domestic interior is a perfect reflection of this taste; and when sliding doors, all along one side, open to a garden, boulders and grass beyond seem to merge with the room itself and thus suggest a natural harmony between nature and the human family.

There exists too in the Japanese cultural tradition a plethora of extravagant conceits, of vulgar art and literature, much of it greatly esteemed in the West. Among the more admirable of these manifestations are the range of colorful Kabuki plays, still performed in Tokyo, the wood-block prints that flourished in the eighteenth and nineteenth centuries, and the boisterous novels of Saikaku (1642–1693) and his school.

The elaborate temples at Nikko belong to a similar tradition of ostentatious display. But on the whole, when it comes to the highly decorated and ornate, we shall find more impressive specimens of Oriental grandeur and ingenuity in China, Burma, and India than in Japan. The best works of art in Japan tend to be plain to the point of austerity.

This applies with particular force to the buildings and practices associated with Shinto, the old indigenous faith of the Japanese. Shinto is a simple religion. It requires only faith in the deities who created the Japanese islands. Its rites are not elaborate; neither is its code of ethics. The typical Shinto shrine is a plain structure, made of wood wholly unadorned. The worshiper washes his hands and rinses out his mouth at a tank before approaching the shrine to pray. This act of cleansing has roots very far back in the past, and there may be a connection here with the addiction that the Japanese, like the ancient Romans, have always had two daily baths. The worshiper's prayer will be short. If he waits to meditate, to speculate on religious truths, he is more likely to do so in a Buddhist temple than at a Shinto shrine. Indeed, strictly speaking Shinto has no priests, but only "shrine attendants," of whom the most distinguished is the emperor himself.

The old and the new exist side by side in Japan, but the Japanese are inclined to think of Tokyo as modern and Kyoto as old. Tokyo was a tiny village (Edo) about three hundred years ago when the Tokugawa shoguns established it as their capital, although the emperor remained in Kyoto. The walls and moats of the Edo castle, in its day one of the greatest fortifications ever built, still survive. With its concentric moats and walls, its thirty-six gates, its population of warriors, it was in effect a city in itself. The outer walls have long been engulfed by the tide of modernization. Much of the network of moats, too, has disappeared. But even today this relic of the Edo castle domain is so extensive as to impose its image on the city of Tokyo. From most districts of the city it is difficult to reach the center without passing the walls and moats.

Today, Tokyo is the largest city in the world, a great, sprawling metropolis, the center of business, industry, and commerce, the capital of Japan.

The emperor and his family live in a newly completed modest residence, set in an area of some 250 acres enclosed by the inner walls. This is not the ancestral home of the emperors of Japan. The imperial family has lived in Tokyo for less than a hundred years. Yet the castle and its domain formed the palace and headquarters of the real rulers of Japan for well over two hundred years. These rulers were the shoguns and their advisers, who governed in the name of the emperors. The latter, enjoying high prestige and very little significant power, lived in the distant western part of Japan in the city of Kyoto.

Old Japan

Kyoto is a very old city, for it was founded in A.D. 794. But it was not the earliest capital of Japan. In very ancient times the death of an emperor meant that his successor would have to build a new palace in another area since death was believed to be a defilement. Thus the earliest records tell us that the imperial capital was often moved; but one of these moves was of particular significance because it involved the planning and construction of a new city on a considerable scale. This was Nara, which was laid out in A.D. 710. Its heyday lasted less than eighty years. In 784 the court moved to a place called Nagaoka; and then, ten years later, another capital was planned and constructed. The name of this latest capital was Heian-kyo, later to be known as Kyoto.

In those days the prestige of China overshadowed Japan like some beneficent mantle. China represented the quintessence of all that was civilized.

Korea was the main channel for Chinese influence reaching Japan. The straits between Japan and Korea were too wide to make armed invasion a facile proposition to any ambitious despot on the Asian mainland, although this had not prevented the Japanese from invading Korea in the fourth century, but the sea passage was sufficiently short to permit steady intercourse between the two countries. Notable in the stream of cultural influence flowing into Japan from China for several centuries had been the ideographic script. This was adopted only by degrees. Being mountainous, Japan was not a land of easy communications. Furthermore, the Japanese spoken language was quite unlike Chinese, and it did not lend itself readily to the new script. However, by the eighth century Chinese ideographs and a whole range of Chinese practices and ideas, including Confucian thought, had been absorbed by the Japanese. The Buddhist religion, too, had entered Japan and after some initial opposition had prospered.

The first emperors were doubtless no more than rude tribal chieftains. A complicated mythology surrounds and obscures their origin. It was said that they were directly descended from Amaterasu, the sun goddess. In later years this became orthodox doctrine, and to doubt it was both impious and unwise. The very soil of the Japanese islands, according to this body of myths, was created by the gods. The indigenous religion was known as "The Way of the Gods," which in Japanese is *Shinto*. The emperors were its high priests. They were themselves, indeed, numbered among the deities whom it revered. So when Buddhism arrived it met an existing native Japanese faith, which was vigorous enough not to be swamped by the newcomer. In fact there was no necessary conflict between the two religions. Buddhism is very tolerant, and it did not demand the abandonment of Shinto. But it brought with it an elaborate structure of speculative theology and much artistic excellence. For this reason, perhaps, it had won the patronage of the imperial household.

When Nara was laid out as the capital, it was designed on the model of a Chinese city, with avenues crossing one another at right angles. On these were built many temples and mansions in the Chinese manner. This was a striking tribute to the Tang dynasty (A.D. 618–906), then at the height of its power and splendor.

Some of the Nara temples have survived. They stand today in the wide environment of a deer park, some of them in close proximity to an amusement park. But it is these buildings that suggest most vividly the glories of the Tang period. For nothing comparable remains in China from that particular age. Among the treasures of Nara is the Shoso-in, a structure of severe and beautiful simplicity in which are preserved the personal belongings, including many gifts from China, of the Japanese imperial family in the eighth century.

It is possible that Nara was abandoned by the imperial household in A.D. 784 because the many Buddhist temples and monasteries in the capital were becoming too powerful in matters of government. At any rate, after a sojourn of ten years at Nagaoka in the same province, the court moved, as we have seen, to Heian-kyo (Kyoto) in A.D. 794. The new palace at Heian-kyo is said to have been built in about five months by 300,000 men working in shifts throughout the twenty-four hours of the day and night. Heian-kyo, like Nara, was laid out on the Chinese metropolitan pattern in rectangular blocks. Modern Kyoto still preserves this form.

There now ensued the Heian period, famous in Japanese history and, indeed, famous in the artistic history of the civilized world. Strictly speaking, the Heian age lasted for nearly four hundred years, until 1185, when the first shogunate, or military government, was firmly established under Yoritomo Minamoto. But its heyday was the ninth, tenth, and eleventh centuries. We can form an entrancingly clear picture of refined life in those days by reading *Genji Monogatari,* written by a court lady in the early eleventh century, and this is only the best known of several elegant chronicles of the time.

Now, Heian culture, although showing many signs of the influence of China, was decidedly not a mere reflection of Chinese models. It was in fact primarily a native, a Japanese, culture. A process of digestion had taken place. The culture imported from China and Korea had been chewed over and assimilated into the body politic of Japan.

We are seeing the same kind of process in operation now, in the middle of the twentieth century. It has been going on, indeed, for the past hundred years, as the stream of European and American ideas and techniques has poured into Japan. The Japanese have always had two qualities in abundance, namely, curiosity and resilience. Curiosity has led them to borrow, often indiscriminately, all kinds of faiths and practices from abroad whenever they have been allowed to receive the full impact of the outside world. Resilience has enabled them to accept, assimilate, and adapt foreign ways without losing their own identity, all appearances to the contrary notwithstanding. What happens is that in course of time—and it may be a long time—imported foreign ways are changed into something distinctively Japanese.

This is what had occurred by the ninth century; and this is why the aristocratic culture of the Heian age differed in many respects from that of China, of which it was nevertheless the descendant. For example, by this time the Japanese had evolved their own beautiful syllabic script, adapted from Chinese ideographs. This flowing Japanese syllabic script did not replace the imported ideographs, but then as now, was supplementary to them.

In the Heian age, Kyoto presented a picture of elegance and refinement, supreme attention being paid to the ceremonious as well as the beautiful. This period was the seedbed of nearly all Japanese good manners and aesthetic instincts of later times.

This culture, no doubt, was understood and enjoyed only by the few, not by the great bulk of the population. As we should expect, the further from the capital, the more uncouth the conditions became. There is much evidence to show that the idea of being sent to some distant province, even in a high position as the emperor's representative, filled a courtier with bitter forebodings. Even the Musashi Plain, on which modern Tokyo stands, was looked upon as a place of exile, separated as it was by many days of travel over mountains and rivers from Kyoto. Further still from the capital, in the wild northeastern part of Japan, a non-Mongolian race, the hairy Ainu, kept up a rearguard action, rather in the manner of the American Indians in the nineteenth century, against the encroachments of the Japanese. It seems certain that at one time the Ainu people were to be found all over Japan and were gradually pushed back to the east and north by the race, or mixture of races, that invaded the islands in antiquity from the Asian continent, and from Southeast Asia, perhaps, as well. Of such ancient events, however, we have no records, only myths, to guide us. In the early Heian age the Ainu caused the Japanese a good deal of trouble, for they were fierce fighters. Those who had to "pacify" them were the Japanese who lived in the rugged countryside between the Musashi Plain and the Sendai area, two hundred miles to the north. These men had already acquired something of a warrior tradition. Their ancestors were famous in literature as the *Azumabito*, or Men of the East, because they were notably braver than the forces raised by the government in the home provinces around Nara and the other early capitals.

In those days, then, the eastern and northern provinces were the "Wild West" of Japan. That area, like America's frontier, was the scene not only of struggles against aboriginal "barbarians" but also of much general banditry and disorder. So it was perhaps inevitable that in time the best fighting men were reputed to come from that part of Japan.

Early in the ninth century these men were commanded in a campaign against the Ainu by a warrior specially appointed by the emperor, who gave him a title that was to become very famous in later years. This title was "Barbarian Subduing Generalissimo," which in Japanese is *Sei-i Tai Shogun*, the shortened form of which is "shogun."

So in the Heian period there is an evident contrast between the elegant, sophisticated world of Kyoto and the rough community of warriors in the provinces, more especially in the east and northeast. In name the whole land was ruled by the hereditary line of "sacred" emperors. In reality the arm of the government was often ineffective in regions distant from the capital.

But in any case the revered sovereigns themselves rarely exercised direct governmental power. This had fallen into the hands of the gifted Fujiwara family, which through intermarriage with the imperial household had gained control of the monarchy. The Fujiwaras never tried to usurp the throne. They never attempted, in the Chinese fashion, to found a new dynasty. Such a blasphemous thought probably never occurred to them. Only an emperor from the direct, original line was regarded as having the innate, hereditary qualifications for what had become first and foremost a priestly, ceremonial office.

The glory of the Fujiwaras lasted for so long, generation after generation, that it must have seemed almost eternal. Most emperors in those years abdicated as soon as their heirs were old enough to take part in palace ceremonies. Retired emperors were treated with the highest respect, and abdication can have meant little to them, seeing that the Fujiwaras occupied the posts of real power.

Eventually, however, the Fujiwaras also found themselves possessed of only the names and forms of authority. Actual governmental power had been taken over by the warrior class. This happened in the twelfth century. It was a development of portentous, even ominous significance for the subsequent history of Japan.

Who were the members of this warrior class? Putting it rather simply, they were descendants, very largely although not entirely, of those who had risen to local eminence in the turbulent provinces far from the capital. Brought in by Fujiwara nobles to keep order in Kyoto and the metropolitan provinces, they made themselves at home there; and at last one warrior household, the Taira family, contrived to reach and hold the reins of power. This family in its turn was overthrown in civil war by another military clan, the Minamoto, whose dominant figure was a severe and extremely capable man called Yoritomo.

Instead of ruling the country in the emperor's name from Kyoto, Yoritomo established a military government in the east, at Kamakura on the shores of Sagami Bay, more than 250 miles from the capital. After a few years he received the title of shogun.

Kamakura was the important center of all government, but the emperors and the Fujiwaras were not subjected to interference if they observed the wishes of Yoritomo and his successors.

Invasions and Seclusions

Yoritomo's power was consolidated in 1185. Thereafter the warrior class ruled Japan for more than seven hundred and fifty years. It could be argued that the dominance of this class persisted, in one form or another, right up to 1945.

The Kamakura government endured for about a century and a half, but during that time Yoritomo's progeny lost the reality of power. This passed to a family of regents. And so the strange duality of Heian days, between emperors and Fujiwara dictators, was reproduced in Kamakura between shoguns and regents.

In the latter half of the thirteenth century, toward the end of the Kamakura period, Japan was twice attacked by invading forces sent by Kublai Khan, the Mongol emperor of China. This menace was beaten off because of the skill and courage of the Japanese warriors and the intervention of a typhoon, which wrecked and scattered the invading fleet. This storm was accepted as heaven-sent. The Japanese called it a *kamikaze,* which means "divine wind."

Some fifty years after these invasions were repelled, the Kamakura government was cast down by civil war, and in course of time a new military administration under a new line of shoguns (the Ashikaga) was set up in the Muromachi district of Kyoto. All this took place before the middle of the fourteenth century. There followed a very disturbed period, of more than two hundred years, in which the country was rarely at peace. Indeed, throughout most of the fourteenth century, there were actually two imperial courts supporting rival emperors, both of them, of course, belonging to the ancient imperial line. The fighting that arose from this cause and the later civil wars that succeeded the union of the rival courts provide a tale of both great savagery and great heroism. The central theme throughout is the continued supremacy of the fighting barons and their supporters. Neither emperors nor Fujiwara nobles could pretend to govern the country, and often the Ashikaga shoguns themselves had little enough real power.

Yet, for all the constant civil war that was taking place, the fourteenth and fifteenth centuries saw the development of such arts as the tea ceremony and flower arrangement; much excellent painting, drama, and landscape gardening; the construction of works of great architectural merit; and a general promotion of aestheticism that affected even the most bellicose and unlettered of the warring barons. Extreme violence and a true instinct for art existed side by side, sometimes within the same breast. This is suggested, perhaps, by a suit of medieval Japanese armor. It is serviceable in terms of bodily protection; it is also grotesquely menacing, with its dark mask often adorned with a contrived, scowling grimace. At the same time, it is undeniably beautiful both in color and general design.

Something must be said here about the kind of man, the samurai, who wore this armor. For he is the spiritual ancestor of the soldiers, sailors, and airmen who fought in the Pacific and in the jungles and hills of Burma and the Philippines.

At its ideal best his code of conduct was not wholly unlike that of the knight of European chivalry. For, again at their best, both codes were affected by the humanizing elements of two great religions, Buddhism and Christianity. Like the French or English knight, the samurai was supposed to respect the weak and aged. It was held that the samurai should be well mannered, for courtesy is a Buddhist precept. Buddhism, like Christianity, has a concept both of heaven and hell. Thus both samurai and knight were taught to regard life as fleeting and dishonor as much worse than death. After this, however, the resemblance, on the ideal plane, comes to an end. The idea of courtly love, so much a part of the chivalrous ideal in medieval Europe, finds little echo in the world of the samurai. Moreover, the samurai never had to face the Christian prohibition of the act of suicide. On the contrary, as everyone knows, hara-kiri is a specifically Japanese phenomenon. The samurai was taught from childhood very precisely how to kill himself should need arise.

Perhaps the most positive tenet in the samurai's ethical code, and one that owed much to Confucian ideas, was that he should be unswervingly loyal to those to whom he owed respect and obedience: his father, his teacher, his feudal superiors. Loyalty was all; loyalty to a person rather than to any principle or ideal. This has been at once the strength and weakness of the Japanese throughout the ages.

This code, however, was often abused. Even loyalty did not invariably prevail. There have been some notable instances of the grossest treachery, especially in Ashikaga days. The warriors could be merciless in their treatment of fallen enemies, irrespective of age or sex. By a curious perversion of Buddhist beliefs, violence could sometimes be exalted for its own sake. Among the teachings of the Zen sects of Buddhism was the justification of direct action as one road to *satori*, or enlightenment. "The sword is the soul of the samurai." This was a cliché in old Japan. It was associated with the Zen ideal of action for action's sake. It led to such hideous conceits as these: that it is not the swordsman but the sword that does the killing, that "the enemy appears and makes himself the victim," that the sword is the embodiment of life and not of death.

The samurai is the hero and villain of Japanese history. He is brave, brutal, faithful, merciless, gentle, coarse, artistic, vulgar, a sensitive lover of nature. At one time or another he has been all these and more. But it is fair to say that he has almost never been a poltroon. First and last he was a fighting man. Other classes in the community—farmers, craftsmen, merchants—carried on with their occupations, leaving fighting to the samurai, although it must be admitted that for centuries Buddhist monks, too, were not slow to take up arms.

In the second half of the sixteenth century some kind of unity was at last imposed on the warring fiefs of Japan. This was achieved through a combination of cunning diplomacy and force of arms by two able men, Nobunaga Oda (1534–1582) and Hideyoshi Toyotomi (1536–1598). The latter was Nobunaga's lieutenant, and he completed the unification of the country. Hideyoshi indeed was a despot with large ambitions. In 1592 and again in 1597 he sent huge armies across the sea to invade and conquer Korea, the further objective being the empire of China itself. These ventures came to nothing. Not even the new weapon in the samurai's hand, the musket, enabled him to consolidate the subjugation of Korea.

The new weapon had been introduced, together with a new religion, some fifty years earlier by the first Europeans to land on Japanese soil, the Portuguese, who came as traders and missionaries. At first this contact with another world appeared most promising. The Japanese welcomed the chance of commerce with the Portuguese, and they did not reject outright the new faith, Christianity, preached by the Jesuit fathers who came on the Portuguese vessels from Macao. In time there were many Christian converts in western Japan. We do not know the exact figure, but it is possible that there were nearly 300,000 Japanese Christians by the end of the sixteenth century.

Nobunaga was friendly in his whole approach to the Europeans; but Hideyoshi, after some wavering, came in the end to look upon the Christian missionaries, if not the traders, as possibly disruptive of the social order. However, in general he left them alone, although some Christians were put to death on his orders.

Hideyoshi died in 1598, leaving a son aged five whom he regarded as his heir as the future effective ruler of Japan. Before his death, Hideyoshi secured a promise from the most powerful of his lords that they would cooperate as guardians of the boy until he became old enough to take over the government. Among these barons, the leading figure was Iyeyasu Tokugawa (1542–1616).

Iyeyasu had been one of Nobunaga's junior allies, and on Nobunaga's death, after some doubts and a short clash of arms, he had joined forces with Hideyoshi. After Hideyoshi died, quarrels soon broke out among his son's guardians, and these led to civil war, from which Iyeyasu emerged victorious, for in a great battle in 1600, he soundly defeated his opponents. This made him the master of Japan for all practical purposes, but he could not feel absolutely secure until he had dealt with Hideyoshi's son, whose supporters established a strong headquarters in the castle at Osaka. It was sixteen years before Iyeyasu could see his banners flutter above the ruins of this fortress, after a complicated siege and a merciless assault. Hideyoshi's son, now a young man of twenty-one, committed suicide along with his mother as the castle fell.

Before the siege of Osaka, Iyeyasu had already obtained imperial appointment as shogun, which he soon passed on to a capable son. The new shogunate was set up in Edo, the modern Tokyo, in the castle that was the heart of the city; and as we have seen, Iyeyasu greatly enlarged and strengthened it.

After the fall of Osaka, Japan entered a long period of almost unbroken peace. Some of the shrewd methods by which Iyeyasu and his Tokugawa descendants maintained their supremacy are worth describing. The territorial lords, or *daimyo* as they were called, were allowed very great latitude in the government of their own fiefs, but they had to spend part of every year in Edo, where much of their time was taken up with ceremonial duties at the shogun's court. When they returned to their own territorial domains, they were compelled to leave their wives and families behind in Edo as virtual hostages. Daimyo marriages had to be approved by the shogunate. No daimyo was permitted to communicate directly with the imperial household in Kyoto, and no daimyo was allowed to pass through Kyoto on his way to and from Edo. The shogun's government employed an army of spies to watch relations between the great lords. In fact Tokugawa Japan was in some ways a forerunner of the modern police state, for although administration was not centralized, the daimyo having much local autonomy, the shogunate was determined to know exactly what was going on in the various parts of the country.

Once the new shogunate was firmly established, the authorities began to enforce, with the greatest severity, the official ban on Christianity that had been nominally operative for several years. A great persecution of Christians followed. So thorough was it that by the middle years of the seventeenth century, the government could believe that the alien faith had been stamped out. Yet, two centuries later it was discovered that certain households in the southwest of Japan had passed on, from father to son through the generations, the doctrines and practices of Catholic Christianity.

As part of the ruthless campaign against Christianity, all dealings with the Portuguese were ended and their ships were forbidden to come to Japan. Foreign trade, in fact, was confined to the Dutch and Chinese at Nagasaki, the Dutch being segregated on the tiny island of Deshima, connected by a closely guarded bridge with the town of Nagasaki. No Japanese was allowed, on pain of death, to leave the country.

So Japan was in this way sealed off from the world. This occurred at a time when the Japanese could have learned a great deal from certain European nations. For this was the age, of course, of the Renaissance, and Japan might have gained many benefits from the rising tide of scientific inquiry in Europe. One notable consequence of this self-imposed national isolation was that the Japanese, who were capable seamen, failed to discover Australia; and so this new continent was colonized by English-speaking men and women from the other end of the globe.

This so-called seclusion policy was certainly very much related to the shogunate's determination to keep a firm grip on the country. For they feared that if there were free contact with foreigners, the barons of the far west, the part of Japan most distant from Edo and closest to Europe, might obtain weapons and supplies from abroad that would enable them in time to challenge the Tokugawa regime.

During two centuries and more of national seclusion, Japanese society, by comparison with the countries of Western Europe, was almost static. Nevertheless, the merchant community in Osaka and Edo became more numerous and more influential in spite of the fact that as a class, merchants were ranked below peasants and craftsmen and far below the various grades of the samurai class. In the long years of peace, the merchants began to live in a certain style, and they became patrons of a flourishing culture of entertainment. This world is revealed to us in color prints; in the Kabuki and puppet theater; in many works of literature, notably novels, verses, and short stories. The standard assessment of wealth was rice. The samurai's stipend from his overlord was calculated and paid in quantities of this crop. But obviously money was the most convenient means of exchange. This the merchants could provide in return for the rice provided or promised by the warrior class. The latter was trained to despise mere monetary calculations. It was inevitable, then, that the merchants, as alert businessmen, should enrich themselves over the years.

In the eighteenth century there grew up a widespread interest in Japan's national history. The shogunate always encouraged the pursuit of learning. The government wanted people to read the Confucian classics and edifying works on history and morals instead of wasting their time at the Kabuki theater and other places of entertainment.

But the study of Japan's own history led certain scholars to wonder why the ancient imperial house should be kept, as it were, in a backwater at Kyoto while the real government ruled from Edo. People began to whisper that the Tokugawa shogunate had only a rather dubious right to keep all political power in its own hands.

There were, too, a few men who looked beyond Japan's shores to the outside world. Some of them became proficient in the Dutch language and so were able to study and explain to others the interesting books and maps that arrived from time to time on Dutch vessels at Nagasaki. So a rudimentary but not inaccurate knowledge of many events and institutions, and of techniques too, in the outside world percolated through to the government and to various individual Japanese who had an itch to know what was going on in foreign lands. Some of these inquisitive men wrote books pointing out that it would be wise to open the country to overseas trade on a large scale so that Japan could become as strong in Asia as England was in Europe. But such views were those of a minority. But they began to acquire relevance in the first half of the nineteenth century as foreign vessels in increasing numbers approached the Japanese islands. In the north the Russians were pushing forward their trading posts in the Kurile Islands and along the shores of the Sea of Okhotsk.

To the west the English were clearly determined to develop their trade with China, by force if necessary. Across the Pacific, to the east, California was being opened up, and Americans were full of plans for a thriving trade with China and Japan. Steam power was beginning to revolutionize the scale and speed of maritime trade.

Western Impact and Wars

In the summer of 1853 four United States naval vessels steamed and sailed into Edo (Tokyo) Bay. Their commander brought with him a letter from President Fillmore to the emperor of Japan.

The "black ships," as they were called by the Japanese, created a great sensation. This was not the first time that foreign ships other than Dutch and Chinese had been seen in Japanese waters in those years, but on the whole they had been rare visitors and had arrived singly, save for a Russian squadron that had anchored in that same year in the Nagasaki roadstead.

The President's letter, brought by Commodore Perry, was a politely phrased request that Japan change her seclusion policy. Having delivered the letter to special envoys sent by the shogun, Perry said that he would return the following year for an answer. He then sailed away, not before having conducted a reconnaissance of Edo Bay, much to the chagrin of the Japanese authorities.

After much heart-searching and agonizing debate, the shogun's government came to the conclusion that the President's desires could not be ignored. Probably the great majority of the samurai class favored armed resistance rather than compliance with the American request, but the shogun's advisers were forced to be more realistic. When Commodore Perry returned, negotiations were opened, and on March 31, 1854, a treaty was signed whereby two ports were made available for American ships. This concession was soon followed by others, not only to the Americans but also to the British, Russians, and Dutch.

The prestige of the shogunate was now undermined, for after all, the shogun's primary function was that he should be "Barbarian Subduing Generalissimo." As a Japanese wrote at that time: "If it [the shogunate] is unable to defy the foreign menace, the words *Sei-i* [barbarian subduing] are nothing but an empty title."

Still, it was fourteen years before the shogunate came to an end. Tokugawa supremacy was overthrown by a coalition of certain western lords and Kyoto nobles. This change of government, achieved in 1868, is known as the Meiji Restoration; for in theory at least, powers long lost by the imperial house were restored to the sixteen-year-old emperor, Mutsuhito, who reigned as Meiji (enlightened rule). The real architects of the new regime were fairly young warriors of great capacity, energy, and alertness of mind. Some of them had contrived to visit Europe before the Restoration took place and had been converted from antiforeign fanaticism to a belief in wholehearted modernization, involving the adoption of many alien institutions and techniques.

The new government was established in Edo, which was now renamed Tokyo, or "Eastern Capital." Emperor Meiji took up residence in the new capital in the foreign Tokugawa stronghold. The new oligarchy began the task of transforming Japan into a modern state, in other words a Westernized industrial state. The national aim was summed up in the slogan "a rich country and a strong army." It was to be achieved within the next fifty years.

How was it done? The short, oversimplified, answer can be given in two words—hard work. This of course was nothing new. The great masses of the Japanese people had always worked hard, as farmers, craftsmen, and merchants. Now the samurai class, too, threw itself into the labor of modernization with remarkable adaptability, considering that the Meiji Restoration soon led to the abolition of their privileges and, indeed, of their whole traditional way of life. Some warriors, to be sure, could not accept this destruction of their world; and they rose in rebellion against the government, not against the emperor. This was entirely suppressed after a short but bitter struggle. And eventually the samurai came to realize that many of his old ideals would not be lost after all. Thanks to general compulsory primary education, these ideals would be taught to the children of the poorest peasants, and on reaching manhood, many of these children, because of compulsory military service, would become devoted soldiers and sailors, ready to die for the Emperor Meiji.

The same basically Confucian, samurai ethics infused the management of the new industries—textile mills, iron foundries, coal mines, and shipbuilding yards—that were turning green fields into deserts of factory roofs, slag heaps, and belching chimneys. Most of the lords of the new industrial empires were men who had been brought up as warriors; and when they exchanged their two swords for the once despised account books of the merchant, they entered business life with the zest of a samurai riding into battle.

Needless to say, there was a minority of nonconformists, and there were even a few rebels who rejected the prevailing national ideology. And at all levels of government there were of course inevitable disagreements and quarrels. But the atmosphere throughout most of the Meiji period (1868–1912) was one of virtual unanimity as to the basic national aim, the modernization of Japan.

One of the obstacles in the path of rapid achievement of this aim was a shortage of capital. Certainly money could be borrowed from foreign countries, but at first the Japanese were chary of raising foreign loans. The man who pays the piper does not always call the tune, but human nature being what it is, he is tempted to do so. In the early years of modernization, then, very little money was borrowed from abroad. Later on, in the twentieth century, it was a different matter, for by that time Japan was strong enough not to worry about the possible political influence of foreign capital. In the nineteenth century, however, the government relied on taxation, on a land tax in particular, as a means of raising capital with which to launch new industries. The land tax hit the peasant hard. In the old days, though subjected to the authority of his territorial lord, he was recognized as possessing the land on which he worked. But the Meiji land tax had to be paid regularly in cash whether harvests were good or bad. The effect was to make more and more debt-ridden peasants into tenants or day-laborers of progressively fewer landowners. The latter paid the tax. His tenants paid high rents in kind, from the crops that they cultivated. In bad years this could mean that the peasant was unable to eat the rice that he himself had planted and reaped. Consequently, after the Meiji Restoration, the condition of the peasantry actually deteriorated in an economic sense.

But for those who could not scrape a living off the land, there was work in the new mills and urban workshops. Thus the countryside came to supply a stream of cheap male and female labor for the expanding cities and towns. So the land tax not only provided most of the capital with which the government could start new enterprises, later selling these at very low prices to private businessmen, but also created a large supply of labor that could be paid low wages.

In a sense, then, the Japanese countryside was sacrificed on the altar of urban industrialization, and indeed this is one road to industrialization for any underdeveloped nation in the modern world. Speaking to the peasants, the nation's rulers can say, in so many words: "You peasants must now tighten your belts for the sake of your descendants. Hard conditions on the land will drive your younger sons and daughters into the factories that will turn out the exports that are going to help change our nation into a modern state. In future years everybody in town and countryside alike will enjoy a rising standard of living. But this process will be relatively slow outside the cities, and you yourselves may not live to derive much benefit from it." This certainly represents the way in which the Meiji oligarchy regarded the problem of the countryside in nineteenth-century Japan.

To marry hard work to efficiency, the government hired foreign experts from many parts of the world to show the Japanese how to run railroads, banks, and hospitals; how to organize a modern army and navy; how to establish and operate a system of posts and telegraph: how to create, in other words, the intricate material structure of an urban technological society.

Japanese were sent abroad to learn all these skills so that

on their return they could replace the foreign experts, who were costing the Ministry of Finance a sizable chunk of its annual budget.

All this took place more smoothly than one might expect. Despite the long years of seclusion, most Japanese had a very practical, inquiring turn of mind. For example, when Japanese officials were shown the engine room and bridge on Perry's flagship, they were not particularly astonished, as the Americans thought they would be, by the machinery, charts, and navigational aids that they saw. For they had some knowledge already, even if it was only theoretical, of such devices. Moreover, a Japanese who visited the United States some seven or eight years after Perry's arrival has told us that the process of American technology did not surprise him. He had read about all that kind of thing in books brought in through Nagasaki by the Dutch. What did strike him as novel and strange were American political ideas and social customs.

Japan's rapid modernization certainly impressed both Europe and America, especially when the Japanese won resounding victories in two wars against China in 1894–1895 and against Russia in 1904–1905. After the defeat of tsarist Russia on land and sea, Japan became indubitably one of the great powers of the world. In a matter of half a century the faith of those who had advocated surrender to Perry's pressure in 1854 seemed wholly vindicated.

Now, together with banks, railroads, filing cabinets, and telephones, nineteenth-century Japan had borrowed and adopted many Western modes in art, literature, music, architecture, and drama. At first it almost seemed as though the Japanese were going to renounce their own cultural heritage. For example, at the very moment when Japanese color prints, greeted with delight by European artists, were having a profound influence on such painters as Toulouse-Lautrec, these fine works were held in low esteem by the Japanese themselves.

But in time there came a reaction against the craze for foreign art and foreign manners and ideas. From the very beginning, the Meiji regime was suspicious of such ideas as political and social democracy and the equality of the sexes. The rulers of Japan wanted people to discard "useless old customs." They wanted them to be up-to-date, practical, technologically skilled. But they certainly did not want the emperor's subjects to go chasing after foreign gods.

The government, it is true, had to make concessions to the demand for some kind of parliament. In 1889 Emperor Meiji bestowed a constitution on his people. This gave limited powers to a diet, or national parliament. But the constitution, much influenced by German example, was a very authoritarian document. It allowed the army and navy to retain great power that was not subject to cabinet control.

The authorities encouraged the police to check and punish the expression of radical ideas. In fact, they erected a kind of grille or sieve through which foreign notions must pass. The intention was to allow through the bars only such ideas as seemed strictly useful and to keep out politically and socially "dangerous thoughts."

By the end of the Meiji period, in 1912, Japan had a colonial empire. This comprised Formosa and the Pescadores, ceded by China in 1895, and Korea, finally annexed in 1910. Port Arthur and Dairen were also in Japanese hands, and so was much of the South Manchurian Railroad. By this time, too, both the Kurile Islands and South Sakhalin were in Japanese possession. All these gains (with the exception of the Kuriles, granted by Russia in the nineteenth century), had been won as a result of the short but bitter wars against China and Russia.

Not unnaturally the Japanese felt an upsurge of confidence after these successes, especially after their defeat of tsarist Russia. Moreover, in the cockpit of international relations Japan had a powerful friend, Great Britain, with whom she was bound in a treaty of alliance. But in the years after 1905, relations with the United States showed signs of deteriorating. For this there were several reasons. The Japanese made it increasingly clear that they intended to dominate South Manchuria economically as well as politically, that they meant to capture as much as possible of the China market for their own exports. Japan's economic expansion across the Yellow Sea was not at all to the liking of Americans trading with China. Americans began to wonder whether "gallant little Japan" might not turn out, after all, to be what the German Kaiser had already called it, namely, the "Yellow Peril." Feelings were even more strongly aroused on the Japanese side when the state of California brought in legislation greatly restricting the sale of land to Japanese immigrants.

Meanwhile, China, by contrast, presented a picture of industrial backwardness, military weakness, and internal confusion. For years this geographical giant had been a prey to foreign interference of every kind. From the Japanese point of view, China was a market and a source of raw materials, ripe for development if only the Chinese would agree to accept Japanese advice in the running of their affairs. To this end Japan presented a set of demands in 1915 to the Chinese president which, if they had been accepted, would have turned China into a Japanese protectorate. It was an ambitious gamble, which did more harm to the Japanese than to the Chinese. The latter rejected the most menacing of the "Twenty-One Demands" amid a general outcry against Japan's action. America in particular was deeply shocked. From this time onward, Japanese-American relations began to take a downhill course.

Yet, in the 1920's Japan pursued, on the whole, a restrained and conciliatory policy toward China. At the same time, there was some progress toward greater political and social democracy inside Japan. The Kuomintang government in Nanking imagined, unwisely, that the Japanese armed forces were losing for good the political influence they had long enjoyed. How mistaken this view was, time was soon to reveal.

The 1930's opened under the cloud of the world depression, affecting Japan very seriously since the American market for Japanese silk collapsed. This not only ruined exporters in Kobe and Yokohama but also brought conditions of near-starvation to millions of peasants. For in Japan the production of silk thread in its early stages, from the care of silkworms onward, was to a great extent a home industry, carried out by the wives and daughters of peasants. This necessary side occupation had saved many a family from actual destitution. And now this was gravely threatened.

There is a grim Japanese proverb that says that a bee will sting a crying child's face. In other words, troubles never come singly. Thus, as if the disaster to the silk market were not enough, the year 1932 saw a failure of the rice crop in no less than eight prefectures in northeast Japan.

Such woes created the kind of bitter discontent that in other nations might have erupted into something approaching a revolution. There was by this time in Japan a rather striking contrast between the living standards of the rich and those of the poor, between the cities like Tokyo, Osaka, and Nagoya and the backward countryside. But police control had efficiently suppressed all revolutionary Marxist activities. The Communists were under a total ban, and indeed most of them were in prison. Socialist parties and groups were under constant observation. Very strict laws existed, and were enforced, against critical or even frivolous comment on the emperor, and this kind of censorship extended to the newspapers, magazines, and movies. All the while, of course, schoolchildren of all ages were being indoctrinated with an ideology that exalted a submissive patriotism as the supreme social virtue.

Nevertheless, the people at large now lost confidence in the capacity of the government, almost entirely composed of diet politicians, to relieve the economic distress caused by the world depression. It was in this atmosphere of resentment and frustration that the people of Japan opened their newspapers one morning in September, 1931, to read that Japanese troops had clashed with Chinese soldiers in the city of Mukden in South Manchuria. The army in Manchuria then proceeded to take the law into its own hands. In a matter of a few months, and with not a great deal of fighting, Japanese forces occupied all Manchuria. This was done without any prior authorization from the Tokyo government, and the military campaign in Manchuria was in fact a source of acute embarrassment not only to many civilian ministers but also to the emperor himself.

However, there was a surge of popular enthusiasm for the army, which was occupying hundreds of miles of territory with great speed and few losses. The politician had never acquired, in the eyes of the ordinary citizen, the glamour that surrounded the soldier, the heir to the samurai. When Japan left the League of Nations, her action having been condemned by that body, the emperor spent some sleepless nights; but the majority of the people probably approved of what had been arranged in Manchuria, namely, the creation of an "independent" state, Manchukuo, a puppet state administered at every level by the Japanese.

A wave of nationalist sentiment swamped Japan in the 1930's and seemed to carry all before it. Public men of temperate views lived under the shadow of the assassin. Over a period of four years, three premiers or former premiers were shot down and killed by nationalist fanatics; and early in 1936, ultranationalist young army officers with more than a thousand troops under their command seized buildings in the center of Tokyo and defied the authorities for four days. This was a stroke aimed against those who were alleged to be giving "evil advice" to the throne. The rebellious young officers protested their extreme loyalty to the emperor. He himself was always shocked by nationalist excesses. Indeed it was largely as a result of his indignation that the military authorities in Tokyo regarded the armed outbreak as a rebellion and treated it accordingly.

In 1937 the friction between Japan and China, acute since the Japanese seizure of Manchuria, burst out into full-scale undeclared war. The fighting spread from North China to Shanghai and the Yangtze valley. At the end of 1937, Nanking was stormed and sacked with a brutality that dismayed and shocked the world. In 1938 other cities, such as Hankow and Canton, fell to the invaders. But the Chinese refused to give in, and Chiang Kai-shek, China's leader, moved his capital to Chungking, far to the west. Japan claimed to be setting up a New Order in East Asia. The phrase was ominous. It was the sort of language that the

European dictators Hitler and Mussolini used. At this time, too, Japan was allied with Germany in an Anti-Comintern Pact.

This alliance was strengthened in 1940 after Nazi Germany's impressive victories in the summer of that year. With Britain apparently facing invasion, with France defeated and seemingly impotent, with Holland under German occupation, the colonial territories of Southeast Asia—Indochina, Malaya and the Dutch East Indies—presented a strong temptation to a nationalist Japan; for they were rich in mineral and food resources much needed by the Japanese.

In July, 1941, the Japanese, who already occupied a few key points in northern Indochina, put irresistible pressure on the French Vichy government to consent to the establishment of Japanese military and naval bases in southern Indochina.

Immediate countermeasures were taken by the United States, Britain, and the Netherlands. The governments of these countries put a virtual stop to further commerce with Japan. One most important result was that Japan could no longer import oil from the Dutch East Indies.

Japan now faced a critical decision in consequence of the intemperate behavior of her military class. She could either submit to a real diplomatic defeat, withdrawing from Indochina and China in exchange for a raising of the trade embargo, or she could defy America, Britain, and Holland and seize the coveted southern regions by force. In the latter event, a knockout blow against the American Pacific fleet, the only force capable of checking the Japanese at that time, would be a necessary first step in any move to capture the lands of Southeast Asia.

The prime minister of the day, Prince Konoye, was eager at all costs to avoid war with America. He was ready, therefore, to envisage a Japanese withdrawal from Indochina and China. But his war minister, General Tojo, could not accept this view, and here General Tojo undoubtedly spoke for the army as a whole. If the army opposed him, no Japanese prime minister in those years could survive. So Konoye resigned in October, 1941, and was succeeded by Tojo.

All this time talks had been going on in Washington between Secretary of State Cordell Hull and Japanese Ambassador Nomura in an effort to reach some settlement acceptable to the United States and Japan.

What both America and Britain needed was time, time in which to build up their strength in the Far East in the Philippines and Malaya. It might have been wise, therefore, if the American government had come to a temporary understanding with Japan, a lifting of the trade embargo for a certain specified period in return for a Japanese withdrawal from southern Indochina. Such an arrangement could have been reached. But in the climate of those years it would have dismayed American public opinion, for it would have been interpreted, correctly enough, as appeasement of Japan; and "appeasement," after what had happened at Munich in 1938, was an ugly word for most Americans. Moreover, the Chinese were restive. They feared that some kind of Japanese-American agreement might be reached at their expense. There was always the fear, too, in Washington that a disillusioned China might come to terms with Japan.

So in November Cordell Hull presented the Japanese with a firmly worded note offering them full economic cooperation, but only in exchange for withdrawal from both Indochina and China. The Japanese, particularly the military leaders, tried to make out that this Hull note was an ultimatum. It was nothing of the sort, but it certainly made it clear that the United States government was determined to stand by China, that only a real reversal of Japan's expansionist course could lead to a raising of the economic embargo.

Thus, Japan adopted the policy of the knockout blow, and this was delivered on December 7, 1941; but the attack on Pearl Harbor was not in fact a knockout blow, for when the assault came, the American aircraft carriers were not in port. However, a similar blow from the skies destroyed General MacArthur's air force in the Philippines, and within the next few days Britain's only two battleships in the Far East were bombed and sunk off Malaya.

Six months later a huge area of continental size, from the frontier of India to the Solomon Islands, had been seized and occupied by the Japanese. Yet even at that time there were a few highly placed Japanese who wondered whether ultimate victory was in fact feasible.

These anxieties increased as the tide, slowly at first, turned against Japan in the Pacific. But it was not really until the late summer of 1944, after the Americans had captured Saipan in the Marianas and the British had defeated the Japanese on the borders of Burma and India, that it became clear to a minority of Japan's leaders that victory was impossible. Defeat became possible, and then probable, as the spring of 1945 turned to summer. Devastating air raids gave the cities of Japan no respite. The shipping losses had become catastrophic. War industries could no longer satisfy the demands made on them. And then in May, 1945, Germany surrendered to the Allies. Defeat was now inevitable, for although the Japanese did not know it, the Russians were preparing to take part in the Far Eastern struggle.

Desperate as the situation was, Japan's military chiefs still believed that there was a chance of inflicting such losses on the enemy in any attempted invasion of Japan proper that a peace short of surrender could be negotiated. The kamikaze suicide planes had done much damage in the Okinawa fighting. Large numbers of these planes, together with dedicated young pilots, were being held in reserve against the expected enemy landings. Japanese generals, remembering their samurai ancestors and their country's history, could not help feeling that the Americans would be driven off, just as the Mongols were in the thirteenth century. So they ignored the Potsdam Declaration of July 26, 1945, in which the Japanese rulers were told to order the unconditional surrender of all their armed forces, the alternative being "prompt and utter destruction."

Eleven days later, August 6, 1945, an atomic bomb was exploded over Hiroshima. Two days later the Russians declared war on Japan, simultaneously invading Manchukuo and Korea. The next day, August 9, an atomic bomb was dropped over Nagasaki. Late that same night, Japan's leaders held a critical meeting in the emperor's presence in the palace air-raid shelter. The question was whether or not to accept the summons to surrender; and on this, remarkably enough, opinion was evenly divided. The emperor gave a casting vote in favor of peace when he declared that Japan would have to accept the Allied demands.

Acceptance, however, was tied to a request for assurances from the Allies that the prerogatives of the emperor would be preserved. The Allies replied that the Japanese people would have to decide on Japan's ultimate form of government, that meanwhile the supreme commander of the Allied powers (General MacArthur) would have full powers of control over the emperor and government of Japan "from the moment of surrender." This answer reopened the desperate debate in Tokyo among those in supreme charge of military and civil affairs. Once again opinion reached a deadlock. Once again the emperor spoke in favor of surrender. This was on August 14, 1945. The next day a nationwide recorded broadcast by the emperor told the Japanese that further fighting would not only result in an ultimate collapse and obliteration of the Japanese nation but would also lead to the total extinction of human civilization.

Two weeks later American troops were in Japan, and the occupation had begun. The official ceremony of surrender took place on September 2 on the deck of the battleship U.S.S. *Missouri* in Tokyo Bay. Some ninety years earlier, Perry's "black ship," the U.S.S. *Mississippi,* had once anchored in the same roadstead.

Contemporary Japan

The occupation lasted from late August, 1945, to the end of April, 1952. It was, on the whole, a surprisingly harmonious affair. The veteran statesman Shigeru Yoshida, premier during much of the occupation and by no means always pro-American, wrote in his memoirs: "Criticism of Americans is a right accorded even to Americans. But in the enumeration of their faults we cannot include their occupation of Japan." Earlier he had admitted that Japan's occupation of various Asian countries became an object of loathing among the peoples of the occupied countries, "and there is none" (he wrote) "to dispute that fact."

During the war, Japanese propaganda had depicted the Americans as terrible enemies who would behave like devils if they ever set foot on Japanese soil. But when the dreaded occupation forces arrived, the Japanese soon saw that the Americans, though conscious of being the victors, were both just and good-hearted. Indeed, the political, economic, legal, and social reforms put in hand by the Japanese government, under pressure from the Americans, were soon welcomed by the great mass of the Japanese people. Very many occupation officials felt a real sense of dedication to their task, which could be summed up in a single clumsy but important word: "democratization." However reserved and suspicious some of them may have felt when they first arrived in Japan, they soon fell under the spell of the country and its people. The Americans had much to give, and their instruction was eagerly sought even when it was not altogether fully understood.

Surrender, followed by occupation, exploded a myth of invincibility. An oppressive if sometimes intoxicating ideology of national expansion faded away before the reality of defeat. The sword, "the soul of the samurai," no longer cast its shadow over the land. Army and navy officers were now discredited in the public eye. All the terrible sacrifices—the resistance to the death in the jungle, the kamikaze pilots crashing their planes to certain death on American and British ships—all these had been in vain. No doubt a few Japanese brooded with hopeless rancor over the failure of the Divine Mission. But for most people it was the future that counted. The war was over. Now the first thing to do was to keep alive, the second to follow American advice in the reconstruction of Japan.

The new way of life, directed from General MacArthur's office in a building opposite the palace moat, seemed in many ways revolutionary; and there was even a moment when it appeared uncertain whether the monarchy would survive.

But it endured, although radically changed. The so-called "divinity" of the emperor disappeared, together with many other traditions. A new constitution gave the emperor merely a formal status as symbol of the unity of the Japanese people. Sovereignty was firmly declared to rest with the people, and the national parliament was stated to be the "highest organ of the state." Article 9 of the constitution proclaimed that Japan would never maintain any kind of armed strength. Pacifism being now very widespread, this article was welcomed warmly by nearly everyone.

"Democracy" became a catchword on everybody's lips. Even old-fashioned extreme right-wing groups sought to escape suppression by mouthing slogans in praise of democracy, freedom, and human rights. Just as the Japanese in the 1870's and 1880's had often seemed to reject their own heritage, so in the late 1940's there was a general rejection of much that was old, stable, and therefore unfashionable. The centers of the larger cities became a babylonian extravaganza in which a tawdry brilliance, financed by the black market, was in marked contrast to extremes of social misery and corruption. Some of the most vulgar and frivolous aspects of Western life found, as they still do, a reflection in postwar Japan. Having been defeated in war, Japan seemed to be defeated again, in the moral sense, during the early years of peace. For freedom all too often became license. Crime flourished. The divorce rate rose. It seemed that the police, once ubiquitous and overbearing bullies, had become lambs.

Despite this confusion, certain apparently innate national qualities remained. Of these the most striking was the habit of hard work. The rebuilding of the shattered cities, for example, was carried out in an untidy, improvised, but very rapid fashion.

Then in the summer of 1950 came the Korean War. This provided boom conditions for Japanese industry. From this time the nation's economy began to put on a productive spurt that was to transform the face of Japan within the next six or seven years.

One very important measure, inspired by the American occupation authorities, was the Japanese land reform. This gave to the peasants, the tenant farmers, the land on which they worked. In other words, nobody was permitted to own more than a certain small acreage of cultivable land. The land reform has changed the economic basis of the average farmer's life. Relieved of the obligation of a high rent, and with a sure demand at a guaranteed price for his crop, the farmer today has at last come into his own. Farming is still very hard work. But the average farmer nowadays in Japan often has a television set in his parlor and a washing machine in the kitchen. The fact that he has money to spare for strictly nonessential consumer goods means that Japan now has a thriving home market for the products of her factories. This state of affairs did not exist in prewar years.

By 1952, the year in which the peace treaty (signed at San Francisco the previous September) came into force, Japan was on the road to total economic recovery. Yet the population in 1952 amounted to nearly 90 million, compared with 70 million in 1937. This great population continues to increase. But by 1952 the birth rate had begun to fall fairly sharply. This trend persists; and it may be that in spite of a decline in the death rate, Japan's total population will start decreasing by the end of this century.

After the occupation came to an end, Japan was still closely tied to the United States. For by a security pact, signed together with the treaty of peace, American forces were allowed to use army, navy, and air bases in Japan. Furthermore, because of the pressures of the Cold War, Japan was urged by Washington to build up her own armed forces, although these were forbidden her by the postwar, American-inspired constitution.

Neither the security pact nor rearmament have been popular in Japan. Economic recovery has led to a certain resurgence of national self-confidence. This has not gone, so far, beyond what is proper and natural. But it means that the Japanese want to be in sole charge of their own fortunes. It was to meet this kind of aspiration that the Americans greatly reduced the number of their bases in Japan. For this same reason they were ready to negotiate a revised security pact on terms more favorable, so it was thought, to Japan's interests.

As for rearmament, popular memories of the horrors of the air attacks and of the harshness and arrogance of the old semimilitary regime are still sharp enough to make most Japanese over age thirty-five dread the very thought of war, even in defense of their homeland. The present defense forces are, of course, different from the old imperial army and navy. They are not taught to die for the emperor. The old brutal, and brutalizing, discipline has not been reintroduced. The defense forces have been organized and trained very largely on the American pattern.

All the same, there is a lack of enthusiasm for these new guardians of the nation. It will take time for them to win the confidence of the Japanese people as a whole. That they will do so, however, can hardly be doubted.

Bearing all this in mind, we can begin to see more clearly why there was some general sympathy in 1960 for the students and young people who demonstrated for many days against the government for having forced through the diet a revised security pact with the United States. The big street demonstrations in Tokyo in May and June, 1960, attracted worldwide attention, particularly because the Japanese government, as a result of the agitation, asked President Eisenhower to postpone his planned visit to Japan. In much of the world's press, this was described as a victory for Moscow and Peking. But strictly from the Japanese standpoint, the President's visit was not the central issue. Later that summer Mr. Eisenhower could have visited Japan with every assurance of a sincerely friendly welcome. What the students and the great processions of Tokyo citizens were asking for was the resignation of the cabinet. Hundreds of foreigners, most of them Americans, watched the demonstrations and processions with anxious interest. Not one of them was physically harmed.

The hullabaloo achieved its aim. The cabinet resigned. Some months later the government party won a handsome victory at the polls. Basically the situation was unchanged. The new pact with America remained in force. Rearmament proceeded as before.

Thus, below the surface storms there is an evident conservatism, a disinclination among the great majority to change the present structure of society. The reason, without doubt, is the economic prosperity, uneven as it may be, of the new Japan.

This prosperity is illustrated by rising curves on production graphs, by swelling figures in tables of statistics. The flourishing export trade of Japan no longer depends, as it did in former days, mainly on the products of the textile mills. The emphasis now is on shipbuilding, heavy machinery, machine tools, electronics, and precision instruments such as cameras. Increasingly, quality is matching quantity. The old phrase "cheap Japanese goods" is losing its former two-edged meaning, for wages, too, are rising, although these are still modest and the working hours are long in many of the smaller factories. But it is now the declared aim of the government to double personal incomes, in terms of true purchasing power, by 1970. There seems no overwhelming obstacle to the achievement of this aim. For productivity continues to rise. Indeed, over the past few years the rate of economic growth in Japan has been the highest in the world.

The general standard of living in terms of food, clothing, shelter, and personal savings is now superior to that of many regions in southern Europe, and it is very much higher than that of any other country in Asia from the Yellow Sea to the Gulf of Suez. The very countryside, once such a contrast to the cities, has been mechanized. Tractors, it is true, are useless in the small rice fields of Japan. But the weeding of the fields is nearly always done with a machine that the Japanese have invented for this purpose, and the threshing of the harvested rice is done by mechanical means. Once the new network of motorable roads is finished, the farmer will be driving his own Japanese-made Toyopet convertible, and within a single generation a landless peasantry will have become a middle-class rural society. Such people detest the idea that their small properties might be collectivized at the bidding of Marxist theorists in Tokyo. They have lost all awareness of belonging to a class known, in Communist jargon, as "the toiling peasant masses."

This brings us to the question of Japan's attitude to China, a question that has loomed large, as we have seen, at other stages of Japan's long history.

A few years ago most Japanese businessmen believed that fortunes could be made if only the mainland China market were open to them, and they tended to blame the Americans for the virtual absence of trade between Japan and mainland China. Later, however, it was the Chinese themselves who put an end, in 1958, to the small trickle of commerce between the two countries.

Japan's economy has prospered in spite of the absence of the once vital China market. But if the national income is to be doubled by 1970, there will have to be larger imports of raw materials. This is certain to lead to renewed demands for unrestricted trade relations with Communist China. All the same, the Japanese realize that the Peking government uses trade as a political weapon. Japan recognizes the Nationalist government in Formosa as the lawful government of China. Peking is likely to allow trade with Japan only when the Japanese withdraw their recognition of the Nationalist government. Most Japanese writers, university professors, journalists, schoolteachers, and students would say that of course Japan ought to recognize the Peking regime as the lawful government of China. For people in these categories, whom we can call the intellectuals of Japan, usually have strong Marxist sympathies, although many of them would firmly deny that they were Communists. Indeed, the Communist Party of Japan does not have more than about 100,000 members.

Many well-educated Japanese, too, feel guilty about China. There are two reasons for this. In the first place, they know, with shame, that Japanese armies inflicted terrible sufferings on the people of China. Secondly, they know that Japanese intellectuals did not dare to protest at the time against this invasion of their neighbor's territory. In fact, worse than this, many writers and teachers climbed onto the band-wagon of nationalism and tried to justify their country's predatory behavior. The only people in Japan who actually defied the authorities and openly opposed the war in China were the few Communists who happened to be out of jail. So an entire generation of middle-aged and elderly journal-ists, scholars, and schoolteachers recall their own silence or opportunism between 1937 and 1945 with real uneasiness and regret.

As for the mass of the population, they too must be aware that Japanese troops committed outrages in China as else-where, for such crimes have been often mentioned in popular magazines and books during the past fifteen years. Finally, there are even some Japanese, of a rather conservative type, who call China a "Red radish." That is to say, if you peel the skin, you find it is white underneath, since whatever color the Peking government may be, the Chinese people have not changed and indeed cannot be changed.

So Communist China is hardly a bogy in the eyes of the average Japanese man and woman. But this does not mean that Japan is in a hurry to recognize the Peking government. There is no very pressing economic reason why she should. And if Japan did recognize Peking, then good relations with America would be subjected to a strain; and good relations with America are important to Japan because much of her economy, diplomacy, and even social structure are linked with the United States.

Soviet Russia, however, is fairly widely regarded in Japan as something of a menace. Ever since 1945 the Russians have barred the waters around Kamchatka, Sakhalin, and the Kurile Islands to Japanese fishermen. These northern seas, rich in salmon and crab, used to contribute not only to the nation's food supply, Japan being one of the world's great fish consumers, but also to Japan's export trade. The Russians, now occupying islands within sight of northern Japan, have entirely sealed off the old fishing grounds. Apart from this grievance, there is another: Japanese who fell into Russian hands in Manchuria and Sakhalin at the end of the Pacific War, in August, 1945, had to endure many hard-ships, and large numbers of them were not allowed to re-turn to Japan for several years. So although Soviet Russia, as the pioneer Communist state, enjoys some prestige among Japanese Marxists, there is in fact no widespread affection for Russia in Japan.

In the context of the Cold War, Japan is in the camp of the Free World and has no desire to be alienated from Amer-ica and Britain. Yet in the typical Japanese attitude to for-eign affairs there is a certain element of neutralism. Japan would like to be the close friend rather than the ally of the United States. The Japanese no doubt would prefer to have the pleasures of friendship without the obligations of an alliance.

There may be times when Americans are tempted to suppose that the Japanese are somewhat ungrateful and unreliable associates. It is wiser, however, to take account of the deep and lasting reconciliation that has taken place between Japan and America since 1945. For there is permanent gratitude in Japan for what America contributed during the occupation years, not in money, not even in techniques, but in helping to reshape Japanese politics and society.

It is not exactly true to say that America introduced Japan to the ways of democracy. A great many Japanese had some idea of what democracy means long before 1945. What America did do was to lift up and cast away some heavy hindrances, such as military domination and emperor worship, that had kept political democracy in a condition of stunted or retarded growth. These hindrances out of the way, America gave Japanese democracy a powerful shot in the arm with such measures as the new constitution and the land reform. More could have been done, perhaps. But from about the year 1948—this was the year of the Berlin blockade —the world situation made it seem desirable to concentrate on the revival of Japan's strength rather than on the reform of her institutions. But the encouragement given to human dignity and freedom by American precept and example was outstanding.

Even today Japanese society is by no means wholly democratic in the Western sense. Side by side with undiluted freedom of action and expression are many survivals from older, less democratic days. A true story can perhaps illustrate the point.

A few years ago, in the early 1950's, a young woman in a Japanese village discovered that a local official, much esteemed in her neighborhood, had deliberately falsified some election returns. She reported the matter to the police, and the official was convicted in court and fined for his offense. The reaction of the village to this affair brought it into the national press. For almost without exception the villagers strongly condemned the woman's behavior: they ceased communication with her; they would neither talk to her nor have any dealings with her; she was ostracized so severely that her life became virtually unbearable. The big Tokyo and Osaka newspapers praised her for her moral courage, for her sense of individual civic responsibility; and they expressed their disgust at the attitude of the villagers. This led to a flood of letters to the newspapers. Many of these praised the woman. But others sympathized with the villagers. They declared that whatever her feelings as an offended citizen, she had no right to subject the local official to the humiliation of public exposure, thereby causing not only the official but also the village community to lose face.

This kind of incident might not arise today. But the idea that the individual must speak out according to the dictates of his conscience, a Christian rather than a Buddhist concept, is still not universally accepted in Japan.

The coexistence of two sets of beliefs, of two cultures, of two ways of life, is a characteristic feature of contemporary Japan. For example, a boy in his junior-high-school years may take up the saxophone as a hobby and play nothing but modern jazz: and to the outward eye he will be completely Westernized. But in a few years he will probably hope that one of his favorite school or university teachers will choose, in cooperation with his parents, the girl whom he is to marry. The boy's sister, on the other hand, may insist on making her own choice of whom she is to marry, despite the fact that to all appearances she seems most demurely traditional, with quiet tastes such as flower arrangement and the tea ceremony.

This duality is well reflected in Japanese radio and television programs. Here swing sessions, quiz contests, and Beethoven concerts share the ether with extracts from Kabuki and Noh, the traditional forms of drama, and with performances on musical instruments dating from the Heian age. As a spectacle on television, baseball, for a great many years the best-liked outdoor sport, is no more popular than traditional Japanese wrestling.

A wealthy executive, equally adjusted to life in New York, London, and Tokyo, will take three weeks off every year in order to practice meditation in a Zen Buddhist temple, not so much to escape from the hubbub of the world (Zen meditation is no rest cure) but rather to make his mind and will more incisive for the business tussles that lie ahead.

A Van Gogh exhibition in Tokyo was attended by thousands of workmen in dungarees and by elderly connoisseurs, city clerks, students, and cabaret hostesses. Yet for all the love of beauty and art, tawdry ugliness also abounds, notably in the appearance of streets and buildings in the cities. An English poet, James Kirkup, has remarked that although the Japanese have a keen awareness of beauty, they have little awareness of what is ugly. Thus the downright hideous can exist side by side with the beautiful. Electric-power pylons, factory chimneys, and garish billboards often half obscure the view of Fuji, the world's most graceful peak. And a Disney-land-type park sullies the peace of Nara.

Yet this double image has its own fascination. Some would say that it adds a piquancy to the interest of the Japanese scene. For it may account for the fact that to foreigners in Japan it is the unexpected that always happens. To a foreigner nothing Japanese is predictable, or, if it is, this means that he himself has become half Japanese.

All the same, the ugly side of Japan—sometimes overlooked in books about that country—would be almost unbearable were it not for the fact the visitor is entranced by the warmth and courtesy of the Japanese people themselves. For they can be incomparable artists in the conduct of human relations, to a degree unimagined in many Western societies. To experience this quality of friendliness, a knowledge of the Japanese language is not essential. In their relationships with each other the Japanese operate to a marked degree by intuition. In their daily conversation they often say only two thirds of what they mean. The rest, though unspoken, is understood.

An American or European may speak Japanese with fluency. He may have expert knowledge of some aspect of Japanese history or politics or aesthetics. But nonetheless he may miss the best that the country has to offer, for if his knowledge is not infused with tolerance and affection, he is sure to be disliked. In this matter the Japanese, rich and poor alike, have certain mental antennae that are proof against the most careful dissimulation.

The Japanese are easy to like, less easy to understand, although they think of themselves as transparently straightforward by comparison with the inscrutable Occidentals of Europe and America. They are a people with a scientific, practical bent who are yet greatly swayed by their emotions, which lie very near the surface. This gives them a peculiarly formidable character for good or ill. This is the reason, finally, why Japan rose so quickly to the position of a great power, why she lost that position, and why, at least in the economic and cultural sense, she is going to regain it.

Korea

KOREA, a small nation on a peninsula in the heart of the Far East, has been since early history a battlefield for the rivalries of Japan, China, and Russia. It is a country of rugged beauty. Sharply upthrust ranges of mountains cut the country lengthwise, leaving little room for cultivation in the valleys. Yet the Korean farmer makes maximum use of his land. The checkerboard patterns of rice paddies extend wherever climate, space, and irrigation will permit.

The Korean's great longing for freedom, his inherent pride and faith in his country, have grown even stronger through the vicissitudes of war, occupation, and now division that have beset him. The Koreans are a vigorous people, not slow to show either pleasure or resentment. Their sense of humor is quick; love of the beauty of their land runs deep in their lives.

A "unified, independent, and democratic nation," though desired by the United Nations, is far from realization. Korea, "a shrimp among whales," as an old Korean proverb says, is still suffering tragically from the cruel game of power politics, a hot spot in the Cold War. After centuries of living under the protection of its "elder-brother" nation, imperial China, it was a restive colony of Japan from 1910 to 1945. Hopeful of complete freedom in a world at peace, the Korean people have seen their land become a divided country, a "front line" in the conflict of East and West, as a result of actions set in motion by worldwide forces.

In 1945 this hitherto unified peninsula was divided by the thirty-eighth parallel, a rigid barrier between two patterns of occupation, between two opposing governments.

The Communist-inspired Korean Democratic People's Republic in the north moved tanks and forces across this line on June 25, 1950. To the rescue of the Republic of Korea in the south came United Nations forces, largely American, and the Korean War was on. After three years, a truce line at an angle to the thirty-eighth parallel but close to it was agreed upon. The United States has committed itself to a firm support of the independence of the Republic of Korea; in case of renewed aggression, it is solemnly pledged to send forces to wage war again in Korea. On the other hand, the Chinese Communist forces to the north are deployed in support of the North Korean regime. It remains an explosive situation. A spark could ignite not just another "brush-fire war," but a nuclear conflagration. Thus Korea epitomizes many of the problems of Asia in the world today.

In Korea today the people are mindful of these problems, but as practical, resilient, and courageous folk they go on about the necessities of their daily life. This life is a changing mixture of the old and the new. Streetcars clang past oxcarts in the city streets. Planes take off from fields where sedan chairs might have passed in olden days. Yet the conservatism of the past has not given way entirely under the impact of technological advances. Life in the agrarian villages still follows the age-old pattern of the seasons, of rice planting and harvesting, of picklemaking before the frost, of wood gathering on snowy hills.

The Koreans are a people separate from the Chinese and Japanese, though they have absorbed and adapted many cultural features from their neighbors. Their origins as a people are shrouded in the distant past. One legend, still revered, says that in 2333 B.C. Tangun, supernaturally conceived by a bear who was transformed into a woman, founded the Korean race. This legend would tend to account for the northern origin of the Korean people. Their language and other aspects of their culture certainly have affinity with those of peoples from the Ural-Altaic regions of Siberia. Another legend tells of Kija, a sage fleeing from oppression in China who brought civilization to the wild tribes of Korea in 1122 B.C. This would indicate the strong and enduring influences of Chinese culture on Korea.

Actual recorded history in Korea goes back two thousand years to the time of a flourishing Chinese colony in Korea. Most of the peninsula and the adjacent parts of Manchuria were held by Korean tribes or kingdoms. One of them, Silla, with its capital in the southeast of the peninsula, in A.D. 668 conquered or absorbed the other kingdoms and gave Korea a stable and enlightened government. The state religion was

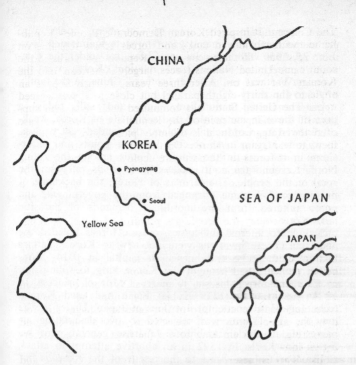

CHINA

KOREA

• Pyongyang

• Seoul

Yellow Sea

SEA OF JAPAN

JAPAN

Buddhism, imported by way of China in previous centuries. Sculptures of this period have an enduring beauty and give evidence of the advanced civilization that prevailed.

Silla's power gradually failed, its court became decadent, and religious rivalry sapped its strength. A new dynasty, Koryo, took control in A.D. 935. It was founded by a dissident Silla general, and it had its capital in west-central Korea. Confucian practices and ethics were dominant in the government, though Buddhism was strong in the life of the people. The close ties with China continued.

Also during this period, cultural advances were achieved. Noteworthy is the high degree of development in ceramic art, known today as Koryo celadon glaze.

In 1392 another general, a remarkable person, revolted and established the Yi dynasty with its capital at Seoul. The first decades of this dynasty were marked by vigorous administrative reform. A state built upon a neo-Confucian philosophical base, with civil servants chosen by examination, exercised effectual control throughout the peninsula. A simple syllable system was developed for writing the Korean language. Long before the time of Gutenberg, books were printed with movable metal type. The state maintained "correct" relations with the rulers of China, for under the Confucian pattern of international relations Korea was the "younger brother" to the "elder brother," China, in the family of Asian nations.

Unfortunately, factionalism, long—and still today—a harmful force in the political and social life of Korea, weakened the state. Confucian scholars, the landed-gentry class, spent time arguing over obscure legalistic points and differences in meaning in the classics. Feuds among the ruling families around the court isolated it from its purpose: the good of the people. The farmers of Korea, the backbone of the economy, became estranged from the government, and many suffered from the inordinate demands of parasitic landlords.

To add to internal difficulties, outside forces invaded the peninsula. These invasions were not new to Korea. Tartars had invaded Koryo and burned its capital in 1014. Mongolian invaders had brought the Koryo king to submission in 1259 and forced his son to marry a Mongol princess. In 1274 and again in 1279 Kublai Khan had used Korean bases and boats to attempt invasions of Japan. Under the Yi dynasty, also, Korea was subjected to two devastating attacks. Hideyoshi, an ambitious Japanese general, sent his forces into Korea in 1592 in an abortive attempt to attack China. The Chinese came to the rescue of the Koreans but in their turn inflicted hardships almost equally severe on the people and their land. At Hideyoshi's death in 1598, the Japanese forces were withdrawn, but legends of their brutality continue in the folklore of Korea. Soon after this tragic period, in 1636, the invading Manchus forced the Korean kings to recognize their power. In view of this chaotic history, it is small wonder that the Koreans in the latter part of the Yi dynasty sought to become a "hermit nation."

The decay of power in Manchu China and the growth of Western influence and of agressiveness in rapidly modernizing Japan forced Korea to open her doors. The first modern treaty for Korea was signed with Japan in 1876. Others quickly followed, including one with the United States in 1882. The government's strength, however, was sapped by internal difficulties as well. Korea's independence as a modern nation was short-lived. In 1894–1895 the Sino-Japanese War established the ascendancy of Japan in Korean affairs, the Russo-Japanese War of 1904–1905 confirmed this, and Korea became a protectorate (1907) and then a colony (1910) of Japan. The Yi dynasty was absorbed into the royal court of Japan, and Japanese governor-generals, always military officers, controlled "Chosen," the Japanese name for their colony.

Japanese rule in Korea was harsh. A high Japanese official characterized the goals of the educational system thus: "The Koreans shall be taught to follow, not to know." They established a police system that strictly controlled the people. The Korean peninsula was a source of raw materials, particularly rice for the growing cities of Japan. Great economic development took place. Partially for militarily strategic purposes, a railroad network was built; mines producing coal, iron-ore tungsten, and gold were opened; and harbors were constructed. The urban centers grew. Yet this was an economic change of exploitation where most of the benefit went to the Japanese and to a few wealthy Koreans. The population increased from an estimated 12 million in 1910 to 24.3 million in 1940. Thus increased economic production was not matched by increased economic well-being for the average Korean. As Japan became involved in its continental adventures—the taking of Manchuria in 1931, embarking on the Chinese War in 1937, the Pacific War in 1941—Korea grew more and more closely knit to Japan's war economy. Bitterly resentful of the actions of their Japanese overlords, they welcomed with joy the freeing of their land from Japanese domination in August, 1945.

This joy was soon tempered, however, by the realization that their land was being divided into two zones for the purposes of accepting the surrender of the Japanese forces, one to be controlled by Russia, the other by America. The thirty-eighth parallel cut through cities and villages, across mountain ridges and rivers. It made a very poor political boundary, but it rapidly became such, as divergent political development took place on each side. Attempts to unify Korea by peaceful means, through conferences in Moscow or Seoul, were not successful. The military means embarked upon by the Communists in the north in 1950 were equally unsuccessful. Korea remains a divided land.

Though Korea has long been unified historically and socially, there are significant geographic differences between the north and south regions. The north is a land of high mountains and limited agricultural area where only one crop may be grown in a year. The south, with winters somewhat less cold, has many fields on the more extensive plains, where winter wheat or barley can be cultivated. Partly as a consequence of this, the population of the south is double that of the north. There are more mineral wealth and hydroelectric-power resources in the north, which had led the Japanese to develop heavy industries there. Most of the industries of the south were food-processing and other consumer-based industries. As a result, the artificial division of Korea has served to accentuate its latent geographical and economic differences. If the complementary parts were ever again united, the economy would be much stronger; but instead, today, both regions are dependent upon large amounts of external economic assistance for survival.

In the north the Communist Party, relying on the help of the Soviet Union and Communist China and working through a political organization that ostensibly includes minority parties, exercises a tight control over the people. In the days before the Korean War, when restrictions were not so rigid, approximately two million Koreans migrated from the north to the south, a fact that bears eloquent testimony to the harshness and unpopularity of the Communist regime. Under tight state control, agricultural cooperatives and state farms regulate the life of the farmers, who make up the bulk of the people. Industrial production has been expanded, and cities and transportation lines rebuilt after their destruction during the Korean War. The leader is Kim Il-sung, a Russian-trained Communist; and many military figures, winnowed through the experiences of the Korean War, have been appointed to high posts in the government.

Military and economic aid have been poured into North Korea from the Soviet Union and her Eastern European satellites. Since their entry into the Korean War, the Chinese Communists have been playing a major military and economic role. There are some indications that North Korea is becoming more and more an economic appendage of the industrially developing area of Manchuria and North China. With a well-equipped army of about 400,000 Korean troops and the ability to call upon Communist China for assistance (readily available from across the Yalu), the North Korean regime is in a strong position. Today it poses a serious threat to South Korea just as it did in 1950.

The American occupying forces in South Korea did not, as the Russians did in the north, quickly develop a local regime to whom they could turn over control. Instead, they tried in vain through conferences to have Korea unified. Finally, in 1947, the United States referred the problems of Korea's political future to the United Nations. After being denied access to the north, the United Nations Temporary Commission on Korea supervised elections for a Korean government in South Korea. Syngman Rhee, who had spent decades in exile in the United States, was elected president of the Republic of Korea, and it was to his regime that General MacArthur gave over control on August 15, 1948. The United States naturally continued to be concerned with Korea, and through the years has furnished large amounts of economic and military assistance.

The supreme crisis for the Republic of Korea came in 1950, when it was invaded from the north. The republic was just beginning to make significant economic and social gains when the war started. The Korean War followed some of the classical patterns of centuries before, when the forces of Hideyoshi and the Chinese met on the Korean peninsula. The North Koreans, equipped with Russian-made tanks, easily cut through the South Korean defenses at the thirty-eighth parallel. After capturing Seoul, they swept south with a major force, going along the classic route toward Pusan in southeast Korea. With the assistance of American forces, the United Nations command was able to regroup some of the South Korean forces and to hold a beachhead around Pusan. From this base and with a landing at Inchon, near Seoul on the west coast, the United Nations and Korean forces were able to roll back the invaders and advance into North Korea. As they approached Manchuria and were putting the North Korean forces to rout, the Chinese Communists threw in massive forces of "volunteers." Again Seoul was lost, but freed once again as the United Nations forces met this new force. Finally a military, and political, stalemate developed, and an uneasy truce was signed.

Syngman Rhee with his courageous stubbornness was a rallying symbol for the Koreans during the war. However, during the years that followed he became less and less able to provide the leadership needed, and was isolated from political realities by a small group around him. Well into his eighties, he ran for president again in the elections of March, 1960. Since his chosen candidate for vice-president, Kipoong Lee, had not been elected in 1956, Rhee's supporters used all sorts of means, including graft and corruption, to assure the election of both Rhee and his running mate. There were riots in some places over the tight police control of the election. In the month that followed, agitation over the flagrant denials of democratic rights increased. Students were particularly active in these movements. On April 19 a march that students led to present a petition to Rhee was fired on by the police. This greatly shocked the country and led to the resignation of Rhee and his departure for Hawaii, to the suicide of Kipoong Lee and his family, and to new elections for a less autocratic form of government. A critical factor in these changes was the attitude of the leaders of the Korean armed forces, who withdrew their support from the politicians who surrounded Rhee and who opposed the use of police power.

On the basis of elections held on July 29, a government headed by John M. Chang was formed. This new democratically inspired government faced many difficulties. The vigorous leadership needed to combat corruption and to provide incentives for economic and social development was lacking. The party in power was riven by personal jealousies and internecine disputes. During the first months there were attempts at reform, but they met with little success.

On May 16, 1961, a group of army officers staged a coup and seized power. Premier Chang was arrested, though Posun Yun, the titular president, was allowed to remain in office. The legislative bodies were dissolved, but elections were promised for 1963. Military officers were placed in the various embassies and ministries. After a short period in the background, a young general, Chunghee Park, emerged as the strong man of the new regime and became chairman of the all-powerful Supreme Council for National Reconstruction. A Five-Year-Plan for economic development was blueprinted. Certain industrialists who were convicted of tax evasion were required to build new factories as payment of their fines, a neat joining of the purposes of the government. There were various other reforms. For example, in the educational system, national examinations for admission and graduation were instituted. There were some moves to improve relations with Japan, particularly for trade and economic investment.

The great desire for a better life on the part of the fast-growing population poses a basic challenge to the new regime. With the necessity for large expenditures for national defense along the "truce line," the government has a continuing need for financial support from the United States. To maintain its rightful position in the modern world, however, it will need to continue in courageous and imaginative action on its own part.

India

Past and Present

ON AUGUST 15, 1947, the people of India achieved sovereignty as a newly independent dominion in the British Commonwealth of Nations. Shortly thereafter they adopted a constitution under which their nation became a republic based upon universal adult suffrage and the parliamentary system. Thus was created the world's most populous democracy, seventh in size among the nations of the world. The birth pangs of the republic were exhilarating but painful, studded with moments of anguish. When independence was granted to India, the subcontinent was divided into two new nations: India and Pakistan. This partition was accompanied by a mass exodus as Muslims hurried north to Pakistan and Hindus fled south to India. Murder, arson, and pillage harried the refugees moving in both directions. Religious fervor had turned men's minds.

The turmoil, the promise, and the pageantry that marked the birth of the two new nations were the modern unfolding of an ancient drama with brilliant-hued contrasts and angry passions. Independence meant accomplishment and expectations in a setting marked by sharp contrasts between the old and the new. Part of the drama lies in the fact that antique symbols and ways of doing things exist side by side with modern scientific and technological installations. Today, in rapid transition between medieval and modern, the story unfolds of how a gifted people threw off foreign rule to become a pivotal state of our time, an emerging industrial giant in the East.

Independence, the culmination of a lengthy development, is also the prologue to a new era, and it raises a host of questions vital to us all. Will India's links with the West grow in strength, or will they weaken? Will her age-old traditions revive, or will they finally be modernized and replaced by Western ways? Will success be achieved in India's epic struggle for rapid economic development? Will parliamentary democracy survive, or will a Communist regime take power? To seek the answers to such questions, we must comprehend the significance of India's past, the implications of British rule and Western influences, and the amalgam that is in the making.

The known human history of the subcontinent stretches back over a period of at least 4,500 years to a time when civilization was in its infancy everywhere. Throughout that vast sweep of time, a rich variety of peoples, carrying distinctive cultures and traditions, have shared the subcontinent or fought to control it. To understand India today we must come to know the India of a fabled past in all its important dimensions.

Physical Background

Study of a globe will make it clear that the South Asian subcontinent is the most prominent landmass in its part of the world, jutting southward from Asia to cleave and control the Indian Ocean. It is larger than all of Europe, excluding the Soviet Union. The subcontinent stretches almost 2,100 miles from north to south and a somewhat greater distance east to west, from the borders of Iran to the frontier with Burma. Great variations in elevation, in climate, and in surface conditions coexist in South Asia. In the north, the icy Himalayas contain the highest peaks in the world. In the northwest there is a large and growing area of desert, whereas in the northeast we find swamps, great rivers, and heavy rainfall.

Portions of the subcontinent lie barely above sea level. Heavy forests, deserts, great valleys, fertile plains, malarial swamps, and open plateaus combine to give the land a richly variegated face. Stark contrasts between the different seasons reinforce the overarching impression of change and variation. Physical and cultural differences among the people of the subcontinent match and seem to reflect the variety of terrain and climate. As if to underline the complexity, the people of South Asia have produced three major religions and several minor religious faiths.

South Asia experiences a wide range of climatic conditions because of its size and location. Variations in tem-

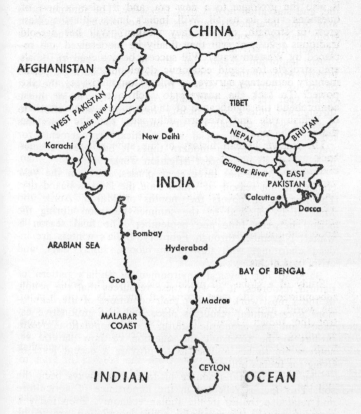

perature, rainfall, and humidity patterns influence vegetation as well as cultivation. The rains in particular are of special importance to man. In South Asia rainfall, with its life-giving supply of water, is controlled by the annual monsoon pattern. Indian agriculture depends to a large extent upon the coming of the rains.

The summer monsoon, bringing the rain, crosses India from west to east. Overland, the rush of wet air turns north-ward and then swings back toward the northwest, more or less following the line of the Ganges toward the Punjab. Most of the rain has fallen by the time this air reaches the southern face of the Himalayas. At times, however, the monsoon air mingles too quickly with dry air coming south from Central Asia. If that happens, the wet monsoon is "dried out" and the much-needed rains fail. Then crops die, and starvation hovers over the scene. The summer rains may bring local floods, but this does not prevent the peasant from making a modest offering at the village shrine so as to ensure their arrival.

An important feature of the monsoon pattern is its brevity. Most of India's annual rainfall comes during a period of six to eight weeks during the summer. During the rest of the year very little rain falls. As a result, a major theme throughout India's long history has been man's effort to conserve water through the dry months. In early times this led to a variety of social and political arrangements for water conservation; in modern times it has been reflected in an emphasis upon great irrigation works.

India's climate has three clear phases. Early in the year comes the hot season, at which time the land is baked dry. The hot season covers the months of March, April, and May. It is followed by the summer monsoon during the period between June and September. The final season is winter, November through February. India's winters are indeed charming, with flowers in bloom, sunny days, and crisp, cool nights.

Basic to her physical environment is India's pattern of natural resources. It is with these resources that the people of India must work to better their conditions of life. Limitations upon natural resources place limits on productive capacity and the economic future. Rapid population growth pushes to the forefront the question of how natural resources are to be used so as to provide a decent level of living for India's millions.

The basic natural resource of India has always been the soil. This fact is reflected in the importance of agriculture and related activities in the Indian economy. Even today a majority of the economically active population are to be found in agriculture or in employment closely connected with agriculture. As population soars, the capability of the Indian land becomes especially important.

The first fact to bear in mind is that much of the soil that can be cultivated in India is already under cultivation. There are no important reserves of cultivable land awaiting development. Perhaps two thirds of the land could be cultivated; however, scarcity of rain limits the land that can actually be used to a lower figure unless expensive irrigation works are installed. Currently almost fifty-three percent of the land area is reported to be under crops or in fallow. Approximately sixteen percent of the total area consists of wasteland or land used for nonagricultural purposes. Forests cover fifteen percent of the total. The remaining sixteen percent includes scrub, pasture, cultivable waste, and firewood patches. The land classified as cultivable waste is largely submarginal and would not repay the cost involved in bringing it into use. Part of the land under cultivation depends upon monsoon rains, which are notoriously unreliable. This good land needs irrigation if its production is to be maintained or improved.

Land use in India falls into one of several major categories. The first is irrigation cultivation, which is quite common in the upper Gangetic plain and in East Punjab. In the past few years the irrigated area has been considerably increased and spread to other parts of the country. Irrigated lands are of special significance because of their dependable production and because yields per acre average high for India.

Dry cultivation is the second major type of land use in India. It is found most commonly in the uplands of the Deccan plateau. Yields per acre are usually rather low, and dry soils have to be put in fallow frequently. By contrast, wet cultivation is practiced in the semitropical lowlands, which receive at least forty inches of rain each year. Wet cultivation in India is usually on an intensive basis and produces more than dry land.

Land use in India is not very efficient, yields are low, and stable water supplies are badly needed in large areas not now so served. A variety of traditional social practices conspire with widespread poverty to perpetuate inefficiency and produce low yields. This is a crucial problem in a land where so many people depend upon the soil for their living.

The subsoil mineral resources of India are on the whole rather good. India produces bauxite, chromite, coal, copper, gold, iron, manganese, mica, salt, and sulfur. In coal, important for industry, India is well situated, with good reserves that lie in easily mined fields. At the present rate of use, India has proven reserves of good coking coal to last almost sixty-five years. Unfortunately, the oil resources of the subcontinent are meager. But there are vast deposits of low-grade coal from which liquid fuels can be distilled. In addition, India can produce large quantities of power alcohol from molasses.

India's industrial-power potential is greatly improved because of important resources in unused hydroelectric waterpower. Recent data suggest that at least twenty-five million additional kilowatt-hours could be developed. To date only a small part of this potential has been captured, but the government of India is building impressive new hydroelectric-power plants.

India is fairly rich in high-grade iron ore and alloy minerals. Fortunately the largest reserves of good iron ore lie in Bihar, not far from the major coal fields. India also has impressive reserves of rock phosphate, from which fertilizers can be produced. Among the strategic minerals, India produces ilmenite, pitchblende, beryls, monazite, and manganese. Indian deposits of bauxite for aluminum are vast, and she has a near monopoly on world production of mica. Good-grade granites, slates, sandstone, and marble are to be found in sufficient quantities for foreseeable needs. Improvements in transport facilities, in extraction processes, and in refinement techniques can be expected to increase the practical importance of these mineral resources.

Races, Languages, and Religions

In the midst of these diverse resources, climatic conditions, and terrain features reside a dense and diversified variety of peoples. Their ancestors infiltrated the subcontinent from Central Asia and from the Middle East and mingled with the original inhabitants of South Asia, who dated from prehistoric times. Present estimates indicate the population of South Asia to be about 565 million. Of the total, approximately 438 million are citizens of India and 94 million inhabit Pakistan. The rest live in Afghanistan, Bhutan, Ceylon, Nepal, and Sikkim. India overshadows her South Asian neighbors completely in respect to population.

Throughout the history of the subcontinent there has been an endless succession of invasions by various peoples. This has resulted in complexity of physical and cultural types and a wide range of ethnic groupings. Certainly the diversity in ethnic and cultural origins is as great as that of Europe. Similarly, there are as many important languages in South Asia as there are in Europe. It is impossible to arrive at clear-cut statements about racial and ethnic types in India because of a great deal of mixing extended over a long period of time. However, a majority of the people are basically Caucasian. Beyond this, little can be said. There is no such thing as a typical Indian.

While ethnic origins may mean little, cultural differences are important. In prehistoric India the dominant cultural type seems to have emerged from the Neolithic era as city builders with settled agriculture. The ruins of the earliest cities in the subcontinent—Mohenjo-Daro and Harappa— have been uncovered in the Indus valley. These great cities are dated between 2500 B.C. and 1500 B.C. The early, dark-skinned people who probably built the cities are usually called Dravidians. Apparently they have continued into the modern era as an important element among the lower classes.

In historical times, 1500 B.C. to 1000 B.C., tribes of Central Asian pastoral people, called Indo-Aryans, migrated into North India. The Aryans spread out slowly across the great north Indian plain in the direction of Benares on the Ganges. Despite considerable conflict between Aryans and the indigenous peoples, there was a blending of cultural traits as well as a steady process of racial intermingling. It was this mixture of Aryan and indigenous traits that produced the complex culture known to us as Hindu civilization.

The Aryan "invasion" was, however, only the first of a long series of invasions. The year 1526 witnessed the last major invasion, when Baber led his Mogul cavalry down into India for the conquest that established the great Mogul dynasty. In the two thousand five hundred years between the last Aryan influx and the coming of the Moguls, there were repeated invasions by Greeks (under Alexander the Great), by Sakas and Kushans from Asia, by Tamerlane and his Mongols, and by Afghan, Persian, and Turkic peoples from southwest Asia. Each invasion or infiltration has added its distinctive bit to the cauldron, laying decorative tiers upon the foundations built by the Dravidians and their Aryan conquerors.

As would be expected, the repeated invasions of north India by different cultural and ethnic bands have greatly increased the linguistic repertory of the subcontinent. Language groupings have served to mark people off from one another, especially on a regional-cultural basis. Each major language occupies a central area whose linguistic borders spread outward to overlap the boundaries of neighboring language areas. The borders between language areas are normally zones of transition, with bilingual populations intermixed. However each major language has its own "homeland."

The major languages fall into several groupings. The most important, both in terms of numbers and in historical significance, is the Indo-Aryan group. From the Pakistan border north of Delhi southward almost to Hyderabad in the Deccan, Indo-Aryan languages are dominant. Each of these languages is related to the group of dialects spoken by the Aryan invaders, one of which later developed into Sanskrit. India has eleven major Indo-Aryan languages, each spoken by a substantial number of people.

First among the Indo-Aryan languages is Hindi, the lingua franca of the northern plains. Hindi serves as a general means of communication in this wide area and has spread outside the area to other parts of India. It has a wider use than any other Indian language. In view of this and because of its cultural significance, Hindi is the official language of the Republic of India. At least 120 million Indians live in the region where Hindi is the standard means of communication. A modified version of Hindi is known as Urdu. Spoken Hindi and Urdu may vary only moderately, but the literary versions of the two are not so easily understood by speakers of either since one borrows its learned vocabulary from Sanskrit, whereas the other, used chiefly by Muslims, borrows from Persian and Arabic and writes in the Perso-Arabic script.

Marathi, also an Indo-European language, is spoken primarily in western India in the region known as Maharashtra. About thirty million Indians are Marathi speakers at present. The Marathi language has well-developed prose and poetry, some of it dating back several centuries. Another important language in western India is Gujarati. It also has a literature many centuries old. In eastern India the major Indo-Aryan tongue is Bengali, spoken by at least twenty-six million people. In modern times, Bengali has experienced the most remarkable revival and development of any language in the group. Its literature, including much prose influenced by Western literary forms, is extensive and has had an important impact on modern Indian thought, literary style, and politics. Oriya, the Indo-Aryan language of the Orissa region, is less well developed as a literary form and probably has no more than thirteen million speakers, whereas Assamese is the mother tongue of six million inhabitants of Assam. In northern India an important language is Panjabi.

There are several important Dravidian languages whose speakers dwell in south India. Four of the Dravidian languages are significant because of their numbers of speakers and their literary influence: Kanarese, Malayalam, Tamil, and Telugu. Together these languages include approximately ninety million speakers who live in the south. They are basically separate from the Indo-Aryan languages of the north. Long-standing political and cultural differences between the "Aryan" north and the "Dravidian" south are reinforced by the separateness of the two language groups.

Sino-Tibetan languages are spoken along the border between India and Tibet, and there is a family of languages called Munda. Though spoken by small numbers of people, this multitude of languages has led to cultural fragmentation in India. In recent years, language loyalty has been an important political factor, with many strident demands for political self-determination for the cultural area of each major language. Recently the government of India has permitted the redrawing of state boundaries so as to satisfy the demands of those who insist that political boundaries should mirror linguistic and cultural boundaries.

Historically, two forces have been at work. The one was regional and local, as discussed above. Language differences reinforced localism. The other was the overarching influence of Hindu culture, carried in the Sanskritic literature, which sought to penetrate and unify the many local variants. Over the centuries Hindu culture has spread among the people of India to provide at least the basis for unification. A major question today is whether such unification has succeeded.

An interesting result of British rule in a land of such diversity is that the English language plays the role of a lingua franca as much as or more than any Indian language. Although speakers of English are a small minority in the population, they are to be found in all of the important cities of India. Up to now, speakers of English have held high prestige positions in government, public life, and the modern professions. Most of the important newspapers and magazines are printed in English. In view of these facts, the Indian constitution lists English as an official language.

Ethnic, cultural, and linguistic diversity is accompanied by significant differences based upon belief in one or another major religion. The partition that produced India and Pakistan is dramatic testimony to the role of religion in public affairs. It reflected the unwillingness of the followers of Islam, i.e., the Muslims, to remain part of a nation in which Hindus would always be the majority. In addition to differences between religions, it is a fact that Hinduism means different things to its followers and creates numerous divisions of sect, caste, or system of belief.

Religion plays a prominent role in public affairs and in social relations in India. Hinduism, Buddhism, Islam, and the Sikh religion dress their followers in quite different social practices and dietary laws as well as marriage regulations and other customs. In India religion has considerable influence on almost all aspects of life. Religion cuts across other loyalties to add to the complexity of the whole.

Hinduism is the leading religion of India. About two thirds of the people of India belong to one or another of its sects or castes. In almost every part of India Hindus outnumber the followers of other religions by a wide majority. The age-old influence of Hinduism is to be seen in every corner of the land. Hinduism contains a central cluster of beliefs upon which most Hindus would agree, but of greater importance is its role as a distinctive way of life. Within Hinduism each caste and sect ideally lives under a specific set of rules that cover their rituals, their style of life, their beliefs, and their approved occupations. Some of the crucial rules are those embodied in the caste system that maintain ritual and social distance between the various compartments of society. However, there are some basic themes that bind Hindus together.

There are some holy days that are held in common by all Hindus regardless of caste, sect, or regional affiliation. Pilgrimage to noted temples, sacred mountains, and holy rivers is widespread. Veneration of the cow, as well as a general respect for all animal life, is a common Hindu trait, as is respect for the Brahman (priestly) caste. Most Hindus would agree that the ancient Hindu holy books, the Vedas, are sacred. Belief in the Hindu doctrine of reincarnation is quite widespread. There is common acceptance of the idea of karma: the sum of the effects created by a person's previous acts. Most Hindus believe that reincarnation reflects the karma each of us has "earned" by our past behavior.

The caste system is a central feature of Hinduism. It separates all Hindus from non-Hindus. It places each Hindu in a compartment that is in some ways separate from the compartments of others who do not share his lot by birth. Each Hindu is born a member of one or another caste, depending upon the caste of his parents. No Hindu may move from one caste to another except by rebirth. The customs and rules of each caste govern many aspects of the life of each caste member. A basic rule of caste forbids marriage outside of one's own caste group. Other rules define the acceptable occupations for each caste and regulate social distance and social contact between members of one caste and another. The rules of social distance are especially important with regard to physical contact and the sharing of food. There are limitations on the kinds of food one is allowed to eat after it has been touched by a member of a lower caste. As a whole, the caste system is organized and ranked in a hierarchical fashion. There are regional variations in the order of rank assigned to the various castes, but despite exceptions the same general rank order holds good for major castes in all parts of India. The Brahman caste is always ranked at or very close to the top of the caste ladder. Everywhere in India one finds the "untouchable" groups, whose members are limited to menial and unclean tasks. In all parts of India these people are at the bottom of the caste system. These patterns are breaking down today, at least in the cities.

In the past each separate caste had a preferred occupation. But the system never operated perfectly, and the modern era has further weakened the occupational significance of caste, leaving it a ritual and social mechanism. For more than a hundred years prominent Indian thinkers have debated caste, and a number of them have condemned it. The constitution forbids any role to caste in public life and sets up legal punishment for discrimination based on caste; but the old ways die slowly, and caste continues to govern basic matters such as marriage, ritual purity, and handling of food.

The development of caste has reflected another widespread characteristic of Hinduism: the ability of Hindu society to accept and absorb new elements into its fold. This is done by assigning them, and their distinctive traits, to a position in the caste system as a new and separate unit. It could be said that there is room for everyone in the Hindu household, but each group has its own separate quarters. The unusual tolerance of Hinduism is shown by the willingness of any one caste to let the other castes govern their members by their own distinctive sets of customs and rules. As a result there has been little uniformity in Hindu society.

India has produced not only Hinduism but also Buddhism, another world religion. Its founder, Gautama Buddha, was born of a petty Hindu ruling family. Dissatisfied with life as he saw it, Gautama retired into meditation and therein secured the enlightenment that he taught as the Middle Path. Upon this foundation the Buddhist faith was built. Before the birth of Christ, Buddhism was an all-India religion that was sending its missionaries into the rest of Asia. Thereafter, although Buddhism became a world religion outside its homeland, its importance in India declined. By the twelfth century A.D. Hinduism was firmly reestablished as the dominant religion of India, and followers of Buddhism were hardly to be found.

India has given birth to two other important religions. One of these, Jainism, was popularized contemporaneously with Buddhism and, like it, was an offshoot of Hindu thinking. Jainism places great emphasis on absolute noninjury to any form of life. Jain monks frequently wear a cloth face cover to prevent inhalation of tiny insects, and few Jains will practice agriculture because of possible injury to insects while cultivating. The other important religion produced in India is quite unlike Jainism. The religion of the Sikhs resulted from a fusion of certain Hindu ideas with ideas picked from Islam. Sikhism came to stress the idea of a militant "brotherhood," united in veneration of a sacred book, the *Granth*. Each Sikh is clearly marked off from his Hindu or Muslim neighbors by several distinctive symbols, such as the long beard and the Sikh turban. The Sikhs have recently agitated for a separate Sikh state within the Indian Union. This reflects the fact that most of the Sikhs live in East Punjab.

The other major religion of the subcontinent developed in the Middle East and first appeared in India during the eighth century. During the eleventh and twelfth centuries Islam was spread through north India by hardy Muslim conquerors. Today there are approximately 140 million Muslims in the subcontinent, of whom over 40 million live in India and the rest in Pakistan and Afghanistan. Between 1200 and the mid-eighteenth century, Muslim rulers were dominant in north and central India. When the British took power in India, it was largely from Muslim hands that the scepter fell. Until 1857 a nominal Mogul emperor "ruled" at Delhi (with British permission) as a slight but visible symbol of the greatness of Islam in India. For years thereafter, Indian Muslims could brood over their loss of power. In a sense, Indian Islam never accepted a future on equal terms with the Hindus who had formerly been ruled by Muslim kings. This fact helped to support dreams of a revived Islamic state.

The separatist tendency in Indian Islam reflects religious as well as political factors. There is a marked difference between Hinduism and Islam. Whereas Hinduism includes polytheistic beliefs with numerous gods, Islam is rigorously monotheistic. There is but one God, Allah, for all Muslims. Islam condemns idol worship, whereas Hindus have expressed their rich feeling for nature in their idols. In Islamic theory there is no room for caste; Islam is supposedly a true brotherhood of the faithful. Each Muslim has a clear and simple creed and a single sacred book, the Koran. Hinduism has none of these features. Hinduism includes a bewildering multiplicity of beliefs, practices, and sects. Centuries of contact between the two religions have done little to soften the contrasts. Despite some intermarriage and conversions from Hinduism to Islam, the differences remained great. In the modern era political and economic considerations strengthened the contrasts and laid the basis for competition and conflict.

India has also been the home of certain minority religions, such as the Parsees. They are the descendants of a group of immigrant Persians and have become an important community in terms of economic and intellectual leadership. There are approximately eight million Christians in India, divided into Catholic and Protestant sects. There is also a small community of indigenous Jews and many groups of hill folk who follow animistic-worship cults.

The Arts and Literature

India has been outstanding in her creativity in the arts. The wonder that was India is based upon an artistic tradition that stretches back to the earliest levels of the Harappa ruins that have been excavated. Since the days of Harappa and Mohenjo-Daro, religious themes have been dominant in all Indian fields of creativity. The impressive and lyric Vedic hymns were religious. The great *Upanishads* of classical Hindu philosophy were concerned with metaphysics. The famous epics *Mahabharata* and *Ramayana* place great emphasis upon ethical understanding. The *Bhagavad-Gita* (Song of the Blessed One), an independent portion of the *Mahabharata,* is a profound statement of Hindu religious thought as well as a moving piece of poetry. Sanskrit drama, which was highly developed, drew most of its themes from religious sources.

The era of the Gupta empire (fourth to seventh centuries A.D.) saw the highest expression of classical Sanskritic culture, art, and literature. Kalidasa, India's greatest dramatist and poet, lived at the Gupta court and embellished the age with his *Shakuntala,* a play that has influenced men such as Goethe in the West. He was also the author of the most famous Sanskrit lyric poem, *Meghaduta* (The Cloud Messenger). In the post-Gupta period, remarkable South Indian poets composed in Tamil. During the medieval period the Rajput courts were adorned by bards who sang tales of Rajput heroes.

As a society in which a hereditary priest class dominated the scene and more or less monopolized literacy, India's literary heritage includes much that is relevant to the religious profession. The sutras, for example, deal with ceremonials, rites, and customary law. Among the sutras are texts on grammar, on metrics, and on astronomy. Panini's Sanskrit grammar, written perhaps by 500 B.C., remains to this day an outstanding achievement. Indian work in mathematics, though less impressive, contributed what we call "Arabic" numerals to the West, as well as the crucial concept of the Zero. The priestly tradition also created a body of law, called the *shastras*. The oldest of these is the famous law code of Manu. It has long been the duty of Brahman pundits to know and explain this law to rulers and other laymen whose lives it was supposed to govern.

Indian art forms have been equally rich and even more variegated in their content and expression. Indian art is to be found at its classical best in magnificent sculpture and in a highly decorative temple architecture. Indian art has also been expressed in splendid handicrafts in cloth, wood, metals, and leather. When the Europeans began to trade with India, it was her handicrafts that were in most demand. There is also a colorful folk-art tradition in rude materials such as clay. Painting has an illustrious history, beginning with the ancient Ajanta cave paintings and coming down through fine schools of Rajput and Mogul painting in North India.

The Muslims brought to India their own literary and artistic traditions. Since the Islamic faith does not permit artistic reproduction of living beings, Muslim art and architecture have stressed complex floral and geometric designs. These designs, including magnificent inlay in stone, are to be seen on fine metalwork and as decorations on mosques and tombs. The famed Taj Mahal, built during the seventeenth century in Agra, represents at its best the grace and skill of Indo-Muslim architects.

India has been the home of impressive classical music and dance. There has also been a strong tradition of folk music and dance. Indian dance and music express in complicated and graceful form the great themes of the Hindu religion. The dance is highly stylized and is accompanied by complicated gestures of symbolic meaning. It takes years to train the classical dancer and musician in their sophisticated arts. Both music and dance are richly rewarding experiences for the spectator, especially since the dance is in fact a fluid drama.

These artistic, literary, and cultural motifs are the product of centuries. The foundations, laid by the Aryans as their culture mingled with that of the Dravidian peoples, became the basis for the tradition that has developed over the centuries. The striking fact is that the early Aryan-with-Dravidian foundation has been able to stamp its imprint on almost everything that has been added subsequently. Hindu art motifs of the last century contain recognizable elements that were present two thousand years ago. There is also an unbroken line of religious speculation and literature.

When the Aryans came to India their society was based on a simple class system consisting of Brahmans (priests), Kshatriyas (warrior-nobles), Vaisyas (respectable cultivators and artisans), and Sudras (menials). Over a period of time the Aryan class system changed and became the rigid caste system that stresses precise gradations, ritual purity, and social distance. On the political side, a number of Aryan kingdoms developed in north India as early as 700 B.C. During the next few centuries the fundamentals of Brahmanic Hinduism were evolved, and the way of life of classical India first received its characteristic shape.

Alexander the Great led a Greek army into northwest India during the fourth century B.C. He stayed only a short time, but the invasion began a period of cultural interchange between north India and western Asia. The first Indian empire was created by King Chandragupta Maurya shortly after

Alexander withdrew. The Mauryan empire spread over much of north and central India, incorporating petty states. Contemporary accounts describe the Mauryan empire as a highly centralized state under a numerous and organized bureaucracy. The agents of the emperor were everywhere. Tight controls were maintained over trade, and spies were used to uncover sedition and unrest. The army was of impressive size, and was used to extend the boundaries of the kingdom. The ruler lived amidst great pomp and ceremony, surrounded by an oligarchy of officials, nobles, priests, and royal relatives.

Chandragupta's grandson, the celebrated Asoka, ruled the empire at its peak. Under him the empire included part of Afghanistan, all of north India (Hindustan), and part of the Deccan. After a bloody war of conquest, Asoka was converted to Buddhism and renounced war. He then devoted himself to Buddhist missionary enterprise and to peaceful construction. His great edicts, carved on rocks and on pillars, show him to have been a pious, just, and enlightened ruler. He insisted upon religious toleration, and his court is said to have been the home of famed poets and artists. However, too much depended upon his unique personality, and after his death, the empire began to disintegrate. There followed a fresh Greek invasion of Sind and the Punjab, but the Greeks were followed by more troublesome invaders from Central Asia, the Sakas and then the Kushans.

Shortly after the beginning of the fourth century A.D., a new empire arose in north India. It reached its peak under the celebrated Chandragupta II, who ruled between A.D. 385 and 413. His capital was the center of classical Sanskritic art and literature, boasting the presence of Kalidasa, the famous poet. Distinguished architects and sculptors embellished the land with beautiful buildings. However, new invasions from Central Asia brought turmoil and the collapse of Gupta power. The end of Gupta power led to a revival of separate warring states. In the post-Gupta period, Buddhism faltered and lost its hold on India.

South India had had only minor contact with the north up to this time, and Hinduized Dravidian kingdoms dominated the peninsula. Important among the south Indian kingdoms were the Cholas in Madras, the Pallavas to their north, and the Keralas in Travancore. The Pallavas and Cholas were enterprising seafarers and traders. Chola ships sailed to Siam and Java, bringing parts of Southeast Asia under Indian cultural influence. They also traded with the Arabs and through them with Rome. Collections of Roman coins have been dug up in the peninsula, proving the early demand for Indian handicrafts in the West.

The revival of Hinduism as the dominant faith in India

was in part the work of south Indian religious leaders. The greatest of these, Shankaracharya, reformed Hinduism and gave it a better organizational structure. He created a powerful all-India order of monks based upon four primary temples that he established in different parts of the country. Shankaracharya brought Hinduism back into contact with the masses by his organizational efforts. Tamil holy men, meanwhile, taught a new emphasis upon the devotional side of the religion. This appealed to the common folk and suited their needs.

This was an important era for strengthening fundamental Hindu traits. This period reinforced the Hindu emphasis upon other-world ends for man. The hermits had made the spiritual quest a matter of deep meditation. Though this attitude became important in Hinduism, the average man could not seek solace in a forest hermitage. The new emphasis upon devotion and on mystic communion with a savior-deity made it possible for the Hindus to participate in their religion in a meaningful fashion. They could accept its world-renouncing ideas without having to abandon their normal earthly obligations.

Islam was brought to India initially by Muslims from the Persian Gulf. At first their effect on India was slight. Later, important Muslim invasions carried Islam into the heart of India. By the end of the twelfth century A.D., the Muslim Khilji dynasty had extended its power to the waters of the Ganges near Delhi. From that time Muslim rulers with capitals in the Delhi region dominated north and central India. In the fourteenth century Muhammad bin Tughlak ruled over a kingdom in India almost as great as Asoka's Mauryan empire.

The most direct effect of the rise of Islam in India was upon the Hindu rulers. The Muslim conquerors replaced them. This affected the Brahmans who had held important posts in Hindu kingdoms; they too were ousted. Political and military positions and the upper levels of administration fell into Muslim hands. The lower levels of administration and the clerical positions, however, tended to remain in Hindu hands. There were not enough literate Muslim conquerors to fill all the lower posts. But advancement to real power depended upon being a Muslim, with the result that a number of Hindus converted to the victorious faith. This was the second important effect of Islam on India.

Hinduism had always assimilated the newcomers, but absorbing Islam proved to be impossible. Hindus, instead, began to convert to the religion of Muhammad. Also, Muslim invaders had not always brought families with them. Muslims began to take Hindu wives, causing them to join the Islamic faith. There grew up in India a Muslim population, partly descended from converts. The two great religions remained separate despite such mingling.

The third major effect of Islam on India was its occasional zealous attack upon Hinduism. Temples were destroyed, Hindu art was hacked away, and Hindus had to pay special taxes. At times Brahmans were persecuted; on occasion there was forced conversion to Islam. Muslim political power implied an attack on the institutions of Hinduism and on Hindu power. In response, Hinduism tightened its ranks to defend itself against the threat.

The effects of Islam were largely confined to those just mentioned because the Muslims had little effect on the Hindu masses in the villages. The Islamic state touched the village only to collect taxes and to ensure law and order. The villager paid taxes, whether to a Muslim ruler or to a Hindu king, with the same spirit of stoic resentment. Hindu children continued to get their education from Brahman teachers, so that they were hardly exposed to Muslim ideas. Government had always been "distant" to the villager, and it remained distant under the new, Muslim, kings.

A long-range effect, which evolved slowly, must be mentioned. Hinduism and Islam, living together, could not avoid subtle interactions. Ideas, values, and artistic tastes in each great community came to be influenced by those of the other community. There are several dramatic examples of this development. Indo-Muslim art and architecture show the reciprocal exchange between Islam and Hinduism. There were religious movements in each religion that borrowed ideas from the other. Hindu reform groups arose that preached against caste and affirmed their belief in one God. Muslim Sufi mystics promoted ideas congenial to their Hindu counterparts. The Sikh religion is dramatic evidence of the ability of Hinduism and Islam to combine in a new form, different in some ways from each parent. The interaction, however, was most impressive in regard to language and literature. Muslim conquest created a new, hybrid, language, Hindustani, and new literary forms that had Indian and Persian antecedents. Though Hindustani was at bottom an Indo-Aryan language, it borrowed many words and idiomatic expressions from Persian and Arabic. These reciprocal tendencies were carried to their extreme during the reign of the greatest of all Muslim rulers in India, Akbar the Great (1556–1605).

Akbar was the grandson of Baber, founder of the Mogul dynasty. Baber's conquests laid the basis for the Mogul empire. However, it was Akbar who pushed the empire well into south India, and it was Akbar who demonstrated political genius by a policy of conciliation toward his Hindu subjects. His policies supported all those tendencies that worked for reciprocal interchange between the two communities, Hindus and Muslims. Akbar realized that a secure Muslim domination over a Hindu majority demanded tolerance and a policy that would give opportunity to the Hindus. He guaranteed full rights for the Hindus, eliminated all discrimination, and employed Hindus as officials in his kingdom. Akbar created a working Hindu-Muslim relationship in India.

The death of the last great Mogul emperor, Aurangzeb, in 1707, marked the beginning of the end for the empire. After 1707 the centralizing power of the emperor was in rapid decline; local governors and petty chieftains began a scramble for power, which broke the unity of India once again. It was this political anarchy and warfare between rivals for power that created the conditions under which the Europeans could take over. As long as the Mogul empire remained effective, the Europeans kept their place. In the middle of the eighteenth century the restraints were gone, and the Europeans carved out a new position for themselves.

Transformation Under British Rule

The first Europeans to visit India were the Portuguese. Vasco da Gama sailed to the Malabar Coast in 1498. The Portuguese were interested in a profitable trade in Oriental commodities to be resold in Europe. They were also interested in defeating Islam and in converting the heathen to Christianity. A monopoly trade would best suit their needs, so they attempted to control the Indian Ocean. For a century the Portuguese virtually dominated the trade of the Indian Ocean from tiny coastal enclaves.

Portuguese successes in the trade with southern Asia served to whet the appetites of European rivals. The merchants of Holland and England were not willing to leave the rich Indies trade in Portuguese hands. The first Dutch expedition went out in 1596, and in a few years, the Dutch East India Company and the English East India Company had been founded. As it turned out, the Dutch concentrated their interest in Java and the Spice Islands. Due to armed Dutch opposition, the English company centered its attention on India. Later, in the decade of the 1660's, the two rivals had to face new competition. The French established the Company of the Indies, which opened trading centers in India to compete with the English and the Dutch.

In the period of virtual anarchy that developed after 1707, the companies assumed a military posture, fortified their trading posts, and began to fish in troubled waters. The French company took the lead in the use of military power to secure commercial privileges. Shortly after 1740 the French company formed alliances with strong men who were trying to create independent kingdoms for themselves in south India. Troops supplied by the French company supported their Indian allies and helped them win thrones. Rewards were given to the company by the grateful aspirants who realized they owed their success to French help.

The English East India Company could not tolerate such an outcome. They knew that French predominance would lead to the freezing out of English commercial interest. Robert Clive, one of the English-company officials, formed counteralliances with rival Indian princes and used the company's native army to destroy the French alliance. The result was the collapse and virtual withdrawal of the French from south Indian affairs. This left the English company in a strong position, with its Indian allies seated upon their thrones.

The English company carried on its most important trade in Bengal, in the north. From that rich and industrious province the English carried valuable cargoes of textiles and raw materials back to Europe. The ruler of Bengal, Siraj-ud-daula, was suspicious of the English and fearful that they might intervene in local affairs as the French had done in the Deccan. When the English strengthened their fortifications around Calcutta, Siraj took offense and seized the town and fort. Robert Clive sailed to Bengal and formed an alliance with disgruntled leaders in the native court. The result was the celebrated Battle of Plassey (1757), an English victory. Siraj-ud-daula was killed, and his throne was occupied by a native officer supported by the English. With this victory began the rapid expansion of British power across India.

By 1818 the English company was the leading territorial and political power in India, having defeated or subdued almost every important Indian ruler. This meant that a company had become a government. In 1813 the English government gave the company a new charter. At that time Parliament insisted that the company's role in India must be primarily administrative. Parliament also strengthened its own control over the company and opened India widely to travel and residence by Europeans. The result was a rapid increase in the number of Europeans going to India. A growing number of them were evangelical missionaries. In the years following, a sense of obligation developed in the ranks of the English in India, accompanied by a desire to reform what were considered to be outmoded Indian ways. With parliamentary backing, the company legislated against Hindu customs that were disapproved. One of these customs, suttee, the burning of the widow on the funeral pyre of her deceased husband, was supposedly enjoined by the Hindu scriptures. Orthodox Hindus viewed British reform legislation against suttee as an objectionable violation of their rights.

Enthusiasm for social reform and the new evangelical fervor stressed the benefits of Western education for Indians. In the charter of 1813, Parliament insisted the company must set aside part of the revenues of India to support education. For some years little was done, and there were divided opinions as to what kind of education should be provided. In 1835 Thomas Babington Macaulay settled the controversy by his vigorous support of Western, secular education in India. From that time forward the number of educated Indians, trained in an English curriculum and in the English language, grew steadily. As their numbers grew, they began to play an important role in the new India that was emerging.

During these same years, the Industrial Revolution was changing the face of England. After 1813 the English interest in India came to be an interest in raw materials that could be used by England's manufacturing system. A secondary interest was what and how much could be sold *to* India. India had been a leading producer of handicrafts, but now she was becoming a supplier of raw materials. British policy favored this change. The peasant was now selling cash crops that entered the world market; his living came increasingly to depend upon the monsoon and on fluctuations in world market conditions and prices. This was an important change for people who had been brought up in a subsistence economy. As in all transitions, some people got hurt in the process. New ideas, new ways of doing things, and a new money economy were converging upon the Indians. There were many who were not at all convinced they liked the new ways.

Meanwhile, British political supremacy continued to spread. Each decade witnessed the annexation of additional Indian states. As a result, the remaining princes became suspicious and hostile. Westernizing practices embittered orthodox Brahmans, who saw their ancient supremacy sharply challenged. Lord Dalhousie, governor-general from 1847 to 1856, pushed the frontiers of the company's territory forward and stressed reforms. When he annexed the kingdom of Oudh, embers of discontent were fanned into flames.

The accumulation of discontent and suspicion led to the mutiny of the native army in 1857. It blazed rapidly, catching the English by surprise. The English put the mutiny down without much difficulty, but considerable bitterness and fear resulted between English and Indians. In London it was decided that misgovernment by the company had been to blame. Parliament acted in 1858 to abolish the government of the company and to place British India under Crown rule through a secretary of state for India, who was a member of the British cabinet.

After 1858 British India was governed directly by Britain. The years following the mutiny witnessed several important trends in imperial policy, each of which contributed to the making of modern India. Chief among the new trends was the administrative unification of India under a centralized and systematic government. Administrative unification was accompanied by legal unification. Systematic codes of civil and criminal procedure were enacted, bringing all Indians under a uniform rule of law. Ideas and practices derived from English law tended to replace native customary law. At the same time, India was increasingly unified by a growing network of railways, highways, and modern postal services.

Western education was pushed more vigorously after the opening of three English-style universities, located in Bombay, Calcutta, and Madras, in 1857. This education produced a new middle class, trained in the English language and familiar with Western values and practices. The Western-educated class was spread all over India, and with common ideas and language contributed to the unification of the land. A number of the new graduates became social reformers, anxious to bring India into line with the ideas of the contemporary West. The printing press, established in all of India's cities, also contributed to the unification of India and to the spread of Western values.

The government of India also engaged in certain public works designed to prevent famine and improve agricultural production. Chief among these was the building of a modern irrigation system. In the irrigated areas, the older reliance on the coming of the monsoon was replaced by the security of a safe water supply. The English further developed production of important cash crops that were wanted in the world market, including jute and cotton. Increasingly, the Indian economy came to be oriented to the needs, as well as the fluctuations, of international trade. By all of these means, the British laid the basis for a modernized and unified nation. However, in two important respects their rule went contrary to the trends just discussed.

In the first place, the British believed that an important cause of the mutiny had been their policy of annexation of Indian princely states. At the end of the mutiny, the Indian princes were promised that their titles and lands would be sacrosanct, under Britain as the paramount power. In the modernizing and unifying post-mutiny era, more than five hundred Indian princes, great and small, were left undisturbed to rule over that part of the subcontinent (roughly one third) that had not been annexed. The British policy of conciliation of the princes, marked by a tender concern for their sentiments, ran counter to the trends described above. The princely states, scattered haphazard across the face of the land, tended to remain as medieval backwaters.

In addition, British rule in the late nineteenth century failed to give any lead to the industrialization of India. Hampered by a laissez faire doctrine that was applied to India even after it had been eroded in England, the government did almost nothing to facilitate industrial growth. In this important respect, the modernization of India lagged far behind world trends. Indian entrepreneurs did begin a small textile industry, and some other factories were established to process agricultural raw materials, but these were minor efforts. The bulk of the Indian population remained in India's myriad villages, using the same antiquated agricultural methods their forefathers had known centuries before. The British bureaucracy that governed India was an administrative body little interested in technological improvement or in welfare-state activity. India was unified and modernized in certain respects but not in others. This legacy must be kept in mind if we are to understand the problems of contemporary India.

A crucial trend after 1857, one that reflects the other trends just noted, was the emergence of Indian nationalism. Western education was doubtless the most important factor in the growth of Indian nationalism because it provided the ideas and aspirations upon which nationalism could be based. Almost all of the early nationalist leaders were graduates of English-style colleges. The political, administrative, and judicial unification achieved under British rule was also an important contributing factor. For the first time in India's history the image of a unified nation under a strong and effective government had appeared. Railways, highways, and the mass media contributed to unification and to the circulation of ideas among the new leaders. All of these changes may be spoken of as prerequisites for nationalism.

Economic changes, already mentioned, furthered the growth of nationalism because the changes worked unevenly to benefit some and to penalize others. English-manufactured goods, for example, pushed the older handicrafts out of existence. Unemployed artisans fell into the ranks of the agricultural laboring class at a time when steady population growth was pressing sharply upon the rural economy. An antiquated agricultural system had to support ever larger numbers of people. As numbers outstripped the capacity of the soil to support them, there developed a steady drift to the towns in search of employment. But the slow pace of Indian industrialization limited the opportunities for gainful employment away from the land. One result was emigration by impoverished Indians to various parts of the British Empire as humble laborers. A second result was the decline of levels of living and a sharp increase in the effects of famines. As population grew, misery increased. This gave impetus to nationalism because many Indian leaders felt that the country was being "exploited" and that the English were gaining the most from the new order.

The conflict between nationalists and the government was given a sense of urgency by virtue of the fact that opportunities for respectable employment in the public services were few. The number of college graduates outstripped the posts open to Indians. Unavailability of work for the educated, noticeable by the end of the nineteenth century, sharpened the sense of injustice in Indian minds. Educated Indians felt they were being excluded from opportunity in their own homeland for the benefit of foreigners. Moreover, British business houses were predominant in important sectors of the Indian economy, and here too the educated Indian felt the effects of discrimination. Indians could secure clerical posts not wanted by the English, but the higher jobs were naturally in English hands.

In 1885 educated Indians formed the Indian National Congress as a forum from which to express their grievances and demands. Their most insistent plea was that government posts at the higher levels be thrown open fairly and fully to educated Indians. Furthermore, they criticized the government as an alien and unresponsive bureaucracy that was not influenced by Indian opinion. They also advocated certain reforms in the system of government. As citizens of the empire they demanded their "birthright," representative government. They argued that if educated Indians could take part in the shaping of public policy, they would be able to reform and improve Indian government and society. They also charged that the British exploited India and that Indian economic interests were bypassed. They wanted representative government so as to be able to change trade, tariff, and fiscal policies that seemed detrimental to Indian interests.

Unfortunately, the government responded to the National Congress with wooden lack of sympathy and with growing mistrust. To the bureaucratic mind, the nationalists were at best petty, carping critics and were possibly seditious. This attitude fed the fires of nationalist discontent. British coolness estranged many of those who wanted to cooperate with the government and brought to the fore a school of extremist leaders. One of these was Bal Gangadhar Tilak, who attacked foreign rule sharply and spoke of driving the British out so that Indians might govern themselves. Government spokesmen maintained that the educated nationalists represented only themselves and did not deserve serious attention.

British criticism was at least partly accurate. Western-educated nationalist leaders were out of touch with the masses of illiterate Indians living in the villages. The interest in openings in civil service and in representative institutions was far removed from the world of the villager. Educated criticisms, published in English-language journals, completely failed to touch the masses. The Congress Party realized it needed mass support to strengthen its hand, but the educated leadership found it difficult to think in mass terms. A few nationalist leaders realized that a national appeal presented in terms of Hindu culture and religion would gain mass support. Beginnings were made in this direction shortly before the turn of the century. Religious nationalism had an important negative by-product. Mass appeals to Hindu sentiment could not avoid wounding Muslim feelings. Religious nationalism could arouse the masses, but it seemed to mean separate Hindu and Muslim nations. The dilemma facing the leaders, most of whom were secular in their own outlook, plagued nationalism in India from that time forward.

By the time of World War I, a virtual stalemate had been reached. The British were unwilling to grant major concessions, and the constitutionalists were losing their following because they had failed to win dramatic gains. The masses still had to be captured, and Hindu-Muslim disagreements had increased despite temporary efforts at mutual adjustment. When the war broke out, nationalism was still of genuine concern to only a small minority of educated Indians. During the war, however, Mohandas K. Gandhi appeared on the nationalist scene, having returned from South Africa, where he had developed his distinctive political tactics in defense of emigrant Hindu civil rights. The doctrine he championed was civil disobedience, or nonviolent noncooperation. Gandhi came from a middle-level Hindu family, and had been trained as a lawyer in England. He had abandoned Western habits and dressed in simple Indian garb. He preached a nationalism that every Hindu could understand and approve. His message was directed specifically to India's unlettered village millions. Gandhi knew that nationalism that did not move the villager had no power. He rose quickly to power in Congress, became its revered leader, and reorganized it so as to base it squarely on village interests and village work.

From 1920 until his death Gandhi was the undisputed leader of Congress. At times other party leaders disagreed with his strategy or tactics, but they did not challenge him. They knew he had an uncanny grasp of the popular mind and could rally popular support as none of them could. His great civil-disobedience campaigns mobilized Indians to action and convinced the British that Congress must be reckoned with. Gandhi's nonviolent creed kept Indian nationalism from falling into the hands of extremists and radicals who would have incited violence. Faced with the pressure he could exert, the government made concessions that moved India ever closer to self-government. The Government of India Act of 1935, the culmination of the harrowing second civil-disobedience campaign, gave the provinces of British India limited self-government and provided Congress leaders with invaluable experience in parliamentary institutions.

The Gandhian years were important to contemporary India because Congress set forth its vision of what independent India should be like. Utopian in tone, the platform and various election manifestoes argued that political independence was essential because it would usher in a new era: independence was to make possible a peaceful social revolution in which rapid economic development would improve conditions of life for India's impoverished millions; economic opportunity was to be accompanied by full social justice; all of the wrongs Indians felt they suffered from were to be removed; the struggle for independence should be supported because it meant a struggle for opportunity. The tendency was to promise dramatic improvements as soon as freedom was won; the effect was to burden Congress with the great weight of unfulfilled hopes of those who believed that independence would automatically make India prosperous and give everyone a new chance in life.

In one important respect, Gandhi failed in his efforts. He was a sincere champion of Hindu-Muslim cooperation, but the inner core of his personality and of his political genius was his Hindu point of view. Despite his efforts, the years prior to independence were years of a widening gap between Muslims and Hindus. The Muslim League, a communal political organization under Muhammad Ali Jinnah, became the chief voice of Muslim nationalism. It moved steadily toward the goal of a separate Muslim nation. The result, of course, was the partition of 1947. It would be childish to blame Gandhi for this because many factors beyond his control came into play. Nonetheless, it seems that his gifted leadership as a Hindu stood between him and his dream of a united India.

Gandhi's lieutenant in the Congress Party during these

years was the English-educated and Westernized Jawaharlal Nehru. Nehru, a young aristocrat, followed Gandhi's lead but adopted his own creed of evolutionary and nonviolent socialism. He placed great faith in this to raise the masses from their poverty. By the time the difficult transition to independence had been made, Nehru stood forth as India's chosen leader. Since independence, he has served continuously as prime minister and as the builder of free India. Unlike Gandhi, who epitomized the essence of a tolerant and humane Hinduism, Pandit Nehru is a convinced secularist opposed to religious orthodoxy. He is, in addition, a cosmopolitan world figure. If Gandhi represented the ability of East and West to coexist by drawing the best from both traditions, Nehru represents the power of Western education to remake the East in its own image.

Each in his own way demonstrated that British rule had changed India. By doing so, it had rung down the curtain on foreign domination of the subcontinent. A century earlier, Thomas Babington Macaulay had predicted that this would probably be the outcome of British education and Indian experience with British government. On August 15, 1947, the transfer of power took place, accompanied by partition. Macaulay's prophecy had been fulfilled.

Modern India

Partition, in accord with an uncompromising Muslim demand, detached from India the adjacent Muslim-majority districts in the northwest and northeast portions of the subcontinent. The Republic of India now consisted of 1,221,283 square miles and in 1961 had a population of 438 million and a continued high population growth. In the decade prior to 1961, India's population increased by 21.5 percent. Continued growth at the present rate would give India approximately 526 million people by 1971. If that happens, it seems almost certain that mass starvation will be the result. This fact highlights in a dramatic manner the desperate problems facing the new republic.

Partition modified India's boundaries. To the northeast, India is now bounded by Burma, East Pakistan, Bhutan, Sikkim, and Nepal. To the north, Tibet has a common boundary with India. To the northwest, India is bordered by West Pakistan. The final boundary between India and Pakistan is not settled to the mutual satisfaction of both nations. Between 1947 and 1949 the two nations fought for control of the former princely state of Kashmir. In 1949 a cease-fire was arranged in Kashmir. The cease-fire line has become the actual boundary, but is still in dispute. Along the border with Tibet there has been recent armed action by Communist China to occupy territory to which India lays firm claim. These advances by the Communist Chinese also threaten Nepal. So far no solution has been reached.

India is a federal republic consisting of fifteen states and seven territories that are administered by the federal government. The Indian government also controls Goa (formerly Portuguese), Pondicherry (formerly French), and Sikkim, to an extent. The government has created a special agency to administer a backward border region known as the Northeast Frontier. The largest urban center in India is Calcutta, with five and a half million inhabitants. The city of Bombay has slightly more than four million residents. Three other Indian cities each have more than one million population: Delhi, Madras, and Hyderabad. In recent decades, India's cities have grown more rapidly in population than has the nation as a whole. This reflects the influx of rural population seeking job opportunities.

India's millions live under conditions that would not be accepted in any advanced nation. Poverty, a relatively backward economy, the growing pressure of population, and rural technological stagnation have all combined to bring this about. Accounts of living conditions that are experienced by masses of people in the industrial tenements (chawls) of Calcutta or Bombay read like medieval horror tales. Thousands sleep on the streets because they have no other home. Despite the efforts of the government of India and of charitable Indians, the lack of funds and widespread illiteracy have seriously hampered the improvement of intolerable conditions. Moreover, seventy-nine percent of the total population live in India's half million compact villages. Because of the lack of decent roads and the shortage of transport equipment, it is very difficult to get to the villages with medicine, information, better seed, or modern implements. The size of the task in dealing with half a million villages is enough to stop all but the most determined agents of progress. Malnutrition and other appalling conditions are reflected in the 1961 census report that the average life expectancy has finally *climbed* to forty-three years. Modern medicines have made this improvement possible, with antibiotics cutting the death rate substantially, but the problem of hunger remains to be faced.

India's government is constantly searching for means to increase economic development. Production is far too little for the needs of the vast population. Too much of India's gross national product is created by agriculture and too little by modern industry. There must be greater diversification so as to reduce Indian dependence upon imports,

and there must be a major increase in the investment of capital. India needs many more skilled laborers,
technicians, and agricultural scientists. The rural economy
requires a technological revolution to raise levels of production per acre, currently among the world's lowest.

Since independence, the government of India has mounted
three major Five-Year Plans, of which the third and most
ambitious is currently under way. Despite these concerted
efforts, the economy is still backward and the rate of growth
of production has been relatively modest. Gains have been
made, but a sizable part of such gains has been eaten up by
the population explosion. The first Five-Year Plan laid emphasis on development of agriculture, on irrigation and hydroelectric power, and on improvements in transportation. The
hydroelectric-power projects, though badly needed, were long-
term developments. Their beneficial effects are just now beginning to be felt. The improvements in production per acre
were heartening but not impressive. The transport system
was improved, but much remains to be done.

The second Five-Year Plan placed greater emphasis on
the development of industry and the diversification of India's
production. Noteworthy gains in industrial capacity were
secured, especially in selected light industries. But India
began from such a modest industrial base that even dramatic
improvements did not mean adequate levels of production
had been achieved. Furthermore, the second plan proved
to be overambitious in terms of India's capital resources.
This meant the plan had to be trimmed. The result was a
slowdown in the pace of growth. As late as 1952, factories
produced less than ten percent of the gross national product
of India. In 1961 less than three percent of the population
was employed in factories. In recent years, as much as two
thirds of India's exports have been raw materials. This suggests the continued lack of industrial growth.

India remains a nation of capital shortage. Per-capita national income at present is estimated to be eighty dollars
per year. Even if the estimate is low, the fact remains that
India's people have almost no surplus that can be put into
productive investment in economic growth. This has made it
difficult for the economy to get over the hump toward sustained and rapid growth. Rates of investment in recent
years have been below the minimum most economists think
is necessary for rapid economic development. Foreign capital assistance is especially important in view of this fact.
This assistance is also important for improving India's ability
to purchase scarce industrial equipment abroad. Because the
Indian economy is underdeveloped, it cannot yet produce

all the capital equipment needed. This limits the ability of the economy to grow and diversify and forces importation of machinery.

The agricultural sector of the Indian economy contributes almost half of India's gross national product, but agriculture is the most backward part of the Indian economy. The typical Indian farm is less than five acres in size. This limited acreage, combined with backward techniques, lack of capital, and absence of efficient farm tools, has resulted in low yields per acre. In 1958 India spent almost 1,500 million rupees (one rupee equals twenty-one cents) on the import of cereals required for food. In 1959 a total of 1,228 million rupees went for imported cereals, and additional sums were spent on other imported foods, plus cotton and jute. These heavy expenditures tax the Indian economy and further limit ability to buy needed machinery abroad. The Five Year Plans have tried to correct this situation by several methods: development of major irrigation works and construction of tube wells, creation of a fertilizer industry, and production of improved farm tools. The plans have also put emphasis on a community-development program that seeks to enlist popular enthusiasm for village-improvement schemes. Between 1956 and 1959 there was a nine-percent increase in area under crops and a fourteen-percent increase in total agricultural production, but the population grew by approximately six percent during the same years.

The third Five-Year Plan devotes considerable resources to industrial development. According to current planning, approximately forty percent of all fixed investment during the next twenty years will go into manufacturing and mining. If current plans and rates of industrial growth continue, India will be an important industrial nation at the end of twenty years. Domestic capital, however, will not suffice to finance the planned growth. If foreign capital is not available, current plans will have to be curtailed sharply. If that happens, the ability of India to escape the vicious circle of low productivity, capital scarcity, and antiquated techniques will be tragically affected. Such an outcome would raise the most serious political problems.

As remarked, prior to independence India's millions were told that freedom would bring social change, economic well-being, and opportunity. India's voters want a better future for their children, and if they cannot see it coming under a parliamentary government, they are free to listen to the promises made by other groups, some of which assure them that any change of government would be for the best, that they have nothing to lose, and that only a totalitarian government can marshal the nation for rapid economic development. Under grave economic conditions, parliamentary government can be made to sound like a luxury.

Indian economic-development planning is based upon the theory of mixed development. This means that government is to play a role in development alongside private enterprise. Certain critical sectors of the economy are reserved primarily for concentrated government effort. Other sectors are left primarily in private hands. The government holds that a mixed economy is necessary in order to secure rapid growth because private enterprise is not sufficiently strong to do the job alone. Furthermore, some parts of the economy require heavy overhead expenditures that private enterprise would find difficult to finance. Great hydroelectric stations, for example, demand an outlay far beyond the capacity of Indian business. Observers feel that the past two or three years of the Indian experience with a mixed economy have shown the idea to be reasonable. The private sector has been gaining strength, and private investment has been on the increase. There is reason to believe that government investment has served to spur the rate of development. The rate of growth is important for political reasons already touched upon.

Economic stagnation plays a potentially dangerous role in India for another reason. It has been remarked that British rule began the process of national unification but failed to complete it. Since independence, the divisive voices of regional, ethnic, and linguistic loyalties have increased. It is not yet an established fact that loyalty to the nation is greater than loyalty to kindred, caste, or community. The abstract idea of national loyalty has everywhere taken a long period of time in which to replace more narrow ties. In India the stresses and strains of economic hardship play a role in regionalism and similar localisms. In a scarcity economy, each person seeks to guarantee his share of limited resources by any means at his command. If this indicates reliance upon group influence, group loyalties will grow at the expense of larger symbols. Poverty is brutish and causes men to fight over their plight. These tensions undercut the larger sense of nation in favor of a local banding together to protect what little one has or hopes to get from others.

The unity of India has been somewhat in jeopardy since independence. Economic frustration increases other kinds of frustrations, the outcome of which can be political turmoil. A popular regime based squarely on the consent of the governed cannot coerce its citizens into blind and unquestioning agreement and therefore runs the risk of overthrow by groups that promise sweeping changes. Thus economic grievances can be very embarrassing for elected representatives.

These remarks on India's economic problem and on the unresolved issue of national unification, two of free India's major problems, raise the question of India's success in the field of politics since independence. To date it may be said that India's record of achievement in political stability and creativity has been more impressive than her record of success with regard to economic growth, social welfare, and educational progress.

On November 26, 1949, after almost three years of debate in the assembly, the Indian constitution was adopted. It is the longest constitutional document in the world and includes 395 articles. The constitution went into effect on January 26, 1950. The constitution vested full sovereignty in the Indian people and provided for a federal republic. The Indian constitution spells out in considerable detail the powers of the union government and the powers given to the governments of the various states. The Indian constitution specifies that all residual powers not specifically granted to the states are to belong to the union government. The list of powers given to the union government includes: foreign affairs, defense, railways, atomic energy, fixing of citizenship, customs duties, banks and banking, and a variety of kinds of taxation. The powers given to the states include: local government, public order, education, public health, and specified kinds of taxation. There is also a list of concurrent powers. In the event of a dispute between the union government and a state government over the exercise of powers, the Supreme Court of India has jurisdiction. Under the constitution, the Supreme Court is the highest tribunal in the land. Like that of the United States, the Indian Supreme Court may declare acts of government to be unconstitutional.

The Indian parliament consists of two houses. The upper house, called the Rajya Sabha, consists of representatives elected by members of the state legislatures. There are also twelve members appointed by the president to represent elements of Indian life that might not otherwise secure representation. Like the British House of Lords, the Indian Rajya Sabha is less powerful than the Lok Sabha, or lower house.

The Lok Sabha consists of representatives elected from territorial electorates by the people of each election district. These are direct elections. Like the British House of Commons, the Lok Sabha has power over money bills. Furthermore, as in the British system, the cabinet, or Council of Ministers, is drawn from the Lok Sabha. The Council of Ministers is responsible to the Lok Sabha. Since the Council of Ministers and its prime minister are the executive center in the Indian system, responsibility to the Lok Sabha makes clear the primary position of the latter in the Indian government. The Lok Sabha must, however, legislate within the framework created by the constitution.

The constitution gives the vote to all adult citizens. There are no property or literacy requirements. India has, as a result, more voters than any other nation in the world. More than 200 million people were entitled to vote in the national election that took place early in 1962. This was the third general election held in India since the constitution went into effect. Parliamentary elections come every five years.

The constitution guarantees a series of fundamental rights to all citizens. These include free assembly for lawful purposes, the right of private property, equality before the law, and the right to constitutional redress. Such rights are spelled out in considerable detail. In addition, there is a section of general principles that are supposed to guide lawmakers in the directions favored by the constitution. These basic principles stress the humane, secular, and welfare interests of the men who wrote the document.

The Congress Party has dominated parliament from the days of the first general election in 1952. At the time of the 1957 elections, Congress won more than seventy percent of the seats at stake. In addition, Congress was the majority party in all but one state legislature. The 1962 elections have given the party two thirds of the seats in parliament. However, its popular vote has been smaller than the proportion of seats it has captured. The opposition votes are scattered among several different parties, which has prevented any single opposition party from winning enough seats to take power.

The prestige of Congress as the party that led India to freedom and the stature of some of its leaders have helped give the party this predominance. The results may, however, have been bad for the development of a parliamentary system. The continuous existence of an important opposition party is often held to be a central feature of parliamentary government. In India there is no important opposition party. The seats not captured by Congress are split among the smaller parties, no one of which has secured an all-India prominence as a real alternative to the Congress. Fortunately, Nehru has gone out of his way to encourage parliamentary opposition to the Congress, and this has minimized the tendency toward a one-party system.

An important fact must be kept in mind regarding parliamentary government in India. Party politics are relatively new there. The voters have had limited experience with parties, and the Indian party system does not work in the same way as Western parties. In India voters tend to line up behind a prominent name to whom they are attached by ties of community, caste, or kinship. Parties tend to be combinations of political leaders and their groups of loyal followers. Party discipline is less well established than in the United States, and disgruntled leaders will move from one coalition to another. As long as parties are primarily collections of factions, they have an instability about them. Thus, even though the Congress Party has dominated parliament through three national elections, no one can accuse it of being monolithic or totalitarian. It is a collection of groups and cliques arrayed under one banner. One can find Congress leaders of conservative viewpoint, middle-of-the-road leaders, and leaders of an evolutionary socialist persuasion.

The art of politics in contemporary India is to create a satisfactory compromise between factions and viewpoints. On this compromise one bases a coalition that is called a party. If the coalition has been put together skillfully, one can win elections. To date Congress has had more success at this than any other political group. However, no one can feel confident that such a coalition will grow into an organic unity. Factional parties based on loose compromises can be erratic and can move in almost any direction within the general limits of the interests and ideas of the collaborating leaders. Strong leadership, such as that provided by Pandit Nehru, can hold a coalition together. It remains to be seen whether lesser men can do the same.

The instability of coalition parties tends to hide another, potentially powerful factor on the Indian scene. There is a covert conflict in contemporary India between the proponents of secular modernism and the supporters of traditionalist and archaic values. The traditionalists distrust the implications of modernization. In their view modernization is a violation of all they hold dear and a threat to their way of life and their power. The modernists are an influential minority and have dominated Indian politics since independence. There is no guarantee that the modernists will continue to have it their own way. As Congress learned long ago, effective mass appeals have to play upon the theme of India's past greatness and the virtues of the older Indian way of life. The tension between modernists and traditionalists contributes to political instability. So far Congress has been able to contain such varied elements in its ranks. After Prime Minister Nehru retires, who will be able to take his place effectively in this delicate task?

Sharply to the left of the Congress Party stands the Communist Party of India. The Communists were able, temporarily, to form a ministry in one of the Indian states and have won seats in several legislatures. So far little or no real political power has fallen into Communist hands, but the Communist appeal to discontented voters at the local level continues. Furthermore, the Communists have allied themselves with other "protest" groups in India, hoping to form a coalition of their own so as to win majorities. Political, regional, and economic frustrations play into Communist hands. How much they can make out of these frustrations remains to be seen.

There are, in addition, several right-wing parties. So far they have not been able to attract much of a following. Some of these splinter groups stand on a frankly religious and communal basis. The traditionalist mentality mentioned above is an area of potential strength for this kind of leadership. So far the traditionalist groups have been organized around narrow local issues and leaders. This has prevented them from securing national importance. But they have undermined the unity of India by their strident agitation in favor of linguistic self-determination. They play upon local fears and jealousies, denouncing rival parties or factions. They too feed upon poverty, frustration, and disillusionment. Since they are not burdened with the responsibilities of office, they can afford to criticize in a negative and destructive manner. At the same time, like the Communists, they can promise to solve India's problems easily if given power.

It is obvious that the years since independence have by no means been free from pressing problems. One crisis after another has confronted the government. In the desperate struggle to modernize and raise levels of living, the republic has faced several immense domestic challenges. Many of these were legacies of the colonial past or of the uneven and unsettling impact of the Western world on India. The existence of these problems and the scarcity of India's developed resources have affected Indian foreign policy. The magnitude of domestic issues has served to limit the effort India can put into international affairs. High-level administrators and men of stature have their hands full at home and can devote little energy to foreign involvements. As would be expected, the tendency has been to avoid serious international commitments.

If practical reasons have favored a policy of minimal involvement in international affairs, nationalist thinking has supported such a view. India's leaders came to power by virtue of their active leadership in the Indian nationalist movement. Many of them spent some years in jail as a result of their anticolonial beliefs. Anticolonial passion has not had time to die out among India's leaders. Involvement in international affairs, particularly alignment with one or another world power bloc, seems to them to suggest the danger of renewed domination of India. Their devotion to the cause of Indian independence has made them unusually sensitive about anything that might compromise their independence. A policy of noninvolvement seems to them to be the most effective guarantee of India's independence.

The legacy of anticolonialism carries with it a lingering suspicion of Western "imperialist" motives. It is easy to point out that such suspicions are ill-founded, but it is difficult to get Indians to believe it. Men view the world in terms of certain biases that have been inculcated in them by their background and by their experiences. India's leaders have a background strongly colored by their anticolonial nationalism, and they look at international affairs in that light. We have every right to disagree with their interpretation, but we cannot afford to overlook their reasons for feeling as they do. As they see it, noninvolvement is the policy best suited to India's position and needs.

Moreover, India's leaders know that the voters can turn them out of office. As practical politicians they wish to be reelected. Prior to independence many promises were made about the bright new era that would dawn when freedom was won. Something has to be done to fulfill those promises. Noninvolvement in international affairs leaves India's leaders free to work for the fulfillment of those promises. If India had resources to spare, it might be feasible to push domestic-welfare programs and an active foreign policy. But India has no resources to spare. In addition, India's leaders are convinced that the best defense against communism is a strong economy and a healthy society. From our point of view, this is not enough. From their point of view, it is the essential requirement. As a result, they stress the tasks they have at home rather than foreign affairs.

It is also a fact that their anticolonial preoccupations cause them to be more aware of and more interested in the elimination of the remnants of colonialism than in the great power struggle between Russia and the United States. Indian foreign policy has, as a result, been confined in good part to anticolonialism. The colonialism that bothers Indians the most is that which involves European domination of non-European peoples. All of these factors condition Indian thinking about international affairs and Indian foreign policy.

Despite its limited power and major unresolved problems at home, India's stature in world politics has grown. In the United Nations India has played a prominent part, partly by speaking for the so-called Afro-Asian bloc. India had an honorable hand in the arrangement of the truce that ended civil war in Korea and more recently played its part in the truce that was created, for a time, in Laos. During the past year India has contributed materially to UN attempts to stabilize the Congo. In the UN, India has functioned as an active mediator and has taken a prominent role in some of the specialized agencies.

Indian foreign policy has stressed several major themes. These include noninvolvement in the Cold War, settlement of international disputes by compromise and conciliation, and support of the United Nations. Indian policy has been expressed in the *Pancha Shila* doctrine, based on nonaggression and noninterference in the affairs of other nations. Late in 1962 the Pancha Shila idea received a rude shock when Communist China invaded India at several points along the lengthy Indo-Tibetan border. The invasion came as a blow to Indians because their government had gone out of its way to try to be friendly with Peking.

After dramatic advances against the Indian army, the Chinese armies chose to announce a unilateral "cease-fire"; some weeks later the Chinese armies began to withdraw toward the line from which they had begun their assaults. Meanwhile, several of India's nonaligned neighbors met in Colombo to try to work out a conciliation plan. To India's surprise, some of the noninvolved Asian nations turned out to be so "neutral" as to be unable to distinguish between Chinese aggression and Indian self-defense. These events highlighted the pitfalls of the policy that India had proclaimed to the world.

The uneasy Himalayan "truce" between India and China persists, leaving unanswered any larger questions of how Indian foreign policy might be revised to take account of the Chinese view of what Pancha Shila means. Meanwhile, the hold of Pancha Shila ideas remains prominent in Indian circles and creates oblique difficulties for a government that needs military aid if it is to protect its territory from further Chinese aggression. Fortunately for India, the Western powers have been quite willing to give military assistance without demanding that India's foreign policy undergo any substantial revisions. Partly for this reason, nonalignment has managed to survive a brief but severe Chinese invasion.

The Chinese invasion put pressure on India in other ways. The most obvious, of course, was the need to revise the Indian budget to allow for development of a solid military force. This has meant stresses on economic-growth efforts and on the hard-hit consumer and taxpayer. The invasion also affected Indo-Pakistan relations. While India faced an invasion from the northeast, Pakistan made distinctly unfriendly noises in the northwest. Under gentle Anglo-American prodding, however, the two governments launched a series of talks over Kashmir and related issues that would otherwise doubtless have remained dormant. Unfortunately, the accommodation talks seemed merely to highlight the basic tensions between India and Pakistan.

Thus China's attack has raised pressures on India and tensions in the region. The rapid advance of Chinese armies has no doubt made the desired impression on the independent nations of Southeast Asia. The progress of the Indian economy has been dislocated, and Indian relationships with her neighbors, nonaligned and otherwise, have had to go through an unsettling experience. It is impossible, as yet, to predict what the outcome for India and Southeast Asia will be, but it is clear that Indian leaders can no longer take a relaxed and optimistic view of Asian events. Noninvolvement is by now realized not to be a magic amulet capable of warding off evil by itself.

Indian occupation of Goa late in 1961, held by Portugal since 1516, has been viewed in the West as a violation of the Indian policy of nonviolence. To this Indians reply that Portugal took Goa by force and that Portugal refused to negotiate a peaceful return of Goa to India. The Indian view is that the nation could wait no longer to wipe out the remnants of colonialism on Indian soil. Moreover, it is argued that occupation of Goa freed part of the Indian army for duty in the region occupied by the Chinese Communists.

India has also been charged with violating the principles of her foreign policy with regard to the former princely state of Kashmir. In reply, the government insists that the ruler of Kashmir joined his kingdom to India in a perfectly legal fashion and that therefore no question of illegality can be raised regarding the steps subsequently taken. This argument is, of course, entirely unacceptable to Pakistan, and the bitter quarrel over Kashmir has had a most deplorable effect on affairs between India and Pakistan. The Kashmir dispute and several other outstanding grievances have resulted in an ill will that is a burden to both countries, making for bad trade relationships and the costs of increased military forces. Relaxation of these tensions would be of benefit to both nations.

The crucial issue with regard to India today, however, is the matter of India's prospects for maintaining a stable government based upon parliamentary practices. If the country can solve enough of the problems she faces—especially problems of rapid economic development—she should be able to maintain a healthy parliamentary democracy, and thus the era of European colonialism will have had an impressive and valuable outcome in the form of political freedom, equal opportunity, secular government, and social justice.

Pakistan

THE APPEARANCE of Pakistan on the map of Asia on August 15, 1947, marked the first attempt in modern times to build a political community on the basis of the common religious beliefs of a people. During the years from 1940 to 1947, the Indian Muslim community, led by Quaid-e-Azam (Great Leader) Muhammad Ali Jinnah, pressed the view that the Muslim-majority areas of the British Indian Empire should achieve independence as a separate political entity from the remaining, Hindu-majority, provinces. The creation of Pakistan therefore was a constitutional affirmation of the Muslim contention that the philosophy and way of life prescribed by their religion, Islam, gave Muslims a national identity distinct and separate from that of their neighbors of other religious faiths.

The sense of social and political identity shared by the Muslims derives from the character of Islam itself. "Islam" means "to submit," and Muslims are those who submit themselves to the will of the One God as revealed to His last prophet, Muhammad of Arabia (A.D. 570–632) in the Holy Koran. The community of Islam therefore is the community of true believers, guided by the Divine Word in all aspects of their existence and distinguished thereby from nonbelievers. Islam teaches the brotherhood and equality of all believers, and great emphasis is placed on the social aspects of religious observance, as in prayer five times daily (and community prayer on Friday), fasting during the month of Ramadan, the giving of alms to the poor, and the pilgrimages to the holy cities of Mecca and Medina. These practices help to remind the Muslim of his ties with fellow believers and to set him apart from those of humankind who have not yet accepted the True Faith.

In the early centuries after the death of Muhammad, the faithful were united in spiritual and temporal allegiance to the caliphs, the successors of the prophet, who were able to preserve the oneness of the Islamic religious and political community. However, as Islam spread in Africa and Asia, the bonds of political unity over these vast territories weakened, until the caliphate became a powerless symbol and finally was eliminated altogether. In consequence, only the Koran itself and Islamic law as interpreted by the *ulama,* the learned, preserved the formal unity of Islam throughout a variety of empires and kingdoms. As sectarian differences arose, increasing importance was given to communal prayer and other external observances, and adherence to the formal requirements of Islamic law became essential if the community was not to disintegrate. This social conservatism became especially important in India where Muslim mysticism and religious speculation tended to become practically indistinguishable from some Hindu beliefs and practices. Only by constant vigilance and emphasis on the primary allegiance of the individual Muslim to the community of Islam was it possible to prevent the absorption of Indian Islam by all-encompassing Hinduism.

Muslim Supremacy in India

Islam came to the Indian subcontinent in strength during the twelfth century, brought by invaders of Turkish stock pouring through the mountain passes of the northwest. Muslim rule was soon established in Delhi, and was gradually extended to the east and south. The Indus valley, as the region closest to the sources of Muslim invaders, eventually became an overwhelmingly Muslim country, its population a mixture of idigenous converts and immigrants from Central Asia, Iran, and the Arab West. In northern and central India, Muslim conquerors established themselves as a ruling class, which together with humbler converts never numbered more than some ten percent of the population. However, in Bengal, where Muslim invaders arrived in the early years of the thirteenth century, Islam received a warm welcome from a native population whose Buddhist faith had only recently been crushed out by a sternly Hindu dynasty. Conversions proceeded through the years, until by the end of the Muslim period eastern Bengal, like the Indus valley, had become a Muslim country. Despite many attempts, the Muslim rulers of north India were unable to extend their political sway into the southernmost portions of the subcontinent until the reign of the Mogul emperor Aurangzeb, in the late seventeenth century. However, this was an ephemeral success, as the empire was crumbling under the attack of rebel forces from within and European merchant adventurers from without. In 1757 supremacy passed to the English East India Company, but the fiction of Muslim rule was preserved for another century until in the aftermath of the great Sepoy Mutiny of 1857 both the company and the Mogul emperor were swept aside.

The overthrow of the last remnant of Muslim political power in the subcontinent was a great shock to the traditional leaders of Indian Islam. Their possession of political power had permitted Muslims the pretense that India was a Muslim land and had enabled them to use the machinery of the state to preserve the identity and integrity of the community. However, with the passing of the empire to the British Crown, the Muslims from being rulers became subjects, a minority outnumbered four to one by their Hindu neighbors, and suspect in the eyes of the British authorities as actively disloyal. The reaction of the orthodox religious and lay leaders of Indian Islam was to withdraw from all association with the infidel rulers and to turn their backs on the new ideas that began to transform India during the Victorian era. In consequence, while non-Muslims hastened to take advantage of Western education and to enter new commercial and governmental careers, the community of Islam was becoming not only an alienated minority but also an economically and educationally backward one.

The Creation of Pakistan

The realization that the community was endangering its very survival in the face of a revived Hinduism and the challenge of European ideas brought to the fore a farsighted leader now revered as the father of Muslim nationalism. Sir Syed Ahmad Khan, a descendant of a Delhi family long in Mogul service, recognized that the time-honored conservative policy of holding fast to the Islamic tradition was no longer in the interest of the community and that unless Islam could absorb and mobilize the spirit of a scientific age, it would be overwhelmed. In particular, unless Indian Muslims took advantage of Western education and strengthened themselves economically, the community would not be able to survive the pressures of the Hindu majority. Accordingly, Sir Syed preached reconciliation with the British and loyalty to the government, warning that until Muslims were strong enough to protect their own interests they would have to rely on special legal and constitutional safeguards and the goodwill of the administration. Although the traditional religious leaders, the ulama, refused to accept them, Sir Syed's political and educational views, propagated primarily through his college at Aligarh (a town south of Delhi in north India), became dominant in the Muslim community; and his insistence that Muslims remain loyal and not support the Indian National Congress set the standard for Muslim political behavior until the period of World War I.

The long-term challenge to the Muslim community discerned by Sir Syed lay in the application of Western political ideas in India. Democratic principles of representation and political responsibility implied the supremacy of the numerical majority, but in tradition-bound India this meant a majority defined permanently in religious terms. The social and cultural differences between Islam and Hinduism were such that however broad the franchise, inevitably and naturally Hindu and Muslim voters would support candidates of their own communities. Only in northwest and northeast India, where Muslims were in a majority, could they expect to elect their own representatives, and even there because of their economic backwardness they would be at a disadvantage. Since Muslims of the Aligarh school of thought were convinced that the distinct economic and social interests of the Muslims, as a backward minority, required special protection, their efforts (through the Muslim League, founded in 1906) were directed toward devising means of guaranteeing Muslim representation in the legislatures and of protecting Muslim rights against infringement by an unsympathetic majority. Accordingly, they did not share the eagerness of the Indian National Congress for the rapid extension of self-government in India, inasmuch as this would mean the transfer of political power from the hands of the British not back to the Muslims but to the Hindu majority.

The political history of British India in the twentieth century is a tale of the gradual breakdown in confidence between the Muslim and Hindu communities. At first the Muslims merely desired guaranteed representation and safeguards until the community should feel able to protect its interests in the normal manner in a democratic political process. Constitutional reforms in 1909 granted them separate electoral rolls, so that Muslims could elect their own representatives. This principle was recognized by the National Congress in 1916, making it possible for the Congress and the Muslim League to join in a postwar campaign for further reforms granting a greater degree of democratic self-government. However, the religious appeals that mobilized the Muslim masses in the name of Islam for the anti-British noncooperation movement of 1920–1922 aroused emotions that could not be controlled by the leaders, until violence between Hindus and Muslims broke the Congress-League alliance. In 1924 the Muslim League, presided over by Muhammad Ali Jinnah—who had refused to support the mass agitation of the preceding years—resolved that separate electorates and partially responsible provincial governments as defined in the reforms of 1919 were inadequate to protect Muslim interests. Therefore, federation with complete provincial autonomy was presented as the Muslim demand, elaborated later by additional safeguards for Muslim representation in the central government. Although these conditions were largely met in the Government of India Act of 1935, complete provincial autonomy placed Muslim minorities at the mercy of the Hindu majorities, and the experiences of congressional provincial rule from 1937 to 1939 convinced the Muslim League that once in power Congress would not respect Muslim interests either in the provinces or in India as a whole. Rather than accept the permanent subordination of Indian Islam to the Hindu majority after the departure of the British power, the Muslim League resolved on March 23, 1940, that India should be partitioned and that the Muslim-majority areas should constitute a completely independent state.

The political basis for the Muslim League's decision to demand a separate state was the "two-nation theory," the belief that Islam and the Islamic way of life united the faithful into one Muslim nation, equal in political rights if not in numbers to the Hindu nation in India. This view of Muslims as a nation had been expressed by Sir Syed Ahmad Khan and also by Sir Muhammad Iqbal, the poet-philosopher who in 1930 first proposed the formation of a Muslim state in northwest India. In 1933 and after, the concept of the Muslim nation was further defined by Chaudhuri Rahmat Ali, then a student at Cambridge University, who coined the name "Pakistan" from elements in the names of the Muslim provinces of the Indian northwest. A variety of other schemes for the reorganization of India to secure autonomy for the various religious and cultural communities were proposed during the 1930's, but until 1937 Muslim political leaders ignored them. Thereafter the Muslim League, led by Jinnah, transformed itself into a mass organization, winning support as the embodiment of the Muslim nation and ultimately being led by circumstances to the acceptance of the goal of independence for the Muslim provinces of both northwest and northeast India. After 1940 mass enthusiasm for Pakistan swept aside those Muslims who still sought to reach a compromise with the Hindus, carrying Jinnah and the League to electoral victory in 1946 and forcing Congress and the British to concede partition and independence.

Problems of the New Nation

The creation of Pakistan out of the Muslim-majority areas of British India produced a state made up of two widely separated geographical regions, the Indus valley in the northwest of the subcontinent and the Ganges-Brahmaputra delta in the northeast. The latter region, now known as East Pakistan, comprises 55,000 square miles of low-lying land intersected by two of Asia's greatest rivers and their distributaries. Rainfall is very high, ranging between sixty and two hundred inches, almost all of which falls between March and October. Since this is also the season of high flow in the rivers, the province is subject to flooding during the summer months, whereas the winter is usually very dry. Although almost two thirds of the total area is cultivated during the rainy season, because of the lack of irrigation facilities the proportion drops to around one fourth during the dry months. The principal crops are rice, jute (the raw material for burlap sacking), and tea, the latter being cultivated in the hill areas of Sylhet (before independence, part of Assam) and in the Chittagong hill tracts near the Burma border. The fertility of the soil and the mildness of the climate have enabled the delta to support a very large population, which has increased more quickly than food production in recent decades. In order to cope with overcrowding on the land and to broaden its economic base, the province is attempting to industrialize, with the manufacture of jute goods, cotton textiles, paper, newsprint, and now fertilizer based on natural gas. Although a vast improvement over 1947, the impact of this industrialization has barely begun to be felt.

Eastern Bengal can claim to be the original home of the Pakistan movement because Dacca, the provincial capital, was the scene in 1906 of the founding of the Muslim League, and during the 1930's the Bengali peasants rallied to the League long before their compatriots of the Indus valley. The political awakening of Bengali Muslims began during the short life (1905–1912) of the province of Eastern Bengal and Assam, a Muslim-majority province created for administrative reasons by the British government of India despite bitter Hindu opposition. It was subsequently abolished without reference to Muslim interests when for the convenience of the administration it was felt essential to placate the Hindus. The Muslim League was organized in part to defend Muslim interests in the province against Hindu attack, and the sudden dissolution of the province despite repeated official assurances alienated Muslim loyalists and set the stage for the subsequent era of Congress-League cooperation in anti-British activity. After the failure of the noncooperation movement revived Hindu-Muslim antagonisms, the grievances of the East Bengal peasantry against Hindu absentee landlords and moneylenders provided the basis for Muslim protest movements that eventually were absorbed by the revitalized Muslim League. Without League supremacy in Bengal it would have been impossible for Jinnah to assert his leadership over the Indian Muslim community and to achieve Pakistan.

Although the partition of Bengal and the exclusion of Hindu-majority districts left East Pakistan with a predominantly Muslim population, there remains a minority of nearly ten million non-Muslims, mostly Hindus. The communal diversity is softened, however, by a high degree of linguistic uniformity, as nearly all East Pakistanis speak Bengali, a language written in a Sanskritic script and with strong literary associations with Hindu nationalism. Despite the fact that the sense of Islamic community provided the basis for the creation of the province, unquestionably many Muslims feel a stronger bond with Bengali Hindus than with Muslims from other areas. This sense of Bengali solidarity has been demonstrated clearly in the state language controversy, in which Bengalis of all communities stood together in resistance to the central government's efforts to impose Urdu as the sole state language. Urdu, written in the Persian script and strongly influenced by Arabic and Persian traditions, had been the language of the Muslim upper classes throughout India and then became the lingua franca of the Muslim revival and of the Pakistan movement. Accordingly, although it was spoken by only a small proportion of the people of the new state of Pakistan, Jinnah and other Muslim League leaders assumed that it would become the national language. Although this was acceptable in West Pakistan, Bengalis insisted that their language should have at least equal status, especially since it is the mother tongue of a majority of Pakistanis. The language issue became symbolic of a complex feeling of both exploitation and neglect of East Pakistan by a West Pakistan-dominated central government, and was finally resolved by agreement that the two languages should have constitutional equality and that English should be continued indefinitely as the governmental language.

Although more than half of the national population is crowded into East Pakistan, the western province, almost 1,000 miles away on the other side of the subcontinent, incorporates by far the greater part of the national territory. West Pakistan includes the Indus valley and its mountain fringes and a coastal mountain-and-desert region extending toward Iran and the Persian Gulf, a total of over 310,000 square miles. Apart from a few valleys in the far north, all of West Pakistan is at best semiarid, with rainfall varying between four and ten inches, most of it falling during the summer months when the Indus and its tributaries (Jhelum, Chenab, Ravi, and Sutlej) are in flood. Only about twenty percent of the total area is cultivated, and more than half of that is dependent on irrigation. Great irrigation works have been constructed during the past century to open up lands in the Indus plain for cultivation, but by now almost all the available water supplies are committed. The water problems of the Indus plain were seriously complicated by the circumstances of independence, resulting in an international frontier being drawn across the existing river-and-canal system. The headwaters of all the rivers upon which West Pakistan is dependent are in India, and until 1960 the two countries were engaged in a bitter dispute about their respective water rights. The ultimate solution, arrived at with the aid of the International Bank, allocates the Indus, Jhelum, and Chenab for the use of Pakistan and the other rivers for India. A huge construction program is now under way to build more dams, barrages, and canals so that by 1970 the entire irrigation system in West Pakistan will be supplied with water from her three rivers. A further serious problem that the Indus Basin Development project hopes to remedy by improved drainage and other measures is the menace of waterlogging and salinity in the irrigated lands.

Before independence, the Indus basin was a food-grains surplus area, and the standard of living of the cultivators in the irrigated areas was quite comfortable in Indian terms. However, increased salinity and waterlogging has decreased fertility and reduced production, whereas the population has been increasing very rapidly (twenty-seven percent between 1951 and 1961), to the present total of forty-three million. The principal crops are wheat, rice, sugar, and cotton; the vast uncultivated desert and mountain areas can be used only for grazing livestock, sheep (for wool), goats, and camels. Even before 1947 a small cotton-textile industry had begun, and since that time the much-expanded textile industry has been supplemented by cement, heavy chemicals, pharmaceuticals, fertilizers, and natural gas. In addition, the province possesses considerable natural resources to provide the basis for further industrialization, including the manufacture of iron and steel. The gap between the rate of investment and industrialization in West Pakistan and that in East Pakistan has been a point of considerable political soreness, but it is difficult to see how it can be overcome for several years.

Although the partition of British India in 1947 left Pakistan with one province in the northeast, the Indus valley was subdivided into several units. However, it is a natural geographical and economic region, and in 1955, after much controversy, a unified province of West Pakistan was created. The former provinces of Sind (in the lower Indus valley), Punjab (the land of the five rivers, between the Indus and Sutlej), the Northwest Frontier (the mountain borderland guarding the famed Khyber Pass and other gateways to Afghanistan), the sparsely populated territory of Baluchistan and four adjacent princely states, and the two Indus valley states of Bahawalpur and Khairpur were merged into one unit. The tribal areas along the Afghan border and four Frontier states retain a special status; they are under the West Pakistan authorities, yet subject to the control of the central government. Opposition to the unification reflected the ethnic diversity underlying the apparent homogeneity of a population ninety-seven percent Muslim. Vast migrations accompanying the partition of the Punjab in 1947 had seen some seven million Muslim peasants, mostly Punjabis, pour into West Pakistan, replacing the departing Hindus and Sikhs. Sindhis resented Punjabi immigration into their area and regarded the subsequent proposals for an integrated Urdu-speaking province as a threat to their ethnic survival. Similar sentiments were expressed among the Pathans of the Frontier, whose sense of cultural pride before independence had been the basis of an anti-Muslim League, pro-Congress nationalist movement. In response to these considerations, minority language rights have been recognized and extensive powers delegated to local and regional authorites to avoid the drawbacks of centralization in such a large province.

The two very diverse regions of Pakistan were bound together in 1947 as a federation of provinces and states, based as an interim measure on the constitutional arrangements of the Government of India Act of 1935. The national legislature, the Constituent Assembly, was faced with the task of working out a permanent constitution, of molding the existing familiar institutions to fit the needs of a geographically divided state and imbuing them with a distinctively Islamic spirit. In the meantime, since Pakistan remained an independent dominion in the Commonwealth, the British Crown was represented by a governor-general (initially Muhammad Ali Jinnah) and the government was carried on by a prime minister (at first Liaquat Ali Khan) and cabinet responsible to the Constituent Assembly. Unfortunately for Pakistan, the authoritative and inspiring leadership of Jinnah was cut short by his death in September, 1948, and the tragedy was compounded three years later by the assassination of Liaquat Ali Khan, Jinnah's lieutenant and undisputed heir as political leader of the new state. Deprived of the guidance of its greatest leaders, Pakistan became increasingly embroiled in constitutional controversies, and as the years passed, the problems of defining the philosophy and structure of the state seemed insoluble.

Philosophically, the constitutional problem was and is one of defining the meaning of Islam. Muslims of all political orientations had supported the independence movement, agreeing that Muslims ought to have a state in which the principles of Islam might be realized in social and political terms. However, the constitutional debate revealed wide disagreement as to the content and application of Islamic principles. The modern-day successors of Sir Syed Ahmad Khan consider Islam, with its emphasis on brotherhood, equality, and justice, to be in effect a moral philosophy of democracy. To them, Pakistan as an Islamic society must be a free society, for Muslims and non-Muslims alike, discovering moral solutions to human problems through reinterpretations of the spirit of the Koran and of the traditions of the prophet. Opposing this view are the traditionalists, the heirs of those ulama who so successfully preserved the identity of the community in the centuries of division following the fall of the caliphate. For them, Islamic principles command a return to the political and social practices of the Arab empires and require a reaffirmation of the guiding role of the ulama as a class. A further, fundamentalist, view calls for a return to the letter of the Koran and the elimination of later, un-Koranic, practices, believing to find in God's word the literal answer to modern social problems and insisting therefore on a strictly authoritarian political order based on the Muslim community alone. The inability of any one school of thought to gain acceptance of its views has meant that constitutional solutions have been uneasy compromises liable to subsequent challenge and a renewal of debate.

The more directly political questions of the structure of the state—the relations between the provinces and between them and the central government—have also been the subject of much controversy. The unification of West Pakistan in 1955 simplified the matter by reducing the number of provinces to two, making it possible to regard the task as one of constructing a federal state out of two equal parts. Although East Pakistani political leaders insisted on the justice of their claim to a majority voice in national affairs, ultimately they agreed to accept an arrangement of constitutional "parity," the two provinces having equal status and equal representation in the national assembly. In return, West Pakistanis conceded the need for special measures to ensure equality of participation by East Pakistanis in the public services and defense forces, in which for historical reasons they have been underrepresented, and for rapid measures of economic advance to remove the gap between the two provinces.

The prolonged constitutional debate seemed at last to have been settled in 1956 when the second Constituent Assembly (elected in 1955 to replace its predecessor, dissolved by the governor-general in late 1954 as "no longer representative") approved a new federal constitution. In substance the new constitution was a modification of the Government of India Act of 1935, incorporating the parity compromises outlined above. Although Pakistan was described as an "Islamic Republic" and the president was required to be a Muslim, in the final analysis the dedication to Islamic principles was rendered innocuous since it was left to the legislatures themselves to determine whether a matter was or was not in keeping with Islam. While this accorded with modernist views, it was displeasing to both traditionalists and fundamentalists since not only Muslim laymen but also non-Muslims would share in determining the character of the Islamic society. As the time for the first general elections approached, the struggle for position among political parties and groups caused the reopening of most of the issues "settled" in the constitution: the role of Islam, the unification of West Pakistan, parity, and provincial autonomy. Political instability in the central government and in both provincial governments brought the parliamentary system into disrepute, until on October 7, 1958, President Iskander Mirza proclaimed martial law, abolished political parties, dismissed all ministers, and abrogated the constitution on the ground that it had proved unworkable under Pakistani conditions.

The imposition of martial law inaugurated a new era in Pakistan. General Muhammad Ayub Khan, the commander-in-chief of the army and also chief martial law administrator,

took over as president on October 27, a date since commemo-
rated as "Revolution Day." The new regime promised to
purge and reform the society, to create conditions under
which a meaningful democracy could exist. Strong action
was taken against smugglers and black marketeers, the public
services were purged of corrupt officers, and former politicians were investigated and in some cases disqualified from
further public office. A variety of special commissions were
appointed to study national problems and make recommendations for reform. In January, 1959, President Ayub
Khan promulgated a land reform for West Pakistan to break
the social and political grip of the old ruling class. Subsequently action was taken to bring Muslim shrines and holy
places under government supervision in order to end corruption and the exploitation of the credulous peasantry by
unscrupulous "holy men." The provincial administrative system, especially in West Pakistan, was decentralized and simplified in order to make it more accessible to the people.
Other reforms were initiated in the fields of law, education,
medicine, agricultural credit and development, and so on.

In his first address to the nation, President Ayub Khan
promised the restoration of democracy, but of a type that
Pakistanis "could understand and work." It was his view
that the British parliamentary system as in effect in Pakistan
since 1947 was too remote from the common man to be
comprehensible and was therefore ineffective. He believed
that the political process should begin at a level appropriate
to the rural, overwhelmingly illiterate character of the population and that representation at higher levels should be indirect, chosen by members of local councils from among
persons with whose abilities they were acquainted. On the
national level, he felt that authority to govern should be
unified in the hands of the president rather than being divided
between the president and a prime minister dependent on the
favor of a legislature. Given Pakistan's physical division and
the diverse interests of the people, he believed that overall
unity of direction was of paramount importance.

President Ayub's political conceptions were embodied in
the Basic Democracies system, established during 1960 on
the basis of elections held in December, 1959, and January,
1960. The Basic Democracies structure is a system of four
tiers of councils, linking the people at the local-government
level ultimately with the provincial government at the top.
The primary unit is the Union Council, with local-government functions, elected by adult franchise and with jurisdiction over some 10,000–12,000 people. Three higher levels
of councils, in ever-widening circles, combine members
drawn from the unions with officials and other private citizens

appointed to serve. The system is closely meshed with the development responsibilities of the administration and is intended both to inform officials of public needs and to acquaint the public with the problems of the administration. Members are elected (at the union level) and appointed on the basis of personal reputation and ability, and they have no political affiliations. The system was greeted with great enthusiasm because for the first time it established a uniform system of local government and administration throughout the country and because of the new emphasis on development and the public responsibilities of the administration.

Popular approval of President Ayub's administration and sanction for him to proceed with the formulation of a new constitution was afforded by a referendum of the newly elected union councillors on February 14, 1960. Rather than reopen the public constitutional debate, the president appointed a commission to make recommendations to aid him in his task. After lengthy and careful deliberation, the new constitution of the Republic of Pakistan was promulgated on March 1, 1962, giving permanent effect to the general pattern in accordance with which Pakistan had been governed since the revolution. In outline, the constitution provides a definite separation and balance of powers between the president and his ministers, the national assembly, and the judiciary. It is therefore a break away from the pattern established by the Government of India Act of 1935 and followed in the constitution of 1956. However, the independent executive with strong powers vis-à-vis the legislature is very reminiscent of the role of the governor-general in British India (especially under the 1919 reforms and before) and indeed of the Islamic concept of the *amir* vested with almost unlimited powers to rule the community under God's law.

The new constitution abandons the attempt made since 1935 to balance the claims of center against provinces in a federal distribution of powers. Instead, a relatively short exclusive list of central powers is set out, and all other matters are left normally to the provinces. However, this is not a true federal system because the national assembly retains the right to legislate concerning any matter "in the national interest," and the president appoints and dismisses provincial governors, who are responsible to him. In case of conflict between the governor, as representative of the president, and the provincial assembly, as representative of the people, the ultimate solution (following, perhaps, a new provincial election) must be the replacement of the governor with someone who can get along with the legislators. Although neither the governor nor his ministers are dependent on the assembly, political realities and governmental efficiency demand a substantial degree of cooperation between them. The degree of actual autonomy to be enjoyed by the provinces will therefore be determined by political circumstances, as has, in fact, always been the case, given the reserved central powers under the previous constitutions.

President Ayub's ideas concerning the meaning of representation are embodied in the electoral provisions of the constitution. The president and the national and provincial assemblies are to be elected by an electoral college made up of 40,000 electors in each province, who in turn are elected by adult franchise. The members of the electoral college in each province are grouped to form 75 national-assembly constituencies and 150 provincial-assembly constituencies. (In addition, in each province there are three special seats in the national assembly and five in the provincial assembly for women.) For the first elections in April and May, 1962, the union councillors elected in 1960 served as the electoral college. There was no presidential election because the referendum of February 14, 1960, had confirmed President Ayub in office until 1965. The newly elected assemblies will also serve until 1965, and thereafter the normal term both of the assemblies and of the president will be five years. However, if the president dissolves the national assembly before the end of its normal term, he too must stand for reelection.

Philosophically, the present constitution is rooted both in President Ayub's suspicion and distrust of conventional politics and in his firm belief in the validity of Islam as a moral determinant of political behavior. His distrust of politics is reflected in the constitutional separation of the executive from the legislature so that the stability of the government will be unaffected by random changes of political opinion. It is further reflected in the provisions for indirect elections and in the constitutional prohibition of political parties except as they may be permitted by law, which stem from the president's belief that public representatives can and should be elected on the basis of their known qualities rather than on the basis of party or other considerations. During the parliamentary era political groupings had few principles, and those few were only dimly related to the public welfare. Above all, the lack of a firmly shared morality binding public representatives to a recognized standard of behavior prevented the development of a sense of responsibility either among the voters or their representatives. President Ayub has indicated since he assumed office his conviction that Islam can provide the necessary cement to bind together the political community and to imbue its various elements with an appropriate sense of responsibility. However, he has repeatedly made clear that in order to do so, Islam must be interpreted in a scientific and realistic spirit and must not be tied to sterile legalisms or outdated practices.

Although Pakistan is no longer described as an "Islamic Republic," the president must be a Muslim, and the constitution declares that no law should be repugnant to Islam. However, it is left to the president and the legislators—including non-Muslims—to determine what is required or forbidden by Islam, and no law can be challenged in the courts on the ground that it is un-Islamic. Similarly, although the constitution declares as "principles of lawmaking" that fundamental rights—such as freedoms of speech, assembly, and religion—should be preserved, an act of the legislature cannot be challenged on the ground that it infringes those rights. The Advisory Council of Islamic Ideology, made up of persons with an understanding and appreciation of Islam and of the economic, political, and other problems of Pakistan, exists to offer advice on the observance of the "principles of lawmaking" when requested, but final responsibility rests with the president and the assemblies. In other words, personal liberties and Islamic principles generally are left to the good conscience of the legislators, on the apparent ground that if the people and their representatives do not believe in the preservation of these principles, it will be of no use to attempt to guarantee them by constitutional phrases. Thus the voice of the people is supreme, and the courts must enforce the law as enacted by the people's representatives. The nature of that law, and accordingly the character of the Pakistani society, whether free or otherwise, will in the long run be determined by the view of Islam taken by the awakening Muslim millions.

The task of forging a new and stable society out of the disparate geographic, ethnic, and philosophic elements of the state has been complicated by Pakistan's strained relations with India. The antipathy between the Muslim League and the National Congress shifted after 1947 from the plane of national politics to that of international tensions. The basic premise of the Pakistan movement, that religious commitment gives Muslims a distinct national identity, conflicts directly with the National Congress belief that Indian nationality embraces equally persons of all faiths. Although Congress accepted the principle of self-determination for Muslim-majority areas in 1947, it was conceded as a necessary evil to be minimized by the partition of Bengal and Punjab and by the retention in association with the Indian Union of as many princely states as possible. Thus in October, 1947, India accepted the accession of the Hindu ruler of Muslim-majority Kashmir without reference to the communal principle of partition, and ultimately repudiated an early pledge to consult the people through a plebiscite on the legal ground that the accession once made was irrevocable. However, Pakistan regards Kashmir as a natural part of her national territory and in 1947–1948 intervened militarily in order to prevent India from occupying the entire state and thus controlling the headwaters of all the rivers of the Indus basin and outflanking West Pakistan strategically. Since the United Nations-sponsored cease-fire of January 1, 1949, Pakistan has never ceased to urge the Kashmiris' right to self-determination, confident that a plebiscite would confirm the two-nation principle. The deadlock between the two countries is especially bitter because Pakistanis feel that the Pakistan movement will not have been fulfilled until this last Muslim-majority area is freed of Indian control, whereas to India the retention of Kashmir is essential to demonstrate her claim to be a secular and non-sectarian state. To Pakistan, India's attitude on the Kashmir question indicates a refusal to accept the implications of partition and a long-term hope of reestablishing Hindu dominance throughout the subcontinent.

Because of the importance of the Kashmir issue to Pakistan, it has become the touchstone by which all else is evaluated. Relations with India can never become normal until the dispute is settled to Pakistan's satisfaction, whatever progress may be made in solving lesser problems. Pakistan's involvement in the Central and Southeast Asia Treaty organizations was intended by her policy makers to bolster her against the threat posed by India, and her foreign policy in general has had the primary aims of asserting Pakistan's independence of India and of persuading other countries of the justice of her case in Kashmir. Pakistan's friends are judged by their attitudes on Kashmir, and in consequence both the Commonwealth of Nations and the United States have been found wanting by Pakistani opinion. While Pakistanis are conscious that their country is smaller and weaker than India, they insist that their views be heard and respected, and they resent any suggestion that Pakistan is in any sense inferior to India. They are confident that justice will eventually prevail in Kashmir and that despite Indian opposition, Pakistan will succeed in creating a lasting and dynamic Islamic social order. Whether that Islamic social order will be sympathetic to the values cherished by the West will be influenced by the degree to which Pakistanis feel that they have been treated justly by the great democracies.

Southeast Asia

The Old World of Southeast Asia

SOUTHEAST ASIA is a convenient term for a wide region comprising a number of countries linked together by certain historical and cultural ties—Burma, Thailand, Cambodia, Laos, Vietnam, Malaya and Singapore, Indonesia, the Philippines, and the British territories in North Borneo. Today as in the past, each one of these countries possesses its own individual character, yet together they have much in common: in their social and cultural background, in ways of life, and in outlook on the world. The roots of present-day ways of living and ways of thinking, in Southeast Asia as elsewhere, lie deeply embedded in the past. And so it is that if we wish to understand something of the ideas, the needs, and the aims of the peoples of Southeast Asia in the world today, we need to know a little of the older world out of which they have come.

In more than one sense the 220 million people of Southeast Asia today are living in a midway position between two worlds. Geographically they are placed between two powerful neighbors, India and China, the giants of the Asian continent; they are also between two great oceans, the Indian and the Pacific. Culturally and economically, today as in the past, they are linked with the neighboring peoples of Asia and also with the peoples of the Western world. Ideologically they live today under the contrasting shades of democratic India and totalitarian China. Historically they stand between their own static, largely self-contained world of the past and our dynamic intercontinental world of today.

A tropical region rich in natural resources, Southeast Asia, though new in terms of modern development, is one of the world's oldest areas of human occupation. Some of the earliest pages in the story of mankind describe how primitive man on the Indonesian island of Java learned to come to terms with the world around him. There and elsewhere in the region man early evolved methods of making the first simple tools that were to be his keys to world civilization.

All the possibilities of civilization arose, as elsewhere, from the discovery of the art of food production, or agriculture; and our general picture of life in early Southeast Asia is one of groups of families living in small villages in areas where comparatively open land made irrigated rice cultivation possible. In other areas a family might clear a space in wooded or jungle land, cultivate it for a year or so, and then move on to another temporary location. Near to coasts and rivers especially, fishing would be an important additional occupation; Southeast Asians in general have always been expert fishermen and boatmen. The typical family home would be a wooden structure raised on piles or stilts above the ground, as it is today in many country parts of the region. An ox or buffalo would find shelter underneath the house, and there too would be stored the family's agricultural implements. Economically the family would be largely self-supporting in food, clothing, and shelter. In ways of living, the general picture is not basically different from that of the remoter rural parts of Southeast Asia today.

In ways of thinking, narrow horizons restricted men's minds. The village community or sometimes a group of villages formed the widest conceivable unit of society. Immediately around it lay a strange world believed to be largely inhabited by the spirits of nature and the souls of the dead, ever-present beings that must be either avoided or placated. A hill or mountain visible from the village would be regarded as particularly sacred, a special abode from which the spirits or gods dominated the surrounding countryside. Animism, this sense of an all-pervasive spirit force in nature, governed much of the conduct of daily life. Rules of behavior based largely on accumulated experience of the spirit world were handed down by word of mouth, often as simple poetry, from one generation to another. The force of ancient local custom determined the obligations and privileges of individuals in the community. The village formed a closed little world of its own.

In the course of thousands of years, many waves of change have swept over the little world of the Southeast Asian village, carrying away much of the old yet leaving much behind. Because of its position on the map, Southeast Asia

BURMA

LAOS

THAILAND

VIETNAM

Rangoon

Bangkok

CAMBODIA

Pnonpenh

Saigon

Andaman Sea

South China Sea

Penang

MALAYA

Medan

Kuching

Singapore

BORNEO

INDIAN OCEAN

I   N   D   O

SUMATRA

Java Sea

Jakarta   JAVA

Surabaya

PHILIPPINES

Sulu Sea

PACIFIC OCEAN

Celebes Sea

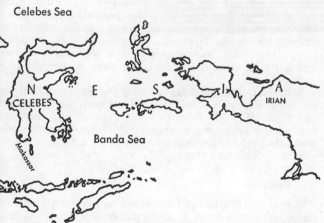

N E S I A

CELEBES

IRIAN

Makassar

Banda Sea

has always been peculiarly exposed to crosscurrents of cultural and commercial influence. As a result, the whole region today may perhaps be compared to a large layer cake in which a number of cultural layers have been superimposed one upon another, each clearly distinguishable but each merging into another.

Indian cultural influence was the first clear layer to be added above the original basis of simple agricultural animism in most of Southeast Asia. And Indian influence originated, as did that of Islam and that of the West in later times, in trade and commerce. From earliest times the economic factor has been of key significance in the international relations of Southeast Asia. In early centuries it was the gold, tin, and valuable woods of the region that drew Indian trading ships to its shores; in later centuries its spices, rice, rubber, and tin have had similar effects on the trading ships of the West. Commercial and cultural influences have always been closely interrelated in the history of the region.

Originating in commercial contacts that began as far back as the sixth century B.C. or earlier, the cultural influence of India definitely began to make itself felt in parts of Southeast Asia by the first century of our era. This was the unplanned consequence of the individual activities of many generations of Indian traders in the seaports of the region; there was no mass immigration of Indian people. New and wider religious, social, and political concepts gradually entered into the mind of Southeast Asia as a result of such contacts. New Southeast Asian states arose under ruling groups whose ideas and techniques closely reflected Indian patterns of law and government, art and religion, literature and life. Under these new rulers the vast majority of the people continued for a long time to retain very much the same outlook on life as before; the lower layer of indigenous culture remained largely unaffected. But gradually, over the course of centuries, Indian cultural and religious ways of thought took root.

Buddhism, the greatest surviving legacy of Indian influence in Southeast Asia today, formed deep roots in Burma and Thailand. With those two countries we may therefore conveniently commence a rapid survey of the world of Southeast Asia as it had become by about 1870, the eve of a century of revolutionary change.

Burma

Burma in 1870 had already begun to move out of its old traditional world. Some of its people, those living in the hilly areas, were even then still largely animists; but the major distinct groups of Burmans, Mons, and Shans were Buddhists with an advanced culture that had achieved a fairly wide diffusion of elementary education and a well-balanced organization of political, social, and religious institutions. Economic structure and techniques remained comparatively simple. The village, still largely self-contained, was the basic unit of social and economic life. The group of some fifteen to twenty villages forming a "circle," or township, under its hereditary local chieftain, was the basic unit of local administration. There was a fairly complex central government functioning under the absolute authority of a king who was still regarded, in the old tradition of Indian monarchy, as semi-divine.

The monarchy drew its main strength from the central plain of Upper Burma, where a large settled population subsisted on a mixed, dry agriculture. Ever since the eleventh century the Burman kings had struggled to impose unity on the whole country by subduing the Mons to the south and the Shans to the north, but with only limited success. Since the sixteenth century they had also made many attempts to conquer the neighboring kingdom of Thailand; but even the capture and destruction of the Thai capital, Ayudhya, in 1767 had not brought that country under Burma's control.

Entrenched in Upper Burma, the monarchy and central government had remained until near the end of the eighteenth century almost completely isolated from the influences of the wider world. Neither the Portuguese, the first Western nation to establish maritime and commercial power in Southeast Asia, nor their European successors, the Dutch, English, and French, had established more than comparatively fleeting contacts with the fringes of the Burman world. There was little to attract them commercially, for Burma in those days had little to offer for export except teakwood, and her export trade was a crown monopoly subject to the whims and extortions of royal officials.

It was a fresh outburst of national expansion that drew the attention of the outside world back to Burma about the end of the eighteenth century. Frustrated in the direction of Thailand, Burma turned westward, overran her borders with Arakan and Assam, and soon came face to face with the rising power of the British in India. Efforts to reach a settlement of border difficulties were defeated by mutual suspicion, and in 1824 Britain and Burma were at war. Two years later, when British forces were within a few days' march of the royal capital, Burma agreed to come to terms, surrendering much of her coastal territory to Britain. But not only did this closer contact fail to establish common ground between the two countries; their relations worsened, and in

1852 they were at war again. As a result, Burma lost what remained of her coastland, including the port of Rangoon.

By 1870, then, Burma had come to be partitioned between two very different and unequal powers, the traditional government of Upper Burma and the British administration of Lower Burma. Whereas the life of the still independent area of Upper Burma remained largely unaltered, the forces of change were already at work in British Burma, now opened to the world. There the old trade restrictions had been replaced by economic freedom; and trade, wealth, and population had increased as a result. The opening up of foreign markets had led to a remarkable expansion of rice production. And social change was following in the wake of economic change. Although except the bustling seaport of Rangoon life in the ordinary villages went on very much as for centuries before, the people of Burma as a whole were standing at the doorway to a new world.

Thailand

Like Burma, Thailand in early times had absorbed a significant element of Indian culture. Buddhism, with its philosophy of acceptance, of calm, gentle self-abnegation, molded the character of its people. As in Burma, too, the faith and ritual of Buddhism were closely linked to the personal majesty of a semidivine absolute monarch and to the ceremonial of his court. The state and all its might were the king's; the yellow-robed monks of Buddhism were his spiritual army.

The Thai people had emerged in the thirteenth century as a national entity under royal rule in the fertile land that bears their name today. In subsequent centuries they extended their influence southward into the Malay Peninsula, but their main external efforts were occupied in a long series of wars with neighboring Burma. The destruction of their old capital, Ayudhya, by the Burmese in 1767 was a severe loss, but it marked a fresh start in the history of the Thais by causing them to found a new capital at Bangkok, nearer the sea and therefore more open to the influences of a larger world.

As in Burma, the external relations of Thailand were regarded as primarily the personal concern of the king. He was the state, and so it seemed natural that he should have a monopoly of the export trade and the first call on all imports. Since the sixteenth century European traders had tried out the possibilities of business with Thailand, especially as buyers of her tin and teakwood, but they found it impossible to get the trade established on a settled basis. Toward the end of the seventeenth century France under Louis XIV had developed closer relations with Thailand through an aid program for the supply of troops and technicians; but before long this had led to a strong reaction against French influence, and from then on Thailand remained extremely suspicious of European motives.

Fresh approaches by the West in the first half of the nineteenth century met with a cool reception. Britain secured limited trading arrangements with Bangkok in 1825, but there was no real change in Thailand's international outlook until the accession of King Mongkut (Rama IV) in 1851. It was he who set the tone of Thailand's foreign policy in the modern age, a policy of judicious concession to the forces of modernization.

Yet Thailand in 1870 retained in large part the traditional attitudes and ways of past centuries. In the minds of the Thai people their country was still a world in itself, a self-sufficient, unchanging world of peaceful rice fields, quiet villages, and local Buddhist monasteries that served as schools and social centers as well as places of worship, a world of long-established social gradings, privileges, and obligations ruled from the distant capital city by a remote, mysterious god-king. If the people of Thailand were at all aware of other lands, it was of China they thought, the homeland of the immigrant tradesmen and shopkeepers of Bangkok and the provincial towns.

But with the coming to power of King Chulalongkorn (Rama V) in 1873, following a five-year regency, Thailand began to move rapidly forward into the modern age.

Laos and Cambodia

To the east and north of Thailand, across the great river Mekong, lies the land of Laos. Its people, Buddhist in religion and closely related to the Thais, settled along the upper waters of the Mekong in the thirteenth century, with Luangprabang as the main center of their kingdom. Three centuries later they had moved their capital southward down the river to Vientiane, but the old town of Luangprabang retained much of its earlier importance and prestige. These two capital towns, old and new, reflected a duality and a weakness that were to persist throughout much of the history of Laos. By the early years of the eighteenth century they had become the centers of two distinct rival kingdoms, neither one strong enough to resist external aggression. Thus by the opening of the nineteenth century both the Laos kingdoms had become dependencies of Thailand; and by 1830 Vientiane, conquered and devastated by the Thais, had ceased to exist as a separate kingdom.

Laos in 1870, then, was a subject state of Thailand, a land of vast jungle and narrow plains, hidden away from the world behind hill and river barriers, untouched by external influences other than those of her immediate neighbors, and known to the West only through the few travel accounts of European explorers.

Cambodia, another eastward neighbor of Thailand, has in past centuries endured a hard struggle for survival. Originally it was one of the major states of early Southeast Asia in terms of both power and civilization. During the period covering the ninth to fourteenth centuries, when Angkor was the capital, a period whose glory is reflected in the majestic wat (temple) and other great buildings of Angkor that still survive today, the people of Cambodia achieved a high level of material and cultural development based on a combination of the Indian traditions inherited from earlier centuries and the local economic and social resources that permitted large-scale rice production. Under continuous pressure from neighboring peoples, especially the Thais, Angkor was abandoned in the fifteenth century in favor of a new capital at Pnompenh, near the banks of the lower Mekong; but this move left the nerve center of Cambodia even more exposed than before. From then on Cambodia was involved in a long struggle to avoid subjection by aggressive neighbors on either side, Thai and Vietnamese. For centuries these competed for control over her, always seeking an opportunity to cut off slices of her territory, so that by the opening of the nineteenth century she was reduced to about half the size she had been in the days of Angkor. The Vietnamese had made the greatest inroads, and infiltration by Vietnamese into Cambodian lands remained a continuing process through the first half of the nineteenth century. Wars, too, continued between Thailand and Vietnam for control of Cambodia until 1845, when a compromise agreement for joint protection was reached. But this balance was soon to be upset by the intervention of a new power factor, France, already established in southern Vietnam. By 1870 the new ruler of Cambodia, King Norodom, had been persuaded to exchange the protection of his powerful neighbors for that offered by a still greater power from the West.

Vietnam

Like the other countries dealt with so far, Vietnam is predominantly Buddhist in religion, but unlike them, she derived her first layer of culture above that of basic animism not from distant India but from neighboring China. As a result, the outlook of the people of Vietnam has been shaped by a mixture of Confucian, Taoist, and Buddhist traditions of thought added to an underlying animism. In political organization, too, Vietnam was for many centuries largely a replica of China. She was ruled by an emperor (regarded by the people as having a direct mandate from heaven) through the agency of a ruling class of mandarins, men who had passed into the civil service through success in a series of stiff competitive examinations in Confucianist learning. But although Chinese cultural penetration has been effective in past centuries, China's occasional attempts at political domination have always met with strong resistance from the Vietnamese ever since they succeeded in throwing off her imperial control in the tenth century.

A persistent feature of the history of the Vietnamese people from the tenth century onward has been their steady southward drive from the Tonkin area, bordering on China, down along the narrow coastal plain to the delta region of the Mekong River (where Saigon now stands) and beyond. This process was still continuing when the situation was suddenly frozen by French intervention, soon after the middle of the last century. Another feature of Vietnam's history, linked to this process, has been an underlying dichotomy between north and south, reflected from the early years of the seventeenth century in a long struggle between two rival families for power behind the imperial throne of Vietnam, and arising partly from a geographical layout that makes Vietnam a country of two separate river-delta regions—those of the Red River in the north and the Mekong in the south —linked by a narrow strip of coastal lowland.

Disunity within Vietnam opened the door to the first stage of European intervention in modern times. Although Portuguese, French, Dutch, and English traders or missionaries had visited the country from time to time, at the opening of the nineteenth century her ruling class as a whole still shared with that of China a firm determination to resist the influence of the West. But the new emperor of Vietnam in 1802 would not have reached the throne without French support, obtained through a missionary bishop, in the civil wars that preceded his accession. France, however, had made no serious effort to exploit this particular situation; and despite her assistance at that time, later emperors of Vietnam reverted to the traditional policy of isolation. In fact Vietnam in the middle years of the nineteenth century shared with China a growing fear of the West and a deep-seated suspicion of Western motives in eastern Asia.

As in China, these feelings found vent in sudden outbursts of violence against Western missionaries and native Christians. A series of such outbursts in the 1850's, involving the deaths of four Catholic missionaries, led to the second stage of French intervention in Vietnam in 1858, when France had a strong naval force in the Far East for co-operation with the British against China. Saigon, the key to the river Mekong, was captured in 1859, and by 1866 France had occupied the major part of southern Vietnam.

Thus by 1870 France had obtained her first foothold in both Cambodia and Vietnam. But her real aims in subsequent years were to be concentrated on the extension of her influence northward into Tonkin and southwest China, with a view to developing the mineral resources of those areas and opening up trade with China as a whole. About the same time, British commercial interests were planning to develop trade routes through Burma into China.

But these moves in power politics had so far made little difference to the life of the Vietnamese people as a whole. The village in Vietnam was still a world in itself, a self-contained social, economic, and administrative unit linked only by the slenderest of ties with the central government and the outside world.

The Malay Peninsula

The Malay Peninsula, extending southward like a spear from the Indochinese mainland, commands the main gateway from the Indian Ocean into the South China Sea. Yet it remained for many centuries a marginal area in relation to the main centers of population and power in Southeast Asia, coming to a greater or lesser extent under the control of more powerful neighbors to north and south. Malaya, largely covered by dense jungle, lacked a natural center of population or point of unity; its people lived in scattered villages on the river banks or along the coast. Singapore, off the southernmost tip of the peninsula, today one of the world's great seaports, was of small significance until the nineteenth century. Malacca, well situated on the narrow waters between the Indian Ocean and the China Sea, became commercially important as a center for the exchange and distribution of goods for Southeast Asia as a whole, but only for a time. After a period of commercial prominence lasting from 1400 for two centuries, Malacca relapsed into comparative insignificance.

More important was the part Malacca played during that period as a cultural distribution center. Early Indian influence, entering the peninsula at several points along the coast, had made a deep impression upon the leaders of the scattered Malay communities; but being unable to establish a single area of concentration, it remained a comparatively thin cultural layer. When a new external influence, that of Islam, arrived in the Malayan area after 1300, it therefore found easy acceptance as a further layer of religion and culture. Moreover, Malacca, emerging as a major exchange port with wide trade connections from about 1400, offered Islamic influence not only a point of concentration for Malaya itself but also a point of departure for further penetration into Indonesia and across to the Philippines.

It was against Malacca, as a key commercial and cultural center, that the Portuguese concentrated their attack when they first came to Southeast Asia; and it was from Malacca, captured in 1511, that they made their further advance eastward to the Indonesian islands, China, and Japan. It was natural that the Dutch in their turn should aim to become masters of Malacca, as they did in 1641. But the main interest of the Dutch in the coming centuries was to lie in Indonesia; and so, from the Western point of view, Malaya now became of secondary importance.

But only for a time. Modern Malaya begins with the founding of a British settlement at Penang on the northwest coast in 1786, a step largely due to the initiative of private traders but also partly reflecting Britain's growing interest in Southeast Asia and China. This was only a first step, to be followed before long by the British settlement of Singapore island in 1819.

A new commercial power from the West now stood at the edge of the world of Malaya. It was a world about which little was known, a sparsely populated country of separate sultanates, small upriver states accessible only by boat or elephant and lacking any cohesive force except that of a lightly held Islamic faith. British policy was to avoid real interference with this static world apart from setting definite limits in 1826 to the extent of Thailand's control. But by its very presence, British rule in the seaports of Singapore, Penang, and Malacca acted as an invitation to new forces of change that would not be likely to halt at the doors of the Malayan world within.

Indonesia

Life in Indonesia in early times, as in other parts of Southeast Asia, centered in tribal and village communities based upon a communal-type organization of agriculture; it was largely dominated by a fundamental animism that has become overlaid, but by no means completely submerged, by later ways of thought. The rise of small states comprising village groupings of varying size under the rule of chieftains or rajas was a consequence of the introduction of Indian political ideas; even then it was not a general development, being confined mainly to the fertile island of Java and to the coastal fringes of other islands. Any real sense of unity among the diverse peoples of this island world had to await the impact of the external forces of a later age.

Java has always been the main power center of Indonesia, with south and east Sumatra as its chief subsidiary. It was largely upon control of these twin bases of power that the Srivijaya empire, under a ruling class inspired by Indian political, religious, and cultural traditions, maintained a general dominance over the whole southern area of Southeast Asia between the ninth century and the thirteenth. Majapahit, a rival Indonesian power which took Srivijaya's place in the fourteenth century, based its strength on East Java.

Economically the preeminence of East Java at that time rested upon her ability to produce and export large quantities of rice, which she exchanged for supplies of pepper from Sumatra and West Java and spices from the Moluccas to the east. This exchange trade gave wealth and independence to the seaports of Java's north coast, thus increasing their attraction to foreign merchants, especially Indian cloth suppliers. Many of the latter came from parts of India such as Gujerat in the northwest, where Islam had now become established; their influence was an important factor in the acceptance of Islam in the seaports of southern Southeast Asia, leading to its ultimate spread through Malaya and most of Indonesia.

Indian merchants who came to Southeast Asia at this time were mainly interested in exchanging their cloth for Indonesian spices. In the same way, the Portuguese, with a rather more aggressive combination of crusading and commercial instincts, first came out to Asia in search of "Christians and spices." Following their conquest of Malacca in 1511, the Portuguese pushed on quickly to the Moluccas, or Spice Islands, the source of supply of the scarcest and therefore most valuable spices: nutmeg and clove. When the Dutch and English first came to Southeast Asia toward the end of the sixteenth century, they too concentrated on Indonesia and the spice trade.

In the end it was the Dutch who captured the spice trade and then went on to establish the first general foreign control of Indonesia as a whole. This was a long process. Playing on the divisions and rivalries among the ruling families of Java, the Dutch gradually succeeded in breaking the power of Mataram, which had emerged as the leading state in the seventeenth century; but it was toward the end of the eighteenth century before they managed to gain mastery over the whole island. Then Holland herself became greatly weakened through involvement in the international wars of the age of the American and French revolutions. For a time (1811–1816) she had to surrender Java and the other main islands of Indonesia to Britain. But with the end of this period of war, the Dutch recovered their former position in Indonesia, and during the first half of the nineteenth century they were able to increase their control and to develop in Java a highly organized system of agricultural production for export, mainly in coffee and sugar.

By 1870 Java and, to a lesser degree, the other islands of Indonesia had already undergone a comparatively long period of European domination. Local rulers in areas of major importance had come into line with the Dutch administration; agricultural production and external trade in general were largely geared to Dutch requirements. Indonesia's relations with the outside world were governed by Dutch interests. But their country's subjection to foreign control did not at that time weigh too heavily on the minds of the Indonesian people. Accustomed to arbitrary rule and feudal exactions, they did not necessarily feel any deep resentment against a remote system of administration that demanded labor services and the cultivation of commercial crops for export in addition to their own rice requirements. If Dutch rule imposed heavy demands on the people and drained off a large proportion of the wealth they created, it brought increased prosperity, order, and security to the countryside, and it left the traditional organization of village life largely untouched.

The Philippine Islands

The vast archipelago of the Philippine Islands includes eleven large islands (two of them, Luzon and Mindanao, of considerable size) and more than six thousand smaller ones. Ferdinand Magellan's voyage across the Pacific in the service of Spain in 1521 brought the West for the first time to this island world. Its scattered population, ethnically the same as the indigenous peoples of Malaya and Indonesia, lived in village communities under elected headmen. In earlier centuries they had been touched only lightly and indirectly by the influence of Indian culture, which, like the later influence of Islam, was probably transmitted from Borneo. By the time of Magellan's arrival in the Philippines, Islam had penetrated as far as the island of Mindanao.

The Philippines was thus the first of the Southeast Asian

countries to come completely under European colonial rule. A Spanish expedition from Mexico founded the colonial capital of Manila in 1571, and it was from Mexico that Spanish control over the islands was exercised for two centuries. The annual galleon that sailed between Manila and Acapulco sold its goods from the Philippines and China in exchange for the Mexican silver dollars that gradually became the common currency of South China and Southeast Asian ports. From Mexico, too, came the feudal system of colonialism already developed by the Spanish in South America. Grants of large tracts of land (*encomiendas*) to Spanish officials and churchmen carried rights concerning jurisdiction, taxation, compulsory labor, and other services.

But the Spanish colonial community of the Philippines was mainly concentrated in and around the city of Manila. Only comparatively few Spanish officials, priests, or soldiers lived among the Filipino people of the countryside. There village life went on with little change. The locally elected leaders of townships and villages retained their traditional status, adding to their customary duties the collection of tax and the organization of labor on behalf of the Spanish regime. In general the influence of the Catholic church, a great landowner, and of the local Spanish priest went much deeper than that of the central administration. Although Christianity made little or no headway among the people of the southern islands already converted to Islam, it was accepted by the great majority of the Filipino people as an additional religious and cultural layer above that of their basic animism.

In accordance with the exclusive mercantilist attitude of European powers toward their colonies, Spain maintained strict political and economic control over the Philippines to the end of the eighteenth century. Then more liberal views began to prevail, especially after the removal of Spanish Mexican control in 1820 had brought the Philippines into direct communication with Spain herself. The opening of Manila and other ports to world trade in the 1830's was the start of a new phase of economic development soon reflected in mounting export figures for agricultural products such as hemp, sugar, tobacco, and coffee. With the growth of trade there emerged a small Filipino middle class increasingly linked by education and political sympathies to the movements of liberal thought in Europe. The opening of the Suez Canal and the increasing use of the steamship only intensified a process of change that was affecting Spanish and Filipino alike. The triumph of liberal revolution in Spain in 1868 was transmitted to the Philippines in the following year, when the Spanish governor announced a series of liberal reforms abolishing press censorship and permitting free discussion of political questions. It seemed in 1870 that Spanish rule in the Philippines was wisely prepared to adapt itself to changing world conditions.

Southeast Asia on the Eve of Change

The face of Southeast Asia in 1870 had changed little from that which it had worn for centuries before. The influence of the West, though gradually increasing since the beginning of the nineteenth century, was still restricted to the outer fringes of the vast inner world of Southeast Asian peasant society. Looking outward from their coastal vantage points were a number of large commercial cities—Rangoon, Bangkok, Singapore, Djakarta, Saigon, Manila—each mirroring in its own way the methods and movements of international commerce. But life in such urban centers was something apart and aloof from that of the vast majority of the population. The isolation of village life was still almost complete. The outside world barely touched it; the state seldom intervened except occasionally in the form of a tax collector or, in Java, an agricultural overseer.

The mind of Southeast Asia, too, showed little change. The ordinary peasant could hardly imagine any other mode of existence than his own. For him the traditional life of village agriculture was not simply one method of subsistence, it was the only conceivable way of living. It was bound up with his whole stock of social and religious ideas: his ancestor worship, his customary duties and benefits, his respect for gods and spirits, his inheritance of story, poetry, and song. The emphasis of traditional society was on a religious rather than a rational view of the world, on personal status rather than impersonal law, on customary obligations rather than individual rights. There was no sense of the importance of the individual; social groups—family, clan, and village—were the significant units of society, each operating within its own framework of collective ownership and labor.

The Southeast Asian peasant in 1870 still farmed primarily for his own subsistence, not with the aim of selling his farm produce in the market. His main concern was to grow just enough food for himself and his family. Beyond that, if he had a surplus of rice he might sell some of it in order to meet specific marginal needs, to obtain cash for some special purpose or to purchase certain goods such as salt, iron, or imported cloth from outside the range of village produce. Otherwise the countryman in general had little use for money. There was practically no local accumulation of capital except by the small Chinese shopkeepers and merchants who handled retail trade and exchange over large parts of Southeast Asia.

The peasant had no idea of economic change because the economic conditions of life for him and his ancestors had remained for so long unchanged. He had no conception of progress; life and thought were equally static. Nor was there anywhere in Southeast Asia an indigenous social and economic class with which ideas of individualism and progress might have been associated. No middle class existed between the small ruling groups above and the mass of the peasant population below.

But if Southeast Asia one hundred years ago remained largely untouched by world change, the nature and speed of change itself had become very different from before. The industrialization of Western Europe, associated historically with the rise of a powerful middle class, the growth of science, and the emergence of the modern nation state, was bringing a whole new world into being, a world of individualism and private enterprise.

Expanding industries in the West created growing demand for raw materials and overseas markets. In response to this demand, long-distance transport was speeded up and communications improved. The steamship answered the call for regularity and speed in sea transport, and the opening of the Suez Canal in 1869 gave the steamship an even faster route between Europe and Asia. The combined results of these innovations were in the end to change the old world of Southeast Asia, for the opening of the Suez Canal to the steamship brought much more direct and frequent contact between the newly industrialized West and the traditional societies of Asia. It helped to bring about that deeper penetration of Western influence that was to generate economic, social, and political revolution in all the countries of Southeast Asia.

After 1870 there was a rapid expansion of Western control in Southeast Asia along with a fuller exploitation, under Western direction, of the region's great potential of natural resources. Western economic interest, hitherto divided between the control of trade and, with the Dutch, the organization of production, now placed its main emphasis on production. Investment of foreign capital stimulated production, which was mainly intended for export. This change of emphasis was accompanied by the advance of Western rule from its coastal footholds into the interior, thus following the earlier example of the Dutch in Java. Dutch direction of agriculture in Java, already successful in stepping up exports of commercial crops such as coffee and sugar, sent the export figures steadily higher after 1870. In all areas there was a general expansion of the old crops such as rice, as well as the development of new ones such as rubber. The region's mineral resources—tin and petroleum, for example—now began to be exploited for the first time systematically. This whole process of development was stimulated by the inward flow of capital and by the improvements in transport and communications both in Southeast Asia itself and throughout the world; it was sustained by Western technological, administrative, and judicial systems. As a consequence of all this, the life of Southeast Asia became now for the first time in history indissolubly linked with world movements; its overall economy became geared to and largely dependent upon world markets.

The modern economic development of Southeast Asia after 1870 required not only capital and direction but also labor and technical skill. These latter the traditional, custombound village communities of the Southeast Asian countryside were not yet ready to offer. Their place was therefore taken by immigrant labor from the human reservoirs of China and India. Once again in her history, Southeast Asia's geographical situation exposed her to a dual flow of social and cultural influences from her great neighbors. Although Indian cultural influences had been predominant in past centuries, imperial China, with her partly Buddhist traditions, her vast territory, and her great economic resources, had always been looked up to by the smaller states of Southeast Asia as a great patron and protector. Communities of Chinese merchants, shopkeepers, and artisans had been established for centuries in some of the commercial centers of Southeast Asia, in Manila, Djakarta, and Bangkok; and in scattered parts of the region, Chinese immigrant groups had long been engaged in specialized forms of agriculture or in tin mining. But the flow of Chinese and Indian immigrants into Southeast Asia in modern times was directly linked with the expansion of Western control after 1870. For them the opening up of the region to Western-directed economic development made it a new world of golden opportunity.

The energy and skill of these immigrant communities constituted an immensely valuable asset for Southeast Asia in her efforts to adapt herself to the standards and aims of modern economic organization. But their presence in fairly large numbers among the indigenous people of the region presented difficult problems of adjustment, problems everywhere associated with plural societies that are composed of several racial elements representing different social, cultural, and political traditions and lacking a common cohesive force. The addition of these new elements to the population greatly accentuated the complexity of the new situation that faced Southeast Asia after 1870.

The New World of Southeast Asia

Burma

In Burma British rule, which was extended over the whole country as a result of the conquest of Upper Burma through renewed war in 1885, attracted an immense flow of Indian immigrants. Burma was in fact administratively a province of British India until 1937. Although many of these immigrants were transients, coming and going as seasonal workers for rice planting, harvesting, or milling, many others settled into the country, particularly in and around Rangoon and in Lower Burma, as merchants, traders, shopkeepers, moneylenders, clerks, or general laborers. Indian capital and labor played a large part in Burma's spectacular economic development, especially in the expansion of rice production, which mounted steadily year by year until the slump of the 1930's. Burma's 1941 rice crop amounted to nearly six million tons, more than half of which was exported. Rising world demand stemming from a general population growth and improvements in transport and communications made Burma the greatest rice-exporting country in the world. Her economic development forged ahead in other directions too. Exploitation of her teak forests and oil and mineral resources became important factors in the national economy. In 1941 rice, timber, and benzine headed Burma's list of key exports.

Chinese immigrants took second place to Indians in commercial life, but they too were economically important as merchants, especially in the rice and timber trades; shopkeepers; and mining workers. Forming a comparatively small immigrant group, unlike the Indians they tended to merge into the rest of the community.

The Burmese people themselves played only a minor part compared with Europeans, Indians, or Chinese in the regeneration of their country's economic life. The vast majority of them remained peasant cultivators, left far behind in the new competition for economic advantage. They gained indirectly from the general increase in wealth, especially during the 1920's, the most prosperous decade in Burma's history; but often they lost through inability to comprehend the workings of a money economy and a strange system of law. Many fell into debt; some were forced to surrender ownership of their land to moneylenders. By 1941 about half of Burma's twelve million acres of cultivated land had passed to the ownership of Indian landlords.

There were other causes for serious social discontent. The abolition of the monarchy in 1885 had removed not only the head of state but also the traditional patron and protector of Buddhism. The vitality of the Buddhist monasteries and the influence of the monks had been undermined by a well-intentioned British policy of withdrawing the former official state patronage of Buddhism and substituting government and government-sponsored secular education for the old monastic schools. The British policy of reaching down to village level for local administration, order, and tax collection had resulted in converting the village headman from an elected leader of the people into an agent of the central government, depriving the village of its traditional autonomy, and draining it of its former social vitality. The Burmese people began to feel themselves trapped in a situation beyond their control, a situation dictated by the overriding interests of a remote impersonal power.

A growing sense of frustration and bewilderment among the Burmese found vent in increasingly open challenges to British rule after World War I. The Indian nationalist movement provided a pattern of aims and methods, except that Burma, lacking India's middle class, found sustenance for her growing nationalism not among business and professional circles but in the countryside among local leaders and village monks. The social and economic roots of Burmese feeling were revealed by occasional outbursts of violence against immigrant Indians and Chinese. Britain made constitutional concessions to this rising nationalism in a series of installments from 1920 on. By 1937 a Burmese government and parliament had obtained a large measure of control over the country's internal affairs, though British control still covered external relations. But the time remaining between 1937 and the coming of the Pacific War was too short to allow the established nationalist leaders to achieve much progress.

The real strength of Burma's national feeling was revealed only when, in the late 1930's, a new generation of young Western-educated Burmese leaders began to harness the forces of the deep upsurge of political-religious emotion in the countryside. This was the Thakin group, the founder members of which, including U Nu, later to become Burma's leading statesman, were at that time students of Rangoon University. Their title of *thakin*, meaning lord, or master, reflected a determination to make the Burmese masters of their own country. This group, which generally favored a policy of democratic socialism, later formed the AFPFL (Anti-Fascist People's Freedom League) Party, which took over leadership of the nationalist movement at the end of the Japanese War.

Soon after the outbreak of war in late 1941, British rule in Burma was overthrown. It was never to be fully restored. For after a short postwar period of adjustment following the defeat of Japan and the ending of war in 1945, Britain gave Burma independence in 1947. Thakin Nu became premier of his country's first independent republican government.

New Burma is a federal republic of five component states, one each for the different ethnic groups of Burmese, Karens, Shans, Kayah, and Kachins. The national flag of Burma symbolizes this structure: a large white star surrounded by five smaller ones. According to the constitution, the government of Burma must always include at least one representative of each of these ethnic groups, who together make up the more than nineteen million population. To weld these various peoples into a single nation remains Burma's most difficult long-term problem. In seeking to solve it, the country's rulers look to a restored and revitalized Buddhism as a most powerful integrating force, while at the same time assuring religious toleration to Christian, Muslim, and animist minorities.

Burma's more immediate difficulties since the war have been mainly economic, though these are inseparable from her social and political problems. Twice fought over between 1942 and 1945, she suffered more heavily from the war than any other Southeast Asian country. Communist rebellion in 1948 retarded her recovery. Her economic dependence on a single commodity, rice, exposed her to the shocks of postwar fluctuation in world demand. An eight-year master plan for economic and social reintegration had to be severely modified because of a steep fall in world prices for rice in 1952. Another basic difficulty was that although widespread elementary education in village schools had given Burma a high percentage of literacy, too few of her people were experienced in the practical problems of leadership and organization in a modern society.

In the face of continuing operations of a wide variety of rebel groups, including Communists, the serene personality of U Nu, premier of Burma for most of the period since independence, has remained a powerful influence for unity. But at more than one moment of national crisis U Nu has had to stand down, and the army has moved in. In September, 1958, and again in March, 1962, General Ne Win and his military colleagues took over the reins of government from the politicians, claiming that the latter had failed to take firm measures against the mounting threat to the country's internal security.

Having recently emerged from colonial rule, Burma's chief desire in her external relations is to go her own way, maintaining an independent neutralist attitude toward all major powers and power blocs. The first country to grant recognition to the Communist government of Peking, she has maintained good relations with China despite difficulties in reaching agreement on frontier problems. A treaty of friendship and nonaggression was signed between the two countries in 1961.

Looking back, the story of the past hundred years forms only a brief chapter in Burma's long history. But it was a chapter packed with momentous change for the Burmese people.

Thailand

Thailand is the only one of the Southeast Asian countries never under colonial rule. This was due partly to rivalry between Britain and France, each protecting Thailand from the other, and partly to the skillful guidance of the Thai monarchy. Thailand's independence was guaranteed under an Anglo-French agreement of 1896, though she was later shorn of some of her outlying territories. Her modern kings of the Chakri dynasty were mainly responsible for holding the colonial powers at arm's length by a program of modernization that brought the country into line with Western ideas of law and government.

In the eyes of his people, King Rama V, who succeeded to the throne in 1873 (after a regency of five years), was a semidivine absolute monarch like all his predecessors. Despite the innovations of King Mongkut before him (1851–1868), Thailand in 1873 was still a traditional Southeast Asian kingdom, feudalistic in structure with hardly anything in the way of modern systems of law, finance, administration, or communications. All that was changed under Rama V. The legal system was modernized; the administration was remodeled along Western lines with the help of American, British, and other foreign advisers; new roads and railways transformed the old system of communications; new treaties with foreign powers revolutionized the country's external relations. Traditional systems of debt slavery and forced labor were ended. New vistas in national education were opened up after 1910 when to the old village monastic schools, similar to those of Burma, was added a modern school system leading up to a university on the Western pattern. To foster national leadership, picked young men were sent abroad for college and university education. A new nation-state was being created.

But all these changes were introduced as favors from above. Rama V and his successors, for all their modernist leanings, retained their right to absolute power. They kept a firm grip on the details of government, sharing the exercise of power to only a limited extent with a small group of ministers, many of them princes of the royal family. Inevitably, however, the process of modernization caught up at length with the monarchy itself. A group of Western-educated middle-class revolutionaries, including lawyers and military officers, seized power in a *coup d'état* in 1932, forcing the king to concede a constitution that provided for a national assembly. This new ruling group proceeded to carry forward the program of modernization where it remained uncompleted, in the legal, administrative, and educational systems. They raised the country's international standing by the revision of treaties so as to bring to an end concessions of legal immunity granted to foreigners in earlier days.

The revolution, having removed power from its traditional basis in the monarchy, placed it firmly in the hands of a new oligarchy. The new national assembly was not representative of the people, half of its membership being nominated by the government. The small group that came to the top through the revolution of 1932, dominated increasingly by its military elements, kept a tight hold on the power they had won. The only significant shifts of power in subsequent years have been from one leading personality to another—as, for example, from Field Marshal Pibul to Field Marshal Sarit in 1957—within the existing framework of oligarchy.

Thailand's political system remained thus halted between monarchy and democracy. No basis for a genuinely democratic system of government had in fact been established. The predominantly peasant population, accustomed for centuries to benevolent despotism and insufficiently educated for the responsibilities of democracy, remained largely unconcerned with the series of political changes centering in the capital. Such national elections as were held met with increasing public indifference, the effect of which was only to encourage the ruling oligarchy to consolidate its power.

Thus the pace of political and social change in Thailand is slow. And it seems likely to remain slow as long as the danger of unrest in neighboring countries and the threat of Communist subversion within appear to justify the "strongman" government that has become the norm in modern Thailand.

A stable and sufficient agricultural economy, combined with the influence of the Buddhist tradition, forms the basis of Thailand's political conservatism. The typical Thai is a small farmer who owns his land and cultivates it on a family basis. Despite population increase, there is no serious pressure on the large amount of fertile land available. From early in the present century, as debt slavery was gradually ended, newly freed peasants were able to strike out on their own as rice farmers merely by taking up land previously unoccupied. This heritage of plentiful land and fertile soil gives the Thai farmer his sturdy independence. Thailand, no less than the Southeast Asian countries then under colonial rule, had to endure Japanese occupation from 1942 to 1945; but she never became a battleground and so managed to avoid its more devastating results.

Like Burma, Thailand lives mainly on her rice exports. Expanding population, increasing specialization in rice production, and growing rice exports—these have been the main factors in Thailand's economic history since 1870. These developments have been linked with the opening up of the country to external trade, a consequent rise in imports, and the widespread use of money. In meeting the rising demand, especially from increasing populations in other Southeast Asian countries such as Malaya, Thailand came second only to Burma as a rice-exporting country. Other lines of economic development with an important bearing on the export trade have been in tin, teakwood, and rubber.

The share of the ordinary Thai in his country's general economic expansion in modern times has been mainly that of a rice farmer. He has taken only a passive part in the development of an exchange economy; he has had little or no part in the rice trade as a miller or exporter, in general trade, or in the tin, teak, and rubber industries. The larger tin mines, opened up early in this century, were under British or Australian ownership; the smaller were operated by Chinese. The capital and management behind the teak trade was mainly British. Rubber planting in southern Thailand, mainly in small holdings, has been shared by Thai and Chinese. The Chinese of Thailand, swollen to about one tenth of the present total population of about twenty-six million as a result of a flood of immigration during the first thirty years of this century, have acquired a dominant commercial position in the country as a whole. Immigration is now very restricted, and the Chinese already in the country tend to become gradually assimilated into the rest of the community. But indispensable as Chinese energy and skill have been to her modern economic development, the fact that an ethnic minority possesses a powerful hold on the country's economy must continue to pose a difficult problem of social and political integration for the people of Thailand.

The presence of an influential Chinese minority within the country has an important bearing on Thailand's foreign policy today. For a century (1850–1949) her survival as an independent state seemed to require a neutralist line, playing off one great power against another, a tradition of policy that still retains some influence. But since the rise of Communist China in 1949, Thailand has taken a definite stand in line with American policy toward communism in East Asia. She has accepted large offers of military and financial aid from the United States that have brought notable improvement in her material conditions—in rice yield, in health services, and in communications. She was one of the original signatories of the American-sponsored Southeast Asian Treaty Organization (SEATO) designed for defense against communism in 1954. Because of her geographically strategic position in relation to both China and the rest of Southeast Asia, Thailand is SEATO's key regional support.

A century of courageous self-Westernization has thus brought the Thai people to a position of leadership in the Southeast Asia of today.

Thailand has no common frontier with China, but she is vulnerable to possible Communist penetration through Laos, her neighbor beyond the river Mekong to the east. This mountainous kingdom, without a railway, with poor roads and unnavigable rivers, lies landlocked between China, Vietnam, Cambodia, Thailand, and Burma. Its population of about three million are predominantly Buddhist-animist peasant farmers living in the mountain valleys or along the alluvial plains of the Mekong, operating their small farms on a family subsistence basis.

In 1893 the French, already installed in Vietnam, drove out the Thai garrisons still holding Laos and declared the country a protectorate. This relationship was recognized and the present frontiers of Laos defined in a series of Franco-Thai treaties between 1893 and 1907. The French colonial protectorate was light. Even though final power was in the hands of the French resident at Vientiane, the king of Laos continued to rule in Luangprabang, the ancient religious and royal capital to the north. There was some development of tin mining and a limited immigration of Vietnamese and Chinese, but otherwise Laos underwent little change until the coming of the Pacific War. Recognized by France after the war as a constitutional monarchy, Laos received installments of self-government in 1949 and 1953, and was finally recognized as an independent state under the 1954 Geneva Agreement on the future of the former French colonial areas in Southeast Asia.

From then on Laos began to occupy a much more prominent place in the world's news. When the Geneva Agreement was signed in 1954, a Communist party, called Pathet Lao, was already in control of the two northernmost provinces of Laos on the borders of North Vietnam and China. In 1957 the royal Laotian government, maintaining a neutralist line in external relations, decided on an attempt to form a united national front with the Communist leaders and to incorporate the rebel forces into the national army. The attempt was unsuccessful. In 1959 there came a violent break between the right and left wings of the ruling group, bringing the grave danger of full-scale civil war. In 1960 the Communists again demanded that they be included in the government. They captured Vientiane in December, but the city was soon retaken in a three-cornered contest between leftists, rightists, and neutralists. By May, 1961, the three warring groups, each led by a Laotian royal prince, had agreed to a cease-fire. Later in the year a new fourteen-nation conference began discussions at Geneva in an effort to bring the various groups in Laos together to form a national government that would keep the country neutral and independent.

In the new world of international rivalry into which Laos has been drawn, her main hope must be to avoid becoming a battleground for even greater forces than those that have trampled her underfoot in recent years. As the Laos people say: "When buffaloes fight, it is the grass that suffers."

Cambodia

Cambodia had already come under the protection of France by 1870. As in Laos, the old system of royal government continued to operate under French indirect control, which was further consolidated in 1884. French companies invested capital in rubber planting; French archaeologists restored the Indian-style buildings of the ancient capital of Angkor. Chinese traders and shopkeepers had already gained control of the country's commercial life. For the indigenous Khmer people of Cambodia, mainly rice cultivators, life went on very much as before.

But the outlook of the small ruling class was gradually changing under Western influence. The youthful King Norodom Sihanouk, who came to the throne in 1941 after a

233

college education in France, guided his country toward the goal of independence during and after the Pacific War. When war ended, he obtained French agreement to measures for introducing democratic self-government; and by 1954, when the Geneva Agreement was signed, Cambodian independence had been recognized. In the following year the king decided to abdicate the throne, retaining the position of head of state.

Despite a series of changes in the government, Norodom's aims continued to direct Cambodian policy. It was a policy of neutralism, under which Cambodia was able to accept aid from fourteen different countries, including the United States, the Soviet Union, and Communist China. Foreign aid financed an ambitious program of development in irrigation, electricity, education, and health for her five million people. American money and skill helped to build a fine highway from the capital, Pnompenh, to a new coastal port, which reduced Cambodia's long dependence upon Thailand and Vietnam for her main lines of communication with the outside world. Occasional frontier disputes with those two countries—nothing new in her long history—failed to upset the even balance that Cambodia had succeeded in establishing in the new world around her.

Vietnam

In terms of human habitation, Vietnam, with its population of about twenty-five million, is a country of two fertile delta areas connected by a long narrow strip of coastal lowland. The great concentrations of population are in the delta regions of the Red River in the north and the Mekong in the south. Hanoi and Saigon are the north and south urban centers of these two granaries of Vietnam.

Already with a foothold in the south by 1870, France first extended trading relations northward and then went on to impose a general control over the whole of the north, with some opposition from China, after 1883. Coal and tin mining were built up, along with small-scale industry, as French capital and organization took over. A small middle class of Vietnamese industrialists and merchants emerged. But rice remained the chief product in northern as well as southern Vietnam. In the north, due to population pressure and the effects of the traditional laws of inheritance, the size of the average peasant holding was extremely small, and so the rice yield was comparatively low. Additional supplies had to be obtained each year from the less densely populated areas of cultivation in the south. There the holdings were larger, and cultivation of rice as well as rubber was partly developed on a plantation basis. As a result, there emerged in the south an influential class of large landlords, French and Vietnamese. Another class, the Chinese merchants and middlemen who had settled in large numbers around Saigon, controlled the expanding export trade, especially in rice.

Although these developments caused little outward change in the countryside, new methods of living and ways of thought began to undermine the foundations of traditional village life. With the spread of the use of money, peasants easily fell into the clutches of Chinese or Indian moneylenders. The number of landless agricultural laborers increased, particularly in the south. Measures introduced by the French to alleviate the harsher effects of economic change were only partially effective. The primary aim of France was to exploit the full potentialities of Vietnam both as a source of supply of raw materials for French industry and as a market for its products. All else was subservient to this purpose, including programs of elementary and technical education at lower levels and a policy of assimilating the upper levels of Vietnamese society to the French cultural tradition.

The French tradition of political and social thought, with its emphasis on human rights and individual freedom, inevitably sowed the seeds of a freedom movement in Vietnam against France herself. The most favorable ground for the growth of such a movement was in the north, with its partly industrialized economy and its traditional exposure to the influence of China, herself sweeping forward into national revolution after 1911. World War I increased French prestige and Vietnamese prosperity, but it also stimulated rising expectations and a growing dissatisfaction with the tight administrative and economic grip that France maintained over Vietnam. But nationalist feeling in Vietnam before World War II remained restricted in general to a small urban minority; it hardly affected the vast peasant majority of the population.

It was the defeat of France by the Germans in Europe, followed by her humiliation at the hands of the Japanese in Asia, that transformed Vietnamese nationalism into a wide popular movement. By the end of the Pacific War a number of nationalist groups had united to form a revolutionary league, the Viet Minh, whose leaders were closely linked by sympathy and training with the Chinese Communists. On the collapse of Japan in 1945, when southern Vietnam was taken over by British forces and the north by Chinese, the Viet Minh proclaimed an independent republic of Vietnam. France, her forces reinstalled in 1946, was prepared to recognize the republic; but it soon became clear that she did not intend it to include southern Vietnam. By the end of 1946, after a surprise attack by the Viet Minh on the French in Hanoi, the whole situation began to degenerate into a long war of attrition. The Viet Minh openly acknowledged itself to be a Communist movement in 1949, and the success of the Chinese Communists in the same year transformed the colonial war in Vietnam into a major international problem. Despite United States military aid, the French lost ground in the struggle, and by May, 1954, they had been finally defeated in the north. A cease-fire agreement reached at Geneva in July, 1954, accepted the *de facto* partition of Vietnam into two separate states.

North Vietnam, under its president, Ho Chi-minh, thus became withdrawn into the Communist camp. Receiving aid from China and Russia, its government claimed in 1960 that the north had recovered from the ravages of war, that mining and industry were expanding, and that the region had achieved self-sufficiency in rice. But 1961 reports of food shortages, industrial difficulties, and unrest indicated that such claims were overoptimistic.

South Vietnam has had a number of difficult problems to face since 1954. Although its president, Ngo Dinh Diem, succeeded in breaking the power of local rebel factions and survived an attempted military coup in late 1960, the security position in the Mekong delta region worsened as a result of the steady infiltration of Communist terrorists and supplies from North Vietnam through Laos. The United States accordingly agreed in 1961 to step up her already considerable aid program to Vietnam. But the country's basic problems were social and economic rather than military. Although rubber exports expanded, exports of rice had fallen away due to population increase and the abandonment of large areas of cultivation during the years of unrest since the Pacific War. Programs of land reform and industrialization were not going ahead fast enough. The success of the experiment of bringing the inhabitants of scattered villages together into new townships for a securer and better life remained uncertain. Early in 1962 the United States and South Vietnam announced a joint economic and social program aimed at raising the standard of living of the Vietnamese and strengthening their country against Communist guerrilla subversion. It was an unfinished war in South Vietnam, a war for the minds of the ordinary people.

Malaya

Modern Malaya has been created out of a combination of Malay social solidarity, Chinese economic enterprise, and

British administrative ability. Nine separate Malay states under Muslim sultans made up a largely undiscovered world in 1870, a world beyond the gates of the British settlements already established at Penang, Malacca, and Singapore. But already through those gates there had passed the first Chinese pioneer tin miners whose rough frontier society was to be the spearhead of revolutionary change in Malaya. Gang warfare between rival mining groups interlinked with feuds between Malay chieftains caused British intervention in 1874. The rulers of four of the Malay states soon accepted British protection, under which modern methods of administrative and economic organization were gradually built up. With the surrender of Thailand's claims over the northern states of the peninsula in 1909, the whole country became opened up to the process of modernization. It was only in the present century that Malaya came into existence as a political entity and its people made their first real mark in the pages of Southeast Asian history.

Malaya's development under British protection was for many years a mundane matter of becoming the world's chief producer of tin and rubber. Along with that came the building up of modern transportation, communication, health, and education systems and a higher average level of income for Malaya's population than that of any other East Asian country. The economic development of the hinterland brought immense prosperity to the free ports of Penang and Singapore, urban centers created mainly by Chinese and Indian immigrants under British rule.

Without the immigration of Chinese and Indian labor and skill into the hinterland itself, Malaya's story would have been very different. The indigenous Malays stood firmly by their own way of life; as a people they were not prepared to provide the type of labor force that the tin mines and rubber plantations required. For them British protection meant the preservation of their rural community life, their ownership of the rice lands, and the prestige of their own traditional ruling class. Sharing indirectly in the general increase of wealth and at the same time protected from the harsher winds of economic change, the Malays were content to forego the direct rewards of commercial and industrial enterprise.

Malaya's new economic classes, engaged at all levels in the tin and rubber industries, in trade and commerce, and in the professions, were mainly Chinese, partly Indian. An almost equal division of the overall population into Malays and Chinese before World War II reflected an approximately even internal balance of power, political and economic, between them. Malay political power was institutionalized in the ruling sultans and their aristocratic state governments, secure behind British protection. Chinese economic power pervaded almost the whole country. The political interests of Chinese and Indians in Malaya were mostly concentrated on their own homelands, each passing through a phase of nationalist revolution. Malaya was the outstanding example in Southeast Asia of a plural society in which a number of different ethnic groups lived alongside one another and yet remained economically, socially, and culturally separate.

The Japanese conquest of Malaya and Singapore in 1941–1942 did nothing to bring the various racial groups together, but by removing the British from the scene it made each of them more self-reliant. Britain's postwar plan, introduced after the Japanese surrender in 1945, for a unified system of government for Malaya as a whole met with strong opposition from the small educated class of Malay leaders and officials who had been at the helm of affairs during the Japanese military occupation. They saw in the preservation of the traditional separate governments under Malay sultans the only practical safeguard for the position of the Malay people in their own land; and in accordance with their wishes, the prewar system was restored in modified form by a new constitution for the Federation of Malaya in 1948.

Six months later the country was at war against an army of Chinese Communist guerrillas operating from within the dense jungle that covers four fifths of the Malay Peninsula. The Communists had built up their organization out of a jungle force formed earlier against the Japanese. They now began a long campaign of terrorizing the scattered Chinese squatters who had opened up land on the edge of the jungle for food during the Japanese occupation, intimidating tin and rubber workers, and killing European managers. Their general plan was to create fear and confusion and thus gradually establish areas of control to be linked eventually in a complete conquest of the country.

The Communist bid for power in Malaya was defeated, though only at heavy cost in life, property, and dollars. By 1960 a sad chapter in Malaya's history, one that really began with the Japanese invasion, had come to an end.

But already a fine new chapter had begun. The country's economy and the people's courage had stood the strain of the long Communist war. The resettlement of squatters in new townships and the regrouping of tin-mine and rubber-estate workers in new villages had helped not only to defeat the guerrillas but also to create a new sense of common purpose. Indeed the battle against the Communists, coming soon after the Pacific War and the Japanese occupation, had brought the people closer together and given them a greater feeling of unity than ever before. Malay, Chinese, and Indian leaders who offered nationalism as the alternative to communism were able to swing the whole country over to their support. So in August, 1957, after the signing of an agreement by which Britain gave up her rights over the Malay states, the 7.25 million people of Malaya became an independent nation. This new free democracy, with its blending of diverse racial elements, could set a pattern for Southeast Asia. Malaya's premier, Tungku Abdul Rahman, has been a leading influence in the trend toward increasing cooperation among the Southeast Asian countries.

Singapore island, a crown colony as distinct from a protected state, remained outside the scope of the revised Malayan constitution of 1948; it made its own way toward a free democratic system of government. The progress of its 1.5 million people (three fourths of them Chinese) in that direction was checked by Communist agitation in industry and the schools; but the island's first free elections were held in 1955; and in 1958, by agreement with Britain, Singapore attained full internal self-government. Yet, despite political separation, Singapore could not be economically divorced from Malaya. Together the two represented an immense potential in industry. Political considerations, especially the threat of communism in Singapore, reinforced the economic argument. As time went on it seemed that a political merger of Singapore and Malaya, with reservation of a limited amount of local self-government for the island, would come by 1963. The natural reluctance of the Malays to see the large Chinese population of Singapore added to that of Malaya seemed likely to be offset by the attractive prospect of a "Greater Malaysia," in which Malaya, Singapore, and the territories of British Borneo would combine to form a new and wider federation.

The North Borneo states of today—Brunei, Sarawak, and British North Borneo—originally began as Malay settlements along the coast. Islam naturally spread to these communities from Malaya and Java; the Muslim sultanate of Brunei dates from the end of the fifteenth century. Sporadic contacts by traders from the West were not followed up until the nineteenth century when the British developed an interest in the northern part of Borneo and the Dutch in the south. The British North Borneo Company, formed in 1882 to consolidate earlier concessions, operated until 1946 when its rights were taken over by the British government. British protection was extended over Brunei and Sarawak by 1890. Chinese immigration was encouraged, as in Malaya, to aid economic development. The discovery of oil in Brunei in 1929 made it the richest of the three territories.

Despite the heavy damage suffered during the Pacific War, the North Borneo states made a remarkable postwar recovery. By 1957 they had begun to think of coming together in some form of federal association. Brunei, historically the parent state, was politically as well as economically the strongest of the three. When the wider movement for a Malaysian federation began, it met with a generally favorable response from all three of the North Borneo territories.

Indonesia

Although Indonesia as a whole had come under general Dutch supervision centuries before, in 1870 the effects of Western administrative and economic organization hardly extended beyond the island of Java. It was not in fact until comparatively recent times that Dutch interests became consolidated in other parts of Indonesia. Even in 1900, although Dutch capital and enterprise were much more active than before, Java was still the main field of Dutch-directed production, mostly in the form of export crops: sugar, tea, and coffee.

After 1900 Dutch control increased in both range and depth so that by about 1930 Indonesia had been carried up to the highest peak of colonialism in Southeast Asia. Rice production expanded rapidly enough to keep pace with a population increase that brought Indonesia's total in 1940 to about seventy million. Sugar, the main export crop, reached the highest levels of output; but with the opening up of Sumatra and other islands to Dutch and other Western capital and enterprise, rubber, oil, and tin also became important items in the Indonesian economy. Between the two world wars, Indonesia outstripped Malaya as a rubber producer. Large-scale state enterprise was applied to the development of communications, irrigation, forestry, and fisheries, as well as to health, welfare, and education programs. The level of exports rose steadily until the coming of the interwar slump in 1930 restricted many of Indonesia's world markets. This was the end of the golden age of Dutch colonialism in Indonesia. To meet the changed situation, the Dutch began to introduce a balanced program of industrialization. Indonesia's trade links with Holland and Europe became weaker after 1930, whereas those with Asian countries became correspondingly stronger. However, this process of economic adjustment was cut short by the coming of the Pacific War.

There is no doubt that Dutch rule brought a great improvement in general living conditions for Indonesians as a whole. It enabled them to think for the first time of the possibility of economic progress. But even in the economic sphere, where the Dutch achievement was outstanding, progress for the ordinary Indonesian was strictly limited. The spread of money here as elsewhere in Southeast Asia often resulted in placing the peasant at the mercy of the local moneylender-shopkeeper, usually a Chinese. The steady growth in population outpaced economic development, thus preventing a general rise in living standards. Seldom could the ordinary Indonesian possibly hope to rise above the status of a small farmer.

Yet he had much to be thankful for. He was protected by enlightened legislation from the harsher effects of economic change around him. As far as the law could see to it, he would not lose possession of his land. Everything was done to conserve his culture, his customs, and his way of life. His native rulers and chieftains retained their positions, weakened though they were, within the Dutch administration. The self-governing institutions of his village remained largely intact.

The conscious aim of the Dutch was to preserve the roots of the Indonesian social and cultural tradition while gradually exposing it to the climate of the twentieth century. They hoped to lead the Indonesians out into the modern world at a steady, carefully controlled pace. But they soon found themselves unable to dictate the speed of the change that they themselves had begun. The machine got out of control; the pace of change left their educational, administrative, and political programs far behind.

The Dutch educational system in Indonesia was good at the elementary level, but at higher levels it remained undeveloped and inadequate. The handful of Indonesians who acquired university or professional training, potential leaders of the country, found few openings in public life or in the largely Dutch-staffed administration. In political development the Dutch ideal was a guided democracy; they aimed at a slow building up of a modern Indonesian democratic system on the foundations of the old traditional village self-government. But it was a painfully slow program. The partly elected National Council (Volksraad) that first met in 1918 had only limited power to influence government decisions. And the unfortunate effect of the rise of an aggressive nationalism among the Indonesians was to cause the Dutch to go even more slowly with their plans for evolving self-government.

Nationalist reaction against Dutch rule was strongest in

the very region where Dutch influence had penetrated most deeply, the island of Java. From its first organized beginnings in 1908 down to 1927, nationalism in Java was a fairly moderate movement. It aimed not at the overthrow of the Dutch but at greater participation by the people of the country in political and national life. The general aim was to break the combined grip of Chinese immigrant traders and Dutch merchants and officials on Indonesia's commerce and administration. After World War I a radical group broke away from the nationalists, formed a Communist party, and in 1927 staged a series of risings. These were suppressed, but unfortunately they caused Indonesian nationalism to be linked with communism in the eyes of the administration; and from then on Dutch policy became reactionary and repressive. By 1934 the leading nationalists, including Sukarno, had been caught and imprisoned. For the hour of their release they had to wait until the Japanese conquest of Indonesia in 1942.

In Indonesia more than in any other Southeast Asian country, the Japanese occupation produced a new sense of national unity. The Japanese themselves did little to encourage it, but it grew underneath their feet. As soon as they knew of Japan's defeat, Sukarno and his colleagues declared Indonesian independence (August, 1945). Holland, herself an occupied country during World War II, was unable to send her forces back into Indonesia until months later. Then followed a series of negotiations punctuated by outbreaks of violence, at the end of which Holland recognized the independence of Indonesia (December, 1949). The long era of Dutch colonialism in Southeast Asia had come to an end.

The first decade of Indonesian independence presented her new rulers with many difficult problems. In the economic sphere were the interlinked problems of shortage of investment capital and technical skill, underindustrialization, and low income levels. Two thirds of a total population of over eighty-five million were crowded on the island of Java. The pressure of population on food resources forced Indonesia, like Malaya, to import rice to supplement her own output. As with other Southeast Asian countries, her economy was heavily dependent upon the demand of overseas markets for her exports of raw materials such as rubber and petroleum. In the sphere of administration, lacking India's legacy of a trained civil service, Indonesia was faced with the immense problem of holding together a vast, complex area that it would be difficult even for an experienced and stable administration to control. Her postwar parliamentary system, with its multiplicity of parties, was extremely unstable.

Linked with both political instability and slow economic growth was the problem of internal security. The authority of the central government in Java was challenged more than once by organized revolts in other islands such as Sumatra and Celebes. Army leaders held a key position in the control of real power, though the political leaders remained at the seat of power. It was the power of personality—the personal magnetism of President Sukarno—that seemed to be the main force holding the Indonesian people together. Sukarno, outstanding leader since the early days of the Indonesian revolution, caught and held the national imagination. Justifiably he claimed to be the mouthpiece of his nation, to "express the aspirations, the longings, and the wishes of the Indonesian people."

The powerful new sense of nationalism among the Indonesians has found expression in various ways: in measures, for example, to curb the economic power and break down the ethnic separatism of the Chinese minority in Indonesia; in the take-over of foreign enterprises and the discouragement of overseas capital investment; and in the campaign for acquisition of the western half of the South Pacific island of New Guinea.

In external affairs Indonesia has held to an independent foreign policy similar to that of India and Burma. Her main outstanding problem of external relations in 1962 was her claim to Dutch-held West New Guinea on the ground that it formed part of the colonial empire that Indonesia had inherited. With United States and United Nations encouragement, talks on this delicate issue were started between Indonesian and Netherlands representatives in March, 1962.

The Philippine Islands

With the collapse of the liberal movement in Spain in 1871, the Philippines came under a reactionary regime that was firmly opposed to any movement for social or economic change. But Filipino national feeling grew out of increasing agrarian unrest, especially on the large estates belonging to the religious orders. The early aim of the nationalist movement was for reforms within the existing colonial system; but as usual, the refusal of the administration to concede moderate reform promoted the rise of a more aggressive nationalism, which aimed at the overthrow of the colonial regime itself. The European-educated leader of the moderates, José Rizal, was executed by the Spanish in 1896 after he had in fact lost his leadership of the nationalist movement to more extreme revolutionary elements. This new nationalist group rose in open revolt against the Spanish regime in 1897, but by the end of the same year they had decided to abandon the struggle.

This was the situation in the Philippines when, on the other side of the world, events occurred that led to war between Spain and the United States. In February, 1898, the American battleship *Maine* was blown up in the harbor of Havana, Cuba, then a Spanish colony. War was declared on Spain in April. An American naval squadron in the Pacific entered Manila Bay before dawn on May 1 and blew the Spanish Philippine fleet to pieces. Manila itself was captured by an American expedition that arrived a few months later. The United States had become a colonial power.

The Filipino nationalists, believing themselves to be the rightful heirs of the Spanish regime, opposed the establishment of American rule for a time, but by 1902 their guerrilla activities had petered out. The United States did its utmost to convince the Filipino people that its firm policy was to prepare them for self-government. In 1916 the U.S. government pledged itself to recognize the independence of the Philippines as soon as a stable Filipino administration could be established. In 1934 the Philippine Commonwealth was set up, with self-government in internal affairs; and the islands were promised full independence in ten years. On July 4, 1946, after the defeat of Japan and the end of the Pacific War, the Philippines was declared an independent republic.

The economic link with the United States played a key role in the emergence of the Philippines as an independent state. From 1909, when free trade between the two countries was begun, most exports from the Philippines had nonduty entry into the United States. This gave a tremendous stimulus to the production of Philippine sugar, tobacco, hemp, and copra (dried coconut, the source of coconut oil) for a wide-open American market. But it also meant that American producers had to face increasing competition from such imports. It was generally assumed that when the Philippines gained independence, her exports would no longer enjoy free entry into the American market. So it was that the Filipino political movement for independence received strong backing from American economic interests, especially after the slump of the early 1930's.

Up to that time, although the movement toward self-government had made great progress, its pace had been irregular. The Nacionalista Party had begun an active campaign for independence after the institution of an elected assembly, with limited powers and on a restricted electorate, in 1907. The American response was seen, between 1912 and 1920, in a speeding up of the process of preparation for self-government. A newly constituted elected assembly was given wider control over internal affairs, and American officials were replaced by Filipinos in the civil service. From 1920, however, the pace became much slower; and it was not until after 1930, when the American sugar and dairy industries came in on the side of Filipino self-government, that the process was speeded up again. The result was seen in the 1934 Commonwealth Act, granting internal self-government, under which Philippine exports were gradually to lose their favorable position in United States markets.

Political independence was one thing, economic self-dependence another. The Philippine economy had become overdependent on a single export crop, sugar, and on a single export market, the United States. There had been no balanced development of trade or industry within the islands. The heavy concentration on commercial agriculture for export had helped to perpetuate and increase landlordism and tenancy; it also necessitated the import of rice. The mass of the Filipino people remained small farmers or agricultural laborers working on land they did not own. Fundamentally their conditions of life had altered little since the days of Spanish rule. The real successors to the Spanish regime were a small class of landowners and businessmen—Chinese, American and mixed Filipino-Chinese-Spanish—associated with the higher levels of the agricultural export economy. Chinese merchants controlled a large share of both internal and external trade.

The other side of the picture of American rule in the Philippines is a fine record of steady progress in education, health, and welfare services; in the development of communications and public works; and, above all, in the building up of a fund of general goodwill. The ties between the peoples of the two countries were cemented by the shared experiences of defeat, destruction, and victory in the Philippines during the Pacific War. Together they shared also the task of postwar rehabilitation. United States financial aid to the Philippines continued after independence in 1946. In external relations the two countries were closely associated in policy and in defense, especially through the Southeast Asia Treaty Organization, founded in 1954.

Most of the problems facing the Philippines in recent years were inherited from the past. The country's economy remained essentially colonial. The problem of increasing the number of small agricultural landowners remained largely unsolved. Low yields per acre, mainly due to lack of capital investment in the land, pointed to the need for wider credit facilities, especially for small farmers. Attempts to protect the tenant cultivator by legislation fixing the share of produce between landlord and tenant were only partially successful. Indebtedness was still widespread among the mass of the Filipino farmers. Agrarian discontent, reflected in the postwar Huk Communist guerrilla movement, was still alive. The country's dependence on the United States market was still strong, and self-sufficiency in rice had not yet been achieved. Personalities seemed to play too prominent a part in political life, and corruption was too prevalent in government services.

For all that, the people of the Philippines could point to one great achievement. In little over half a century they had advanced from a subject colonial society to a free democratic nation. They stood as an example for the whole of Asia of the principle of peaceful change through democracy. National elections in 1953, 1957, and 1961 demonstrated the value and the vitality of the parliamentary democratic system in the Philippines. In 1953 the votes of the nation replaced the Liberals by the Nacionalistas, with the popular Magsaysay as new president. After Magsaysay's tragic death in a plane crash in 1957, Carlos García, a seasoned political figure in both internal and foreign affairs, was chosen president. Then in 1961 the Liberals came back into power under their new presidential leader, Macapagal. Thus the balance of political power has swung freely to and fro according to the prevailing will of the people. At the same time, it must be said that the two main parties have not differed greatly in fundamental policy. Internally, both have aimed at increasing rice production, raising living standards, and curbing corruption. In external relations both have remained closely aligned to the policy of the United States and other anti-Communist Western powers.

* * *

Looking back from the vantage point of the 1960's, the colonial period appears as only a short phase in Southeast Asia's long history. Colonialism as a systematic planned process did not really get started in Southeast Asia, except for Java, until 1870, and then it lasted for only about seventy years.

But during that short period colonialism set off a whole series of changes that affect the lives of the people of Southeast Asia today. Those changes amount to a whole revolution, the revolution of modernization. Modernization meant many things to Southeast Asia; it was a complex process started off primarily by the application of Western scientific and technological ideas and methods to Southeast Asian societies. It meant the organization of material development and economic growth, the construction of Western systems of administration and communication, and the introduction of modern education, health, and welfare services. Concurrently with such material developments, it meant the introduction and spread of Western social and political, along with religious and cultural, ideas.

Modernization, like all change, brought both gains and losses for the people of Southeast Asia. It brought immense possibilities of material and mental development; but inevitably it also disturbed the equilibrium of the traditional societies, upset their cultural and social patterns, and weakened their established institutions. And the effects of these changes were all the more drastic since they took place at high speed during a short period of colonial ascendancy.

These revolutionary changes were not peculiar to the former colonial areas of Southeast Asia. They were part of the general process of modernization that has affected all the countries of Asia, a process resulting from the impact of the West. Colonialism was simply this process of modernization under a special set of conditions. It was a special case, a transitional phase, of the same broad historical experience that has been shared by all countries involved in the meeting of East and West.

The process of modernization is an unfinished revolution in Southeast Asia, just as it is in such countries as China and Japan. Colonialism started the countries of Southeast Asia off on the road to social transformation; now they go forward on their own. For them, as for other countries on the road to modernization, the key problem is the accumulation of capital for industrialization, a problem that in its turn involves a whole process of social transformation, the creation of a new society.

Colonialism brought about a new historical situation in Southeast Asia. Today its role may seem to have been that of the explosive force needed to revolutionize the economic, social, and mental habits of the 200 million people of the region. But future generations may perhaps see its historic function as that of bringing the peoples of Southeast Asia more closely together than ever before within a common framework of existence. Itself born of a world of international rivalries, colonialism may have laid the foundations for international cooperation among the countries of Southeast Asia. In addition to SEATO, such developments as the Association of Southeast Asia, formed in 1961 by Thailand, Malaya, and the Philippines; the movement for a Greater Malaysia; and the joint project between Thailand, Laos, Cambodia, and South Vietnam for the development of the lower Mekong River all begin to point in the direction of greater Southeast Asian unity.

Asia
In the Modern World

FROM THE perspective of the 1960's it seems odd that Westerners only a few years ago spoke of "the unchanging East." The cliché was, of course, never wholly accurate: Asia has never been motionless. In earlier chapters we have read of the rise and fall of empires, of the gradual adaptation of older civilizations to new circumstances, and of the quickened pace of change in the past century as Western values and technologies spread eastward. But never have changes in Asia been so rapid and pervasive as they are today. The new forces astir in Asia touch the lives of ordinary villagers just as they do the shape of governments. They undermine traditional attitudes; they open new horizons; they are profoundly unsettling and sometimes profoundly exciting. The new patterns in Asia affect not only Asians, however; their impact reaches across the world, and can be ignored by other peoples only at their peril. For Americans, the opportunities and the difficulties of working out mutually satisfying relations with contemporary Asia constitute one of the great challenges of our generation.

Before World War II the West knew an Asia that consisted of a huge but weak China, a vigorous but harshly militant Japan, a few smaller independent countries, and the political dependencies included in colonial empires. After the war the face of Asia was transformed. As we have seen, three major changes symbolized the new situation. Defeated Japan came under firm civilian control and moved rapidly to social and economic resurgence. After a period of turbulence, mainland China fell under Communist control, as did the neighboring areas of North Korea and North Vietnam. And rising tides of nationalism signaled virtually the end of the colonial period. The Philippines became independent in 1946, India and Pakistan in 1947, Burma and Ceylon in 1948, and Indonesia in 1949. The subsequent independence of Laos, Cambodia, South Vietnam, and Malaya virtually completed the process by which the peoples of Asia have become responsible for determining their own ways of life under their own leaders, free and able to speak for themselves both at home and in the larger arenas of world politics.

Nor was the transformation solely political. Asia after World War II simmered with expectation of social and economic improvement. Why else have political independence? After generations in which Asia had largely missed the advances that had come to the West in the train of the Industrial Revolution, many Asians no longer accepted as inevitable or inescapable certain traditional social restrictions of endemic poverty, illiteracy, and disease. In recent years commerce and industry had grown in major Asian cities and in many market towns. Even rural villages had become more closely knit into regional and national economies. Increased social mobility was already evident, along with the promise of more extensive educational facilities, public health, and agricultural and urban development. The stage was set, it seemed, for further rapid modernization.

In the years immediately following World War II there was a tendency in the West, including the United States, to oversimplify the issues and problems facing many Asian peoples as they were launched into their new epoch. It was imagined that the newly independent Asian countries could speedily create democratic governments in the image of Western parliamentary institutions and could get on with the business of social and economic welfare. This was expecting a great deal. Several Asian countries had very limited experience with indigenous political processes, and most suffered from a paucity of natural resources and available skills in relation to the needs of their populations.

In Search of Progress

By the early 1960's most Asian countries had made the transition from what has been called first-generation nationalism to second-generation nationalism. In retrospect, the first-generation variety seemed ennobling and unifying. During that period nationalist forces in colonial countries could ignore some of their own differences and unite in opposition of the alien ruler. Many things wrong with society could be blamed on the foreigner, and great improvements could be promised. The high values of human dignity and democratic equality could be adduced in favor of self-rule.

Second-generation nationalism came to these countries after they gained political independence and when local leaders began to bear full responsibility for national policies. Their goal was to release national energies for constructive purposes. They saw the prospect of fuller and more effective utilization of national resources than the prior alien power had achieved. At the same time, some of them recognized that divergent views would find expression in competing political movements. When new classes and groups entered politics, the question was whether these would be integrated into the national political framework or would form an entering wedge for the disorganization and violence that lead either to immobilization or to chaos.

Some countries were well prepared for the second-generation stage. In India, for example, political life had grown vigorous during the British period and the administrative structure was sufficiently strong to function effectively after independence. By contrast, Pakistan, as a new nation carved out of what had been India, found it necessary to create a national government from scratch. In Indonesia the nationalist inheritors of power included only a handful of university graduates.

Given the variety of political and administrative preparation in different countries, the mixed record of self-rule in postwar Asia has perhaps been no surprise. The returns are not yet all in; it would be premature to call certain democratic experiments successful and others unsuccessful. Nevertheless, there have been great contrasts. S.W.R.D. Bandaranaike, the late Prime Minister of Ceylon, once commented that the British two-party system was unsuited to countries in which political parties are not divided solely on political and economic issues but are strongly influenced by such considerations as race and religion. He identified Burma and Indonesia as examples of countries where the weakening of the party system had led to the establishment of some form of military dictatorship.* In similar vein, President Muhammad Ayub Khan of Pakistan said in a speech broadcast from Dacca in 1959 that past experience has shown that what appeared to be a Western-type democracy could not be transplanted or imposed upon a soil that was not prepared for its healthy nourishment and growth. There were certain basic requirements of the Western democratic structure which did not exist in his country, he said. Western

* *Times* (London), April 20, 1959, p. 9.

democracy presupposes a high degree of social and political awareness and mass literacy, enabling the people to know the value of their vote in terms of broad national policies, and an advanced system of mass communication for speedy and accurate dissemination of information on a wide variety of themes of individual and general interest.

On the other hand, since World War II fairly effective representational government has so far been the lot of such countries as Japan, the Philippines, Thailand, Malaya, and India. In India the parliament and state legislature have, in fact, been chosen by the world's largest electorate: more than 100 million voters participated in the 1962 general elections, the third general election since the country became independent in 1947.

In fact, many Asian peoples are struggling to find the form of political life that best suits them as they seek to share more fully in modern social and technological advances. Some countries suffer deep cultural or other divisions. How can they achieve and sustain national unity? Many have limited numbers of democratically oriented leaders. Will the numbers of such leaders expand, or will the present leaderships contract into small, closed groups concerned more with holding power than with building new societies? Can open, constructive political systems succeed, or will some of the emerging countries fall back on some sort of traditionally oriented autocratic system or succumb to a modern totalitarianism of the left?

Such questions as these are life and death issues for many Asian states in these formative years. They also have a wider meaning, for the West must be concerned with the future shape of Asia. Our stake in the success of stable and progressive political institutions is great.

To wrestle with the problems of political organizations is, however, only one of the manifold tasks facing this generation of Asian leaders. They are as ardently committed to the dream of vigorous and sustained economic growth. Prime Minister Nehru once commented that "the main objective is to increase production and thereby find progressively fuller employment for our people. We want to become an industrialized nation with greater production, greater income, more national and per-capita income, and independent and self-developing economy. The overall result we desire . . . is to break through the barrier of poverty and bring about better life, more happiness and prosperity for the millions of our people and, at the same time, try to organize a more egalitarian basis for society in India." * Asians of many coun-

* R. K. Karanjia, *The Mind of Mr. Nehru* (London: George Allen and Unwin, Ltd., 1960), p. 56.

tries would echo his words. Conscious of having missed the benefits of the original Industrial Revolution, they would like to leapfrog as many as possible of the stages by which the West found its way into the twentieth century. They know that the resources available for these tasks are as meager as the hopes of their people are great.

It follows that the developmental efforts of Asian states constitute in many respects both the most difficult and the most constructive of all their works. Many approaches are being tried. Japan's astonishing advances have come about through strong state encouragement and support of private enterprise. Taiwan's dramatic agricultural achievements can be credited substantially to the work of an imaginative Sino-American cooperative organization called the Joint Commission on Rural Reconstruction. India, where the per-capita income of the majority of the people is less than one dollar per week, has made slow but steady progress under the discipline of a series of Five-Year Plans that started in 1951 and are directed toward the goal of doubling per-capita incomes by sometime in the 1970's.

Whatever the approach used, the task has many similar components from one country to the next. Perceptive leaders have come to recognize the political and social requisites of development, the need to organize human talents, the essentiality of agricultural reform, the importance of capital formation, and the complexities of industrialization. If all the developing countries want more and better educational and public health facilities, as they do, there is also general need for improved agricultural practices, including wider use of fertilizers and hybrid seed, more effective water use, better credit and marketing mechanisms, and the like. Most countries also need better power and transportation resources, factories to fuel industrial development, stronger administrations and banking systems, and more effort devoted to science and creative technology. In short, Asians are finding that to enter the modern world effectively, they must make unprecedented efforts, straining their talents, their energies, and their resources.

In many Asian countries there is now free discussion of one of the most perplexing problems that a developing people can face. This is the ratio of resources to population, and the limiting effect of rapidly growing populations on developmental efforts. Asian populations are growing very rapidly indeed. In 1941 the old India, for example, had 388 million people. By 1961 the same territory, which now comprises India and Pakistan, held 532 million, an addition equivalent to four fifths of the population of the United States in 1960. Similar increases have been recorded in other Asian countries. Moreover, it has been predicted that current population figures will be doubled before the end of this century, just one generation from now.

Ironically, much of the present explosive growth in population results not from rising birth rates but from rapidly declining death rates brought about by improved medical care, nutrition, sanitation, and public-health practices. The simple and inexpensive application of DDT, for example, has virtually eliminated one of the great killers, malaria, from large areas of Asia. Improvement of infant and maternal mortality rates has further influenced the recent spectacular increase in population growth rates.

It is no wonder, then, that some governments have begun exploring the possibilities of achieving population control through family planning or other means. Japan's concentrated effort since World War II to stabilize the size of its population resulted in the most rapid decline of birth rates in history between 1947 and 1956. India has officially adopted family planning policies and has incorporated population stabilization programs in its five-year development plans. Several other Asian countries have become increasingly hospitable to family planning programs, sometimes privately conducted with official encouragement. Over the coming generation the population question seems certain to draw even closer attention in countries where the increases are cutting into the benefits of economic advance available to individual citizens.

If modern-minded Asians fret at ever-growing populations, they see other difficulties in the persistence of traditional, generally static patterns of social organization. Changes are coming; indeed, they must come. Even ordinary economic growth requires skills and mobility unknown in the old, largely self-sufficient rural communities. Without men and women steeped in new kinds of learning and possessed of new dimensions of understanding, how can nations create and manage advancing money (as contrasted to subsistence) economies, growing technologies, and all the complexities associated with modern communications, transportation, and industrialization? But economic growth is only one of the reasons underlying today's tremendous desire in Asia for more and better educational opportunities, for improved status of women, for broader and more effective social and cultural institutions in the rapidly growing cities, and for many other evidences of modernization. These are the ambitions that reveal what kinds of people today's Asians want to be and the sorts of values that they, like us, find worthwhile in the twentieth century. The question is how to achieve these changes in good time without undue social disruption. Just as stable and progressive political systems and effective economic development are wanted, so social modernization is one of the great objectives of large parts of contemporary Asia.

Help from Outside

If Asian countries had to rely solely on their own resources and skills to carry forward the vital processes of modernization, the outlook would be bleak indeed. It is true that some countries have had little outside assistance at crucial periods. Take prewar authoritarian Japan as an example or, to some extent, Communist China, though the latter has received Soviet economic and military aid. But not even the totalitarian controls necessary to squeeze developmental capital out of the current consumption of impoverished peoples are necessarily effective, as was shown by the collapse of Communist China's vaunted "great leap forward." Countries that nurture liberal systems of government based on the consent of the governed, and whose incomes per capita range from less than $100 to $300 per year, certainly cannot deny the current needs of their peoples in their search for the trail from present poverty to future prosperity. The tasks are monumental, the resources terribly limited.

Fortunately, we live in a generation that understands, probably better than any previous generation, that "either the benefits of modern civilization in living levels and human dignity will be generalized, so that they no longer will be almost exclusively enjoyed by the peoples of the West where they originated, or they will be lost even to the peoples of the West." [*] Substantial quantities of technical and economic assistance have flowed to the developing countries in the years since World War II from international organizations, European nations, Canada, and, recently, Japan. Government and private assistance from the United States has been particularly important.

International assistance takes many forms. Apart from military aid (which the United States, at least, provides to its Asian allies and to certain other nations [†] specifically for mutual-defense purposes), most aid is classified either as technical or economic. The former includes such nation-

[*] Eugene Staley, *The Future of Underdeveloped Countries* (rev. ed.; New York: Harper & Row, Publishers, Inc., 1961), p. 9.

[†] Asian areas receiving United States military aid in 1963 included Korea, Japan, the Republic of China, Philippines, South Vietnam, Laos, Cambodia, Thailand, Indonesia, Burma, India, Pakistan, Iran, Turkey, and Jordan.

building programs as education and the training of specialists as well as the creation and strengthening of significant public institutions, from rural extension agencies to police or tax administrations. Economic assistance relates to infusions of capital and credit to build factories, refineries, roads, bridges, railroads, harbors, dams, and other facilities; to provide foreign exchange for needed raw materials and manufactures; and to help meet budgetary or other financing crises.

Clearly, foreign assistance can only assist local efforts; the main test in each country will be its own resourcefulness. But foreign aid can add the extra margin that is essential to make local efforts pay off. We must also remember that the relationship between donor and recipient can often be complex and difficult, just as it may be in private transactions. Donors expect certain standards, and recipient countries are sometimes ill-equipped to utilize certain types of aid effectively and yet too nationalistic, proud, or sensitive to want to reveal their deficiences to foreign experts. Such problems are natural enough and may frustrate some persons enough to effect their opposition to the concepts of foreign aid. On the other hand, many early difficulties have been surmounted. In the larger interest, Americans are well advised not to turn away from those that remain but to solve them.

Among world organizations, the International Bank for Reconstruction and Development (World Bank) has, since it was founded in 1945, assumed the leading role in development lending. By 1961 it had made development loans totaling some $2 billion to Asian countries. Its distinguished first president, American Eugene R. Black, who retired in 1962, made the I.B.R.D. not only banker to the world but also an international negotiator. It was the bank, for example, that after eight years of effort brought India and Pakistan to agreement on division of the usable waters of the Indus River basin and arranged for several Western countries, including the United States, to contribute to the Indus Basin Development Fund for the construction of necessary dams, canals, and other works.

An I.B.R.D. affiliate, the International Development Association, was established in 1960 to promote economic development by providing loans on more flexible terms than conventional loans. Another affiliate, the International Finance Corporation, aids development through investing funds and encouraging other private and public institutions to invest funds in private enterprises in less developed countries. Yet another world financial institution that substantially helps developing countries is the International Monetary Fund, whose mechanisms for promoting financial cooperation and exchange stability have repeatedly helped rescue shaky national financial systems.

Other types of aid are given Asian countries by a variety of specialized agencies related to the United Nations. Some of these offer dramatic illustrations of how the world community can organize major efforts to meet urgent needs. The World Health Organization, for example, has succeeded in stamping out malaria in some countries. It also organizes services for the control of tuberculosis and communicable diseases, establishes rural health training and nursing services, sets up machinery for the collection of vital statistics, promotes rural sanitation, and emphasizes preventive and social medicine, including health education. The Food and Agriculture Organization works with governments in developing more efficient use of land, conserving water and forest resources, improving plant production, introducing new crops, and encouraging better breeding and care of livestock.

Two other United Nations-related agencies of particular importance to the developing countries of Asia are the International Labor Organization and the United Nations Educational, Scientific, and Cultural Organization (UNESCO). The former, which was founded after World War I, advises and assists governments in setting standards of work and pay, in vocational training, and in improving overall employment of manpower. UNESCO's concerns with Asia include a major project in East-West understanding and many programs to advise governments on education, secure adequate textbooks, and encourage cultural exchanges.

In addition to the multiple activities of the specialized agencies, the United Nations organization itself contributes substantially to the development of Asian countries through such mechanisms as the Technical Assistance Program, the Special Fund for Economic Development, and the Economic Commission for Asia and the Far East.

In years past, some Asians have argued that the bulk of their needed assistance should be channeled through international organizations because they feared individual donor countries might attach political conditions to their aid. Longer experience with Western aid programs has calmed these anxieties, however, and Western parliaments and congresses have continued to prefer to appropriate major foreign-assistance funds through channels under their direct control. Thus it remains true that the bulk of foreign aid reaches Asian countries through direct contributions from individual countries.

As Europe's postwar prosperity has grown, European

countries have gradually met a larger share of the foreign-aid needs in Asia. Great Britain and Germany have substantially expanded their aid programs, and contributions have also come from France, Italy, Norway, Sweden, Switzerland, and other countries. Canada and Japan have also become important contributors. Measured against relative national income, however, few countries have yet made efforts either in amounts or in flexibility of terms to match those of the United States. Even fewer, including the United States, have yet reached aid appropriations of one percent of national income, the standard against which many people, including Director Paul Hoffman of the United Nations Special Fund, believe the efforts of the more affluent countries should be measured.*

A word should be said about Communist-bloc aid to Asia. Since the mid-1950's, when the good effects of Western economic assistance began to be visible, both the Soviet Union and Communist China have also given assistance to nonaligned countries. By the early 1960's these programs had become substantial, largely in the form of credit for specific projects. The Soviet Union has poured military as well as economic assistance into such countries as Indonesia and Afghanistan. For India, Soviet aid has been almost exclusively economic, ranging from help on very favorable terms for a major steel mill to credit for a heavy machinery plant, a thermal electric power station, and pharmaceutical factories. There have also been gifts of tractors and other agricultural machinery, transport vehicles, and an automatic telephone exchange. Communist China has offered credit—often accepting commodities in repayment—for assistance to such countries as Cambodia, Ceylon, and Nepal. Analysis of Sino-Soviet aid programs suggests that these efforts, like Communist-bloc commercial transactions, are conducted in accordance with the statement made by Mr. Khrushchev in 1955 that "We value trade less for economic reasons and more for political reasons." †

United States interest in helping other peoples has, as we have suggested, not been limited to governmental efforts. Hundreds of private organizations, large and small, are working in Asian countries; it follows that thousands of Americans are intimately involved. To catalog the organizations doing outstanding and significant work would be as difficult as to pick out a few meriting special mention, but the range is suggested by the work of such bodies as CARE, the

* Paul Hoffman, *World Without Want* (New York: Harper & Row, Publishers, Inc., 1962).

† *The Communist Economic Threat* (Washington: Department of State publication No. 6777), p. 2.

American Friends Service Committee, Church World Service, mission organizations, the Institute of International Education, the Rockefeller and Ford foundations, the Asia Foundation, private banks, and our universities and colleges with their multiplicity of training, extension, analytical, and advisory services. Private programs have certain advantages. They are sometimes freer to take risks, to pioneer in untested directions, and to establish friendly and cooperative relations with a wider range of Asian groups and individuals than may be possible in official government programs. Working within total budgets of thousands or millions of dollars rather than billions, the private organizations tend to emphasize research and educational programs for the development of basic social and economic institutions and of trained leadership, as well as assistance in meeting emergency basic needs.

The United States government strongly encourages private efforts, but it has also developed larger official programs to help meet some of the most pressing and important of the vast needs of emergent countries. United States government assistance takes several forms. We contribute our share, of course, to United Nations and other international programs. In recent years a much expanded Food for Peace program has added an important dimension to development in Asia and other continents. After the surplus food grains and other commodities that we provide are sold in local markets, we make a considerable part of the local currency proceeds available to the recipient government for development purposes. From 1955 to 1962 the United States government donated $6.8 billion to this program. In addition, the United States in recent years has directed about three fourths of its total direct foreign-aid outlays to Asia and the Middle East: about $1 billion per year in military assistance and $2 billion in technical and economic assistance. These large figures reflect the great importance of Asia and our national conviction that our own interests will be well served if its extremely low-income peoples manage to get on their way successfully or that they will be damaged if Asian development efforts should break down in failure.

Although the American aid effort seems considerable, we must remember that it is only marginal in relation to the numbers of people in the receiving countries, the need to improve their lot, and the efforts that these countries themselves are making. United States direct economic aid, including Food for Peace, has recently averaged $3.30 per person per year in receiving countries, hardly enough to enrich those nations fast. (This is merely an average. The range is from $.05 per capita to $12.13.) Because our limited aid funds are subject to many competing demands, the United States seeks to make allocations not only on the basis of specific projects but also with a view to overall national development programs so that we can be confident that each dollar spent does in fact help the recipient nation toward a better future.

Nor does the United States necessarily separate itself from other donors. The United States and other Free World donors sometimes coordinate their aid to an Asian nation that has successfully integrated its own development program. Recent participation in consortia organized by the World Bank to assist Pakistan and India, for example, has enabled us to encourage other countries' contributions by agreeing to match them.

Multinational cooperation can be a good principle not only for donors but also for recipients, as a number of Asian countries have discovered. The Colombo Plan, for example, has become a useful mart for the exchange of information, experts, and agreements on particular projects. Multilateral programs of continuing interest include the lower Mekong valley scheme, which if pursued in peaceful times would involve Vietnam, Cambodia, Laos, and Thailand, and the Asian Highway project, which ultimately would link Saigon and Singapore by road with Europe.

As we have repeatedly observed, foreign aid is no cure-all for the difficulties that beset Asian peoples today. Nor is it a perfect instrument even for the limited role it can play effectively. Through the lessons of experience and earlier mistakes, many improvements have been made in its administration, but much in both the concept and the operation of foreign aid remains to be improved as donor *and* recipient countries deepen their understanding of the processes of development and the part that foreign aid can play. Meanwhile, it is well to remember some basic facts. If the 1960's and the 1970's are to be truly more productive than earlier decades, and if the peoples of Asia are to win better shares in the munificence that man has learned to produce, then the affluent countries will have to continue their efforts and carry an effective share of the burden of development. Success is in their interest as much as in the interest of the recipients.

International Relations

So far we have focused on the domestic problems and opportunities with which Asian countries must deal. Their external relations are almost equally significant, for the profound changes that followed World War II transformed the international relations of almost every Asian nation. Asians have vastly widened their horizons. Even such long-independent nations as Japan and Thailand have played new roles since the founding of the United Nations. In former colonial countries the changes have been staggering. Before World War II, Indonesia knew the Netherlands, but very little about its own Southeast Asian neighbors and other countries of the West. India, Ceylon, Burma, and Malaya were oriented toward Great Britain; Laos, Cambodia, and Vietnam toward France; and the Philippines toward the United States. None of these, of course, controlled their foreign relations, nor did any have effective relations with other Asian countries.

The great postwar changes were symbolized at the Asian Relations Conference that was held in New Delhi in 1947. "A watershed of history," Jawaharlal Nehru called it, because for the first time delegations from all Asian states (except Japan, then under Allied occupation) met together to consider the future of their continent. Although unofficial, the delegations were filled with men and women who then or subsequently held high posts in their national governments. From that watershed onward, Asian states have played increasingly active roles in regional and worldwide affairs.

By the early 1950's major patterns of Asian international relations had become clear. After its recovery from defeat in World War II, Japan rejoined the world community as a peace-loving nation. China, weakened and divided by the long Japanese war, succumbed thereafter to Communist control and became a threat to the security of its neighbors. Communist regimes took over North Korea and North Vietnam. A bitter Communist effort to extend control to South Korea was stemmed in a bloody three-year war. Faced with the threat of further Communist aggression, certain Asian nations allied themselves with Western powers for mutual security; these included Japan, South Korea, the government of the Republic of China, the Philippines, Thailand, Pakistan, Iran, and Turkey. Others saw advantages to their welfare and security in not attaching themselves to any international security system except to the degree represented in their membership in the United Nations. These nations, which came to form a loosely knit group in the United Nations along with certain Arab, African, and other nonaligned states, included Indonesia, Laos, Cambodia, Burma, India, and Afghanistan. The aligned and the nonaligned nations differed little, however, in their fidelity to the major non-Communist proposition that the world we want to see is a community of independent and freely cooperating states, each committed to its own freedom and to that of other nations.

To identify Asian nations only by their attitudes toward the overriding global struggle of our age would, however, be to distort their own priorities. The fact is that many of them perceive more pressing problems with, if not greater threats from, their immediate neighbors. Their widening world has begun to include regional economic and political cooperation, yet Asian international relations are also characterized by area disputes that drain resources and energies from other, more constructive, tasks.

The West has been well aware of the grave and persistent difficulties between India and Pakistan that grew mostly out of the partition of 1947 and culminated in the dispute over Kashmir. The two countries have much in common, and more that is complementary, and thoughtful persons in both have striven for improved relations. Yet, whatever the other dangers in the uneasy postwar period, some voices in each country have repeatedly described the other as the principal enemy, at least until the Chinese Communist attack on India. But this is only one example. Pakistan and Afghanistan have twice broken diplomatic relations and disrupted the transit trade that normally passes through Pakistan to landlocked Afghanistan. Thailand and Cambodia, having experienced battle over a disputed temple, finally took their dispute to the International Court of Justice for resolution. Difficulties between Cambodia and South Vietnam grew in the course of the latter's bitter struggle against Communist infiltration and subversion.

And so it goes. In this postcolonial age, Asian countries are getting to know one another, but they have yet to learn to live comfortably with one another. Indeed, some of them seem to have seen in the world struggle between the Communist and Western powers an opportunity to look to one or the other or both for help in their own regional struggles with neighboring Asian nations.

In wider world issues, the experiences of emerging Asian states have quite naturally colored their views and approaches. They greatly value freedom and human dignity, but some, having achieved independence through revolution against Western ruling powers, have been seemingly more attracted by the recently revolutionary countries, e.g. the Soviet Union, even though totalitarian, than by the older American revolution. For similar reasons, they have identified themselves with the even more recent freedom movements in Africa. On colonial issues, on "color" and on other issues that seem to accent the differences between the affluent white Western countries and other peoples, most Asian states express similar views, though with varying intensity. On other kinds of issues there is no more unanimity among Asian nations than among other members of the United Nations.

As this is written, the eruption of large-scale Sino-Indian fighting is too recent to be assessed properly, but it immediately stands out as a possible turning point in Asian international relations. When the largest of the nonaligned countries is attacked by the Communist neighbor with which only a few years earlier it had signed the "Five Principles" of peaceful coexistence, the effects would seem bound to be felt not only in India but also in many other Asian countries. The exposure of Communist China as a disturbing and disruptive force possessing steadily growing military power puts into new perspective not only other nations' direct relations with Peking but also the Chinese-oriented Communist parties functioning in non-Communist countries. It has become clear that Peking's policies have created some of the most perplexing problems that confront other Asian countries and the rest of the world. Major reorientations would not be outside the realm of possibility.

The American Stake in Asia

When global victory crowned the vast Allied effort in World War II, the American people wanted nothing so much as to liquidate the potent military force they had mobilized and to return to the ordinary pursuits of peace. It was a dream we tried to realize by standing comparatively aloof from early postwar crises. In Asia the crisis in China engaged only limited American efforts, and we were able to avoid involvement in the bloodbath attending the partition of India. But America shortly learned that it must rebuild its strength in order to cope with the Moscow-Peking Communist axis. The emergence of Communist China as a hostile, aggressive, and expansionist power made it clear that the United States must exert its economic, political, and military strength to help bring Asia into equilibrium. Failure to act would have given Asia to the Communists through default. Successful action would bring the Asian community of nations through a trying period of transition, helping them toward the political stability and economic health they need for survival.

It was in pursuit of this realization that the United States by 1950 was fighting to save Korea from aggression. The same understanding led to our protection of Taiwan and our military assistance to South Vietnam, Laos, and other nations, including, in 1962, India. The American security stake in Asia has been demonstrated to be real and important enough to justify major efforts when needed.

In the larger sense, going beyond the sharply defined questions of military security, the United States pursues in Asia its unchanging basic policy objective of a world populated by nations free to determine their own forms of government and to conduct their affairs peacefully with other nations, possessed of governments that respond to the will of the people.

As we have seen, American policy in Asia really has three major dimensions. Against the brooding threat of Soviet and Chinese Communist aggression we provide a security screen on which our allies count and that can also be useful to other countries, as was demonstrated by the prompt American response to Indian appeals for assistance to its efforts to repel Communist Chinese invaders in late 1962. Through our diplomacy and other instruments such as extensive aid programs, we make major efforts to help Asian countries get on their feet and strengthen themselves against subversion and disruption from within. Finally, although we possess fewer effective instruments for this task, we strive to help Asian countries to ameliorate the area disputes that sap and divert their energies. We have often used our position as mediator to help others to settle disputes, as between Indonesia and the Netherlands, India and Pakistan, and Thailand and Cambodia. Yet we recognize the limits of our influence in this field.

On issues of global import, we have both sought Asian support and acted to bolster the Asian nations in international forums such as the United Nations. The number and diversity of issues that come to the Security Council, the General Assembly, and other organs of the United Nations underline the importance to us of strong, viable relations with the Asian nations.

Although American self-interest is a basic factor in our relations with Asian states, and must always be so, we must also remember that the American philosophy of international relations recognizes that mutuality of interest lies at the heart of good relations between countries. Furthermore, the American spirit has historically transcended purely selfish considerations and has extended the hand of help to those who need it. On this and on the desire of sensitive Asians to reciprocate rest the strength of our ties with Asia. As Asia modernizes, its huge size and potential will come ever more into play in world affairs. For Americans of the coming generation, few international issues are likely to be more fundamental than relations with Asia.

263

Resources for Teaching
and Further Study

THE NEED for studying about Asia has been emphasized elsewhere on many occasions, but it is worth noting again that this area of the world is important to Americans not only because of its contemporary significance in relation to our national interests in a period of acute international tensions, but also because its civilizations are in themselves worthy of our attention for their contributions through the centuries to universal human knowledge and experience and to our own Western traditions. Indeed, the second consideration may well be the more important educationally.

The urgent need for Americans to understand the Asian peoples and their civilizations makes all the more vital the availability of adequate resources for teaching and further study about this area. The observations that follow are intended to be helpful to the teacher, to the serious student, and to the interested adult who desires to learn more about Asia. They constitute suggestive rather than exhaustive listings of possibilities, and many more might have been added, space permitting.

The most important resource is, of course, the teacher. Like other adult Americans, however, most teachers have had little opportunity to inform themselves about Asia because they are products of an educational system that is, by tradition and for understandable reasons, largely Europe-centered and has generally ignored the non-Western world; however, increasing numbers of colleges and universities are beginning to develop course offerings on the major Asian civilizations and their contemporary development. The participation of teachers is specifically encouraged. The Asia Society, the Japan Society, and The Asia Foundation have for several years supported summer programs for teachers and other community leaders. Each winter a listing of these programs for the following summer is issued by The Asia Society, available on request from their offices at 112 East 64th Street, New York 21, New York.

A growing number of similar opportunities are being developed under other auspices. The East-West Center at the University of Hawaii in Honolulu, for example, has a national program of scholarships in Asian studies for teachers. There are summer-session and school-year plans of study, the latter followed by a summer in Asia. In another instance, the state of New York is developing varied approaches to meet the needs of teachers in Asian and other non-European fields of study. These approaches include summer institutes, academic-year seminars of independent reading, and other programs; further information is available from the Office of the Consultant in Foreign Area Studies, State Education Department, Albany, New York.

After a teacher has acquired essential background on a particular area of Asia through study in programs of this sort, opportunities for further study and experience in that area are the logical next step. The Department of Health, Education and Welfare's Office of Education (Teacher Exchange Section, Washington 25, D.C.) administers a summer institute for secondary-school social-studies teachers in India. Information concerning opportunities for teaching assignments in Asia may be obtained from the Committee on International Relations of the National Education Association, 1201 16th Street, N.W., Washington, D.C.

The Peace Corps offers still another avenue for experience in Asian countries. Opportunities for summer travel in Asia are also increasing; *Overseas: The Magazine of Educational Exchange* (Institute of International Education, 800 Second Avenue, New York, New York) each spring publishes a guide to such opportunities.

Next to the teacher, the most important resource is the printed word. Rich and varied possibilities are given in the bibliography of this book.

There are a number of other valuable sources of information and help that should be mentioned. A general reference source to groups active in Asian affairs is *American Institutions and Organizations Interested in Asia*, edited by Ward Morehouse (New York: Taplinger Publishing Co., Inc.; 2nd rev. ed., 1961). Bibliographies are available from The

Asia Society, the Japan Society (same address as The Asia Society), the World Confederation of Organizations of the Teaching Professions (1227 16th Street, Washington, D.C.), the American Historical Association's Service Center for Teachers of History (400 A Street, S.E., Washington, D.C.), the Association for Asian Studies (P.O. Box 606, Ann Arbor, Michigan), and the American Universities Field Staff (366 Madison Avenue, New York 17, New York).

Periodicals and magazines are valuable sources of information, especially on current developments in Asia. The principal American scholarly periodicals dealing with Asia are the *Journal of Asian Studies,* published by the Association for Asian Studies, *Pacific Affairs* (University of British Columbia, Vancouver, Canada), and *Asian Survey* (Institute of International Studies, University of California, Berkeley). Although some articles in these journals are of a fairly specialized nature, others treat topics of current and general interest to teachers and other adult readers; also helpful for teachers and students are the book-review sections, which provide critical comments on recently published books about Asia. In addition to American periodicals on Asia, there are numerous others published in Europe and Asia that contain useful material, and many general periodicals such as *Foreign Affairs* (Council on Foreign Relations, Inc., 58 East 68th Street, New York 21, New York) and *Social Education* (National Council for the Social Studies, 1201 16th Street, N.W., Washington, D.C.) also include articles or even special issues on Asian countries or topics.

There are several sources of periodical material for students that are eminently useful and that should be far more widely available than they are. Among these are the reports of the American Universities Field Staff, Inc., by specially qualified area specialists; the American Geographical Society's *Focus* (Broadway and 156th Street, New York 32, New York); the Headline Series of the Foreign Policy Association— World Affairs Center (345 East 46th Street, New York 17, New York); and *Current History* (1822 Ludlow Street, Philadelphia 3, Pennsylvania); and the booklets of the Foreign Relations Project of the North Central Association of Colleges and Secondary Schools (Suite 832, First National Bank Building, Chicago 3, Illinois), several of which deal with Asian regions and countries.

Two newsletters that contain helpful information for the teacher are the bimonthly *Orient-Occident,* providing continuing reports on the UNESCO ten-year major project for mutual appreciation of Eastern and Western cultural values (UNESCO, Place de Fontenoy, Paris, France) and the quarterly *Newsletter* of the Association for Asian Studies.

There are several packets of helpful materials for teachers. The Japan Society and The Asia Society, for example, have packets on Japan, Southeast Asia, and India and the adjacent countries of South Asia for moderate cost. These packets contain bibliographies, pamphlet materials, film lists, classroom pictures, maps, teacher guides, reprints of articles, and other helpful materials.

Official publications of the embassies and information offices of Asian countries in the United States constitute another resource for teaching about the area. Such publications tend to reflect official viewpoints, and complete dependence on such materials is rarely sufficient for securing a well-rounded perspective on a particular country and its problems. These materials can, however, usefully supplement other sources of information, and most Asian embassies will supply on request single copies of informative leaflets and illustrated pamphlets. Embassies may be addressed simply Embassy of (name of country), Washington, D.C. The Japanese government (write the Information Office of the Japanese Consulate General, 235 East 42nd Street, New York 17, New York) has perhaps the most balanced and extensive information program in the United States of any Asian country. Indian Information Services (3 East 64th Street, New York 21, New York) also has varied materials, including a film library.

There is a growing number of films on Asia, and the problem for the individual teacher lies in selecting the particular one most suited to his immediate purpose. A helpful guide is *Films on Asia: Selected List,* available from The Asia Society. There is no comparable guide to filmstrips and slides, but the packets mentioned earlier contain some suggestions. From the UNESCO Publications Center (801 Third Avenue, New York 22, New York) it is possible to secure sets of color slides of Asian art with explanatory booklets, as well as other audio-visual materials.

Asian cultures have rich and varied traditions in the arts, and it is important for students to look beyond immediate political and economic problems to these areas of life that tell so much about the values and sensibilities of another people. Fortunately, American museums are exceptionally well endowed with collections of Asian art. A guide to American museum resources in Asian art is being prepared by The Asia Society. It is also possible at very moderate cost to bring the artistic achievements of Asian peoples into the school or community through circulating exhibitions of art and other Asian subjects; among organizations circulating such exhibitions are the Japan Society, The Asia Society, the Smithsonian Institution (Washington 25, D.C.), and the

American Federation of Arts (41 East 65th Street, New York 21, New York).

Asia is the source of several music traditions that match classical Western music in complexity and sophistication, and the variety of folk music is almost limitless. Recordings of this music are becoming more widely available in the United States, and lists of Asian music on record and tape will be found in the packets of materials noted above. An album of Asian music especially designed for use in schools is now in preparation at Indiana University. Further information is available from the Indiana University Audio-Visual Center, Bloomington, Indiana.

Among the many other resources that secondary-school teachers might find helpful is "Teaching About Asia," by Hyman Kublin, in *The Social Studies and the Social Sciences* (New York: Harcourt, Brace & World, Inc., 1962). A volume along related lines that likewise contains useful suggestions is *High School Social Studies Perspectives* (Boston: Houghton Mifflin Company, 1962); the relevant chapters on East Asia and India and Pakistan are by Allan B. Cole and Norman D. Palmer.

Asia, of course, is not a cultural, political, or historical unit, but rather a complex of varied traditions and contemporary circumstances, their principal point in common being geographical propinquity. This suggests that the logical point of departure in any introductory study of the area is geography and that what should follow in the proper study of Asia is concentration in depth on individual countries, including at least one of major world significance in its historical development such as India, China, or Japan.

Experienced teachers develop methods and devices that are effective and consistent with their own philosophies and styles of teaching. There is little that would be of value to such teachers that can be added here regarding specific ways of organizing material and presenting it to students. What these paragraphs have sought to do is to point the way—by indicating some of the varied and abundant resources for further study on Asia—to teachers, as well as serious students and other individuals who are simply interested in a vast, complex, and fascinating part of the world about which most of us know all too little.

Bibliography

Asterisk (*) denotes paperbound books in print at the time of publication.

ASIA

General

Clyde, Paul H. *The Far East: A History of the Impact of the West on Eastern Asia.* 3rd ed. New York: Prentice-Hall, Inc., 1958.

Cooke, Dwight. *There Is No Asia.* New York: Doubleday & Company, Inc., 1954.

Dean, Vera Micheles. *The Nature of the Non-Western World.* New York: The New American Library of World Literature, Inc. (Mentor Books*), 1957.

Fradier, Jacques. *East-West Toward Mutual Understanding.* Paris: UNESCO, 1958.

Latourette, Kenneth Scott. *Christianity in a Revolutionary Age.* 2 vols. New York: Harper & Row, Publishers, Inc., 1958, 1959.

Reischauer, Edwin O., and John K. Fairbank. *East Asia: The Great Tradition.* Boston: Houghton Mifflin Company, 1960.

Romein, J. M. and J. E. *The Asian Century.* Translated by R. T. Clark. Berkeley, Calif.: University of California Press, 1962; London: George Allen and Unwin, Ltd., 1962.

Rosinger, Lawrence K., et al. (eds.). *The State of Asia: A Contemporary Survey.* New York: Alfred A. Knopf, Inc., 1951.

Staley, Eugene. *The Future of Underdeveloped Countries.* New York: Harper & Row, Publishers, Inc., 1954; London: Oxford

University Press, 1954; New York: Frederick A. Praeger, Inc.,* 1961.
Taylor, George, and Franz Michael. *The Far East in the Modern World*. New York: Holt, Rinehart and Winston, Inc., 1956; London: Methuen & Co. Ltd., 1957.
Thorp, Willard (ed.). *The United States and the Far East*. 2nd ed. New York: Prentice-Hall, Inc., 1962.
Ward, Barbara. *The Interplay of East and West*. New York: W. W. Norton & Company, Inc.,* 1957; London: George Allen and Unwin, Ltd., 1957.

Geography

Ginsburg, Norton, et al. *The Pattern of Asia*. New York: Prentice-Hall, Inc., 1958; London: Bailey Bros. & Swinfen Ltd., 1958.
Spencer, Joseph E. *Asia, East by South: A Cultural Geography*. New York: John Wiley & Sons, Inc., 1954; London: Chapman & Hall Ltd., 1955.

Government and Politics

Almond, G. A., and J. S. Coleman (eds.). *Politics of the Developing Areas*. Princeton, N.J.: Princeton University Press, 1960; London: Oxford University Press, 1960.
Barnett, A. Doak (ed.). *Communist Strategies in Asia*. New York: Frederick A. Praeger, Inc.,* 1963.
Buss, Claude A. *The Far East: A History of Recent and Contemporary International Relations in East Asia*. New York and London: The Macmillan Company, 1955.
Montgomery, John D. *The Politics of Foreign Aid*. New York: Frederick A. Praeger, Inc.,* 1962.
Reischauer, Edwin O. *Wanted: An Asian Policy*. New York: Alfred A. Knopf, Inc., 1955.
Rostow, W. W., and R. W. Hatch. *American Policy in Asia*. New York: John Wiley & Sons, Inc., 1955; London: Chapman & Hall Ltd., 1955.

Literature

Ceadel, Eric B. (ed.). *Literatures of the East: An Appreciation*. London: John Murray Ltd., 1953; New York: Grove Press, 1959.
Clifford, William, and Daniel L. Milton (eds.). *A Treasury of Modern Asian Stories*. New York: The New American Library of World Literature, Inc. (Mentor Books*), 1961.
Yohannan, John D. *A Treasury of Asian Literature*. New York: The John Day Company, Inc., 1956; London: Phoenix House Ltd., 1958; New York: The New American Library of World Literature, Inc. (Mentor Books*), 1958.

Religion and Philosophy

Burtt, E. A. (ed.). *The Teachings of the Compassionate Buddha*.

New York: The New American Library of World Literature, Inc. (Mentor Books*), 1955.

Conze, Edward. *Buddhism: Its Essence and Development.* New York: Harper & Row, Publishers, Inc. (Torchbooks*), 1959.

Gaer, Joseph. *How the Great Religions Began.* Rev. ed. New York: Dodd, Mead & Company, 1956; The New American Library of World Literature, Inc. (Signet Books*), 1958.

Pickthall, Mohammed Marmaduke (trans.). *The Meaning of the Glorious Koran.* London: George Allen and Unwin, Ltd., 1930; New York: Alfred A. Knopf, Inc., 1931; The New American Library of World Literature, Inc. (Mentor Books*), 1953.

Prabhavananda, Swami, and Christopher Isherwood (trans.). *The Song of God: Bhagavad-Gita.* London: Phoenix House Ltd., 1947; New York: Harper & Row, Publishers, Inc., 1951; The New American Library of World Literature (Mentor Books*), 1954.

Smith, Huston. *The Religions of Man.* New York: Harper & Row, Publishers, Inc., 1958; The New American Library of World Literature, Inc. (Mentor Books*), 1959.

Smith, Wilfred Cantwell. *Islam in Modern History.* Princeton, N.J.: Princeton University Press, 1957; London: Oxford University Press, 1958; New York: The New American Library of World Literature, Inc. (Mentor Books*), 1959.

Stace, Walter T. *The Teachings of the Mystics.* New York: The New American Library of World Literature, Inc. (Mentor Books*), 1960.

Ware, James R. (trans.). *The Sayings of Confucius.* New York: The New American Library of World Literature, Inc. (Mentor Books*), 1955.

Watts, Alan W. *The Way of Zen.* New York: Pantheon Books, Inc., 1957; London: Thames and Hudson, 1957; New York: The New American Library of World Literature, Inc. (Mentor Books*), 1959.

CHINA

General

Bodde, Derk. *China's Gifts to the West.* Washington, D.C.: American Council on Education, 1942.

————. *Chinese Ideas in the West.* Washington, D.C.: American Council on Education, 1948.

Chai, Ch'u and Winberg. *The Changing Society of China.* New York: The New American Library of World Literature, Inc. (Mentor Books*), 1962.

Cressey, George B. *Land of the 500 Million.* New York: McGraw-Hill Book Company, Inc., 1955; London: McGraw-Hill Publishing Co. Ltd., 1956.

Hart, Henry H. *Venetian Adventurer.* Stanford, Calif.: Stanford

University Press, 1942; London: Oxford University Press, 1942.

Hu Chang-tu, et al. *China: Its People, Its Society, Its Culture*, ed. Hsiao Hsia. New Haven, Conn.: HRAF Press—Human Relations Area Files, 1960.

Hucker, Charles O. *China: A Critical Bibliography*. Tucson, Ariz.: University of Arizona Press, 1962.

Latourette, Kenneth Scott. *A History of Christian Missions in China*. New York: The Macmillan Company, 1929; London: The Society for Promoting Christian Knowledge and The Sheldon Press, 1929.

Needham, Joseph. *Science and Civilisation in China*. 2 vols. Cambridge, Eng.: Cambridge University Press, 1954, 1956.

Rugoff, Milton (ed.). *The Travels of Marco Polo*. New York: The New American Library of World Literature, Inc. (Signet Classics*), 1961.

Art

Sickman, Laurence. *Painting and Sculpture*. Baltimore, Md.: Penguin Books, Inc., 1956; London: Penguin Books Ltd., 1956.

Soper, Alexander C. *Architecture*. Baltimore, Md.: Penguin Books, Inc., 1956; London: Penguin Books Ltd., 1956.

Willetts, William. *Chinese Art*. New York: George Braziller, Inc., 1958; London: Penguin Books Ltd., 1958; Baltimore, Md.: Penguin Books, Inc., 1958.

Communist Regime

Barnett, A. Doak. *Communist China and Asia*. New York: Harper & Row, Publishers, Inc., 1960; London: Oxford University Press, 1960; New York: Alfred A. Knopf, Inc. (Vintage Books*), 1961.

———. *Communist China in Perspective*. New York: Frederick A. Praeger, Inc.,* 1962.

Callis, Helmut G. *China: Confucian and Communist*. New York: Holt, Rinehart and Winston, Inc., 1959.

Faure, Edgar. *The Serpent and the Tortoise: Problems of the New China*. Trans. by Lovett F. Edwards. New York: St Martin's Press, Inc., 1958; London: Macmillan & Co. Ltd., 1958.

Wint, Guy. *Common Sense About China*. New York: The Macmillan Company, 1960; London: Victor Gollancz Ltd., 1960.

History

Bodde, Derk. *China's Cultural Tradition: What and Whither?* New York: Holt, Rinehart and Winston, Inc., 1957.

Clyde, Paul H. *The Far East: A History of the Impact of the West on Eastern Asia*. 3rd ed. New York: Prentice-Hall, Inc., 1958.

Creel, H. G. *Chinese Thought from Confucius to Mao Tse-tung*. Chicago: University of Chicago Press, 1953; London: Eyre

& Spottiswoode Ltd., 1954; New York: The New American Library of World Literature, Inc. (Mentor Books*), 1960.

Fairbank, John K. *The United States and China.* Rev. ed. Cambridge, Mass.: Harvard University Press, 1958; London: Oxford University Press, 1958; New York: The Viking Press, Inc. (Compass Books*), 1958.

Goodrich, L. Carrington. *A Short History of the Chinese People.* 3rd ed. New York: Harper & Row, Publishers, Inc. (Torchbooks*), 1959.

———— and Henry C. Fenn. *A Syllabus of the History of Chinese Civilization and Culture.* 6th ed. New York: Bookman Associates, Inc., 1959.

Grousset, René. *The Rise and Splendor of the Chinese Empire.* London: Geoffrey Bles Ltd., 1952; Berkeley, Calif.: University of California Press,* 1953.

Latourette, Kenneth Scott. *A Short History of the Far East.* Rev. ed. London: Macmillan & Co. Ltd., 1951; New York: The Macmillan Company, 1952.

Reischauer, Edwin O., and John K. Fairbank. *East Asia: The Great Tradition.* Boston: Houghton Mifflin Company, 1960.

Rowe, D. N. *Modern China: A Brief History.* Princeton, N.J.: D. Van Nostrand Co., Inc. (Anvil Books*), 1959; London: D. Van Nostrand Company Ltd., 1960.

Literature and Philosophy

Cranmer-Byng, L. (ed. and trans.). *A Lute of Jade.* London: John Murray Ltd., 1959.

Fremantle, Anne (ed.), *Mao Tse-tung: An Anthology of His Writings.* New York: The New American Library of World Literature, Inc. (Mentor Books*), 1962.

Hersey, John. *A Single Pebble.* New York: Alfred A. Knopf, Inc., 1956; London: Hamish Hamilton Ltd., 1956; New York: Bantam Books, Inc.,* 1961.

Lao-tzu. *The Way and Its Power.* Trans. by Arthur Waley. London: George Allen and Unwin, Ltd., 1956; New York: The Macmillan Company, 1957; Grove Press (Evergreen Books*), 1958.

Lin Yu-tang. *Famous Chinese Short Stories.* New York: The John Day Company, Inc., 1952; Washington Square Press, Inc.,* 1961.

———— (ed. and trans.). *The Wisdom of Confucius.* New York: Random House, Inc., 1938; London: Hamish Hamilton Ltd., 1938.

Nivison, David, and A. F. Wright (eds.). *Confucianism in Action.* Stanford, Calif.: Stanford University Press, 1959; London: Oxford University Press, 1959.

Shih ching. *The Book of Songs.* Ed. and trans. by Arthur Waley. Boston: Houghton Mifflin Company, 1937; London: George Allen and Unwin, Ltd., 1937.

Shui hu chuan. *All Men Are Brothers.* Trans. by Pearl S. Buck. 2 vols. New York: The John Day Company, Inc., 1933; London: Methuen & Co. Ltd., 1933.

Waley, Arthur (trans.). *The Analects of Confucius*. London: George Allen and Unwin, Ltd., 1938; New York: The Macmillan Company, 1939; Alfred A. Knopf, Inc. (Vintage Books*), 1960.

————. *Yuan Mei, Eighteenth-Century Chinese Poet*. New York: The Macmillan Company, 1957; London: George Allen and Unwin, Ltd., 1957; New York: Grove Press (Evergreen Books*), 1958.

Wang Chi-chen (trans.). *Traditional Chinese Tales*. New York: Columbia University Press, 1944; London: Oxford University Press, 1944.

White, Theodore. *The Mountain Road*. New York: William Sloane Associates, Inc., 1958; London: Cassell & Co. Ltd., 1958; New York: The New American Library of World Literature, Inc. (Signet Books*), 1960.

Wu Chêng-ên. *The Aventures of Monkey*. New York: The John Day Company, Inc., 1944.

INDIA

General

Basham, A. L. *The Wonder That Was India*. London: Sidgwick & Jackson Ltd., 1954; New York: The Macmillan Company, 1955; Grove Press (Evergreen Books*), 1959.

Brown, W. Norman. *The United States and India and Pakistan*. Cambridge, Mass.: Harvard University Press, 1953; London: Oxford University Press, 1953.

Dean, Vera Micheles. *New Patterns of Democracy in India*. Cambridge, Mass.: Harvard University Press, 1959; London: Oxford University Press, 1960.

Fischer, Louis. *The Life of Mahatma Gandhi*. New York: Harper & Row, Publishers, Inc., 1950; London: Jonathan Cape Limited, 1951; New York: The Crowell-Collier Publishing Co. (Collier Books*), 1962.

Gandhi, Mohandas. *Gandhi, An Autobiography*. Trans. by Mahadev Desai. Boston: Beacon Press,* 1957; London: The Mayflower Group of Publishers, 1957.

Harrison, Selig S. *India: The Most Dangerous Decades*. Princeton, N.J.: Princeton University Press, 1960; London: Oxford University Press, 1960.

Lamb, Beatrice Pitney. *India: A World in Transition*. New York: Frederick A. Praeger, Inc., 1963.

Nehru, Jawaharlal. *The Discovery of India,* ed. Robert I. Crane. New York: Doubleday & Company, Inc. (Anchor Books*), 1960.

Rawlinson, H. G. *India: A Short Cultural History*. London: Cresset Press Ltd., 1952; New York: Frederick A. Praeger, Inc., 1953.

Rosinger, Lawrence K. *India and the United States.* New York: The Macmillan Company, 1950; London: George Allen and Unwin, Ltd., 1951.
Spear, Percival. *India: A Modern History.* Ann Arbor, Mich.: The University of Michigan Press, 1961.
Talbot, Phillips S. (ed.). *South Asia in the World Today.* Chicago: University of Chicago Press, 1950; Cambridge, Eng.: Cambridge University Press, 1950.
———— and S. L. Poplai. *India and America: A Study of Their Relations.* New York: Harper & Row, Publishers, Inc., 1958.
Tinker, Hugh. *India and Pakistan: A Political Analysis.* New York: Frederick A. Praeger, Inc.,* 1962.
Wallbank, T. Walter. *A Short History of India and Pakistan.* New York: The New American Library of World Literature, Inc. (Mentor Books*), 1958.

Art

Archer, W. G. *The Loves of Krishna in Indian Painting and Poetry.* New York: The Macmillan Company, 1957; London: George Allen and Unwin, Ltd., 1957; New York: Grove Press, 1958.
Rowland, Benjamin. *The Art and Architecture of India.* Baltimore, Md.: Penguin Books, Inc., 1953; London: Penguin Books Ltd., 1953.
UNESCO. *India, Paintings from Ajanta Caves.* Greenwich, Conn.: New York Graphic Society Publishers, Ltd., 1954.

Literature

Chakravarty, Amiya (ed.). *A Tagore Reader.* New York: The Macmillan Company, 1961; London: Macmillan & Co. Ltd., 1961.
Markandaya, Kamala. *Nectar in a Sieve.* London: Putnam & Co. Ltd., 1954; New York: The John Day Company, Inc., 1955; The New American Library of World Literature, Inc. (Signet Books*), 1956.
Mukerji, Dhan Gopal. *My Brother's Face.* New York: E. P. Dutton and Company, Inc., 1924.
Narayan, R. K. *The Financial Expert.* London: Methuen & Co. Ltd., 1952; East Lansing, Mich.: Michigan State University Press, 1953; New York: The Noonday Press,* 1959.
Singh, Khushwant. *Mano Majra.* New York: Grove Press, 1956.

Religion and Philosophy

Morgan, Kenneth W. (ed.). *The Religion of the Hindus.* New York: The Ronald Press Company, 1953.
Zimmer, Heinrich, and Joseph Campbell (eds.). *The Philosophies of India.* New York: The World Publishing Company (Meridian Books*), 1956.

JAPAN

General

Allen, G. C. *Japan's Economic Recovery.* New York and London: Oxford University Press, 1958.

Benedict, Ruth. *The Chrysanthemum and the Sword: Patterns of Japanese Culture.* Boston: Houghton Mifflin Company, 1946; London: Martin Secker & Warburg Ltd., 1947.

Borton, Hugh, et al. *Japan Between East and West.* New York: Harper & Row, Publishers, Inc., 1957; London: Oxford University Press, 1958.

————. *Japan's Modern Century.* New York: The Ronald Press Company, 1955.

Dening, Esler. *Japan.* London: Ernest Benn Limited, 1960; New York: Frederick A. Praeger, Inc.,* 1961.

Kirkup, James. *These Horned Islands.* New York: The Macmillan Company, 1962; London: William Collins Sons & Co. Ltd., 1962.

Lockwood, W. W. *The Economic Development of Japan.* Princeton, N.J.: Princeton University Press, 1954; London: Oxford University Press, 1955.

Maki, John M. *Government and Politics in Japan.* New York: Frederick A. Praeger, Inc.,* 1962; London: Thames and Hudson, 1962.

Maraini, Fosco. *Meeting with Japan.* Trans. by Eric Mosbacher. New York: The Viking Press, Inc., 1959; London: Hutchinson & Co. Limited, 1959.

Reischauer, Edwin O. *The United States and Japan.* Rev. ed. Cambridge, Mass.: Harvard University Press, 1957; London: Oxford University Press, 1957; New York: The Viking Press, Inc. (Compass Books*), 1962.

Storry, Richard. *History of Modern Japan.* Gloucester, Mass.: Peter Smith, 1960; Baltimore, Md.: Penguin Books, Inc.,* 1960.

Sykes, John. *A Japanese Family.* London: Paul Hamlyn Ltd., 1957.

Yanaga, Chitoshi. *Japanese People and Politics.* New York: John Wiley & Sons, Inc., 1956.

Art and Music

Mahm, William P. *Japanese Music and Musical Instruments.* Rutland, Vt.: Charles E. Tuttle Co., Inc., 1959; London: Mark Paterson & Co., Ltd., 1959.

Michener, James A. *The Floating World.* New York: Random House, Inc., 1954; London: Martin Secker & Warburg Ltd., 1955.

Paine, R. T., and Alexander Soper. *The Art and Architecture of Japan.* Baltimore, Md.: Penguin Books, Inc., 1955; London: Penguin Books Ltd., 1955.

Warner, Langdon. *The Enduring Art of Japan.* New York: Grove Press (Evergreen Books*), 1957.

Reischauer, Edwin O. *Japan Past and Present*. Rev. ed. New York: Alfred A. Knopf, Inc., 1952.
———— and John K. Fairbank. *East Asia: The Great Tradition*. Boston: Houghton Mifflin Company, 1960.
Richie, Donald. *The Land and People of Japan*. New York: The Macmillan Company, 1958; London: A. & C. Black Limited, 1959.
Sansom, G. B. *A History of Japan*. 3 vols. Stanford, Calif.: Stanford University Press, 1958.
————. *Japan: A Short Cultural History*. Rev. ed. New York: Appleton-Century-Crofts, 1962.
————. *The Western World and Japan*. New York: Alfred A. Knopf, Inc., 1950; London: Cresset Press Ltd., 1950.
Webb, Herschel. *An Introduction to Japan*. 2nd ed. New York: Columbia University Press,* 1957; London: Oxford University Press, 1957.

Literature

Ernst, Earle. *The Kabuki Theatre*. New York: Oxford University Press, 1956; London: Martin Secker & Warburg Ltd., 1956; New York: Grove Press (Evergreen Books*), 1959.
Keene, Donald. *Anthology of Japanese Literature from the Earliest Era to the Mid-Nineteenth Century*. New York: Grove Press (Evergreen Books*), 1955; London: George Allen and Unwin, Ltd., 1956.
————. *Japanese Literature: An Introduction for Western Readers*. London: John Murray Ltd., 1953; New York: Grove Press (Evergreen Books*), 1955.
———— (ed.). *Modern Japanese Literature*. New York: Grove Press (Evergreen Books*), 1956; London: Thames and Hudson, 1957.
Ooka, Shohei. *Fires on the Plain*. Trans. by Ivan Morris. New York: Alfred A. Knopf, Inc., 1957; London: Martin Secker & Warburg Ltd., 1957.
Shikibu, Murasaki. *The Tale of Genji*. Trans. by Arthur Waley. London: George Allen and Unwin, Ltd., 1952; New York: Doubleday & Company, Inc., 1959.
Tanizaki, Junichiro. *Some Prefer Nettles*. Trans. by Edward G. Seidensticker. New York: Alfred A. Knopf, Inc., 1955; London: Martin Secker & Warburg Ltd., 1956; New York: Berkley Publishing Corporation,* 1960.
Tsunoda, Ryusaku, et al. (comps.). *Sources of the Japanese Tradition*. New York: Columbia University Press, 1958; London: Oxford University Press, 1958.

•

KOREA

Chong, In-sop (ed. and trans.). *Folk Tales from Korea*. London: Routledge & Kegan Paul Ltd., 1952.

McCune, Evelyn. *The Arts of Korea*. Rutland, Vt.: Charles E. Tuttle Co., Inc., 1961.

McCune, G. M., and A. L. Grey. *Korea Today*. Cambridge, Mass.: Harvard University Press, 1950; London: George Allen and Unwin, Ltd., 1950.

McCune, Shannon. *Korea's Heritage: A Regional and Social Geography*. Rutland, Vt.: Charles E. Tuttle Co., Inc., 1956.

Osgood, Cornelius. *The Koreans and Their Culture*. New York: The Ronald Press Company, 1951.

PAKISTAN

Andrus, J. Russell, and Azizali F. Mohammed. *The Economy of Pakistan*. Stanford, Calif.: Stanford University Press, 1958; London: Oxford University Press, 1958.

Bolitho, Hector. *Jinnah, Creator of Pakistan*. London: John Murray Ltd., 1954; New York: The Macmillan Company, 1955.

Callard, Keith. *Pakistan: A Political Study*. New York: The Macmillan Company, 1957; London: George Allen and Unwin, Ltd., 1957.

Chakravarty, Amiya (ed.). *A Tagore Reader*. New York: The Macmillan Company, 1961; London: Macmillan & Co. Ltd., 1961.

Kabir, Humayun, et al. (eds.). *Green and Gold*. New York: New Directions, 1959.

Liaquat Ali Khan. *Pakistan, The Heart of Asia*. Cambridge, Mass.: Harvard University Press, 1950.

Qureshi, I. H. *The Pakistani Way of Life*. New York: Frederick A. Praeger, Inc., 1956; London: William Heinemann Ltd., 1956.

Saiyid, M. H. *Mohammed Ali Jinnah: A Political Study*. 2nd ed. Lahore, Pak.: Muhammad Ashraf, 1953.

Smith, Wilfred Cantwell. *Islam in Modern History*. Princeton, N.J.: Princeton University Press, 1957; London: Oxford University Press, 1958; New York: The New American Library of World Literature, Inc. (Mentor Books*), 1959.

SOUTHEAST ASIA

General

Buss, Claude A. *Southeast Asia and the World Today*. Princeton, N.J.: D. Van Nostrand Co., Inc. (Anvil Books*), 1958; London: D. Van Nostrand Company Ltd., 1959.

DuBois, Cora. *Social Forces in Southeast Asia*. Minneapolis, Minn.: University of Minnesota Press, 1949; London: Oxford University Press, 1949.

Emerson, Rupert. *Representative Government in Southeast Asia*.

Cambridge, Mass.: Harvard University Press, 1955; London: George Allen and Unwin, Ltd., 1955.

Fifield, Russell H. *The Diplomacy of Southeast Asia: 1945–1958*. New York: Harper & Row, Publishers, Inc., 1958.

Hall, D. G. E. *A History of South-East Asia*. New York: St Martin's Press, Inc., 1955; London: Macmillan & Co. Ltd., 1955.

Harrison, Brian. *South-East Asia: A Short History*. New York: St Martin's Press, Inc., 1954; London: Macmillan & Co. Ltd., 1954.

Kahin, George (ed.). *Governments and Politics of Southeast Asia*. Ithaca, N.Y.: Cornell University Press, 1959; London: Oxford University Press, 1959.

Thompson, Virginia, and Richard Adloff. *Minority Problems in Southeast Asia*. Stanford, Calif.: Stanford University Press, 1955; London: Oxford University Press, 1955.

Vandenbosch, Amry, and R. A. Butwell. *Southeast Asia Among the World Powers*. Lexington, Ky.: University of Kentucky Press, 1957.

Burma and Malaya

Cady, John F. *A History of Modern Burma*. Ithaca, N.Y.: Cornell University Press, 1958; London: Oxford University Press, 1958.

Christian, John L. *Modern Burma: A Survey of Political and Economic Development*. Berkeley, Calif.: University of California Press, 1942; Cambridge, Eng.: Cambridge University Press, 1942.

Ginsburg, Norton, et al. *Malaya*. Seattle, Wash.: University of Washington Press, 1958.

Hall, D. G. E. *Burma*. New York: Holt, Rinehart and Winston, Inc., 1950; London: Hutchinson & Co. Limited, 1950.

Trager, Frank N. *Building a Welfare State in Burma, 1948–1956*. New York: American Institute of Pacific Relations, Inc., 1958.

Indochina

Blanchard, W., et al. *Thailand*. New Haven, Conn.: HRAF Press —Human Relations Area Files, 1958.

Brodrick, Alan H. *Little Vehicle: Cambodia and Laos*. London: Hutchinson & Co. Limited, 1949.

Busch, Noel Fairchild. *Thailand: An Introduction to Modern Siam*. Princeton, N.J.: D. Van Nostrand Co., Inc., 1959; London: D. Van Nostrand Company Ltd., 1960.

Buttinger, Joseph. *The Smaller Dragon: A Political History of Vietnam*. New York: Frederick A. Praeger, Inc., 1958; London: Stevens & Sons Limited, 1958.

Chakrabongse, Chula (Prince Chula of Thailand). *Lords of Life*. London: Alvin Redman Limited, 1960; New York: Taplinger Publishing Co., Inc., 1961.

Fall, Bernard. *The Two Vietnams: A Political History*. New York: Frederick A. Praeger, Inc., 1963.

Hammer, Ellen J. *The Struggle for Indochina*. Stanford, Calif.: Stanford University Press, 1954; London: Oxford University Press, 1954.

Le Bar, Frank M., and Adrienne Suddard (eds.). *Laos: Its People, Its Society, Its Culture*. New Haven, Conn.: HRAF Press—Human Relations Area Files, 1960.

Newman, Bernard. *Report on Indo-China*. London: Robert Hale Ltd., 1953; New York: Frederick A. Praeger, Inc., 1954.

Steinberg, David J., et al. *Cambodia: Its People, Its Society, Its Culture*. New Haven, Conn.: HRAF Press—Human Relations Area Files, 1957.

Indonesia

Kahin, George. *Nationalism and Revolution in Indonesia*. Ithaca, N.Y.: Cornell University Press, 1952.

Mintz, Jeanne S. *Indonesia: A Profile*. Princeton, N.J.: D. Van Nostrand Co., Inc., 1961.

Palmier, Leslie. *Indonesia and the Dutch*. New York and London: Oxford University Press, 1962.

Woodman, Dorothy. *The Republic of Indonesia*. London: Cresset Press Ltd., 1955; New York: Philosophical Library, Inc., 1956.

Philippines

Bernstein, David. *The Philippine Story*. New York: Farrar, Straus & Company, Inc., 1947.

Grunder, Garel A., and William E. Livezey. *The Philippines and the United States*. Norman, Okla.: University of Oklahoma Press, 1951.

Smith, R. A. *Philippine Freedom, 1946–1958*. New York: Columbia University Press, 1958; London: Oxford University Press, 1958.

Vaughan, Josephine B. *The Land and People of the Philippines*. Philadelphia: J. B. Lippincott Company, 1956.

INDEX

Afghanistan, Pakistan and, 261
Ainu people, 113, 120
Akbar the Great, 171-72
Alexander the Great in India, 161, 168
Ali, Chaudhuri Rahmat, 196
Ali Khan, Liaquat, 201
Aryans, invasion of India by, 161, 168
Asian Asia, defined, 52-55
Asian Relations Congress (New Delhi), 260
Asoka, 169
Ayub Khan, Muhammad, 203, 205, 250

Baber, 161, 171
Bandaranaike, S. W. R. D., 250
Black, Eugene R., 255
Borneo, 239-40
Boxer Rebellion, 101
Buddha, Gautama (Siddhartha Gautama), 19, 165
Buddhism
  in Burma, 212, 213
  in China, 20, 21, 75, 80-84
  in India, 19, 165, 169

in Japan, 20, 21, 84, 117-18, 123, 145
in Korea, 149
in Laos, 215
origin of, 19-20
in Thailand, 214
in Vietnam, 216
Zen (Ch'an), 20, 84, 123, 145
Bunraku theater, 31, 32
Burma
  British rule of, 213, 226-28
  kingdom of, 212-13
  since independence, 228-29

Cambodia, 215-16, 233-34
  Thailand and, 261
  Vietnam and, 261
Caste system in India, 164-65, 168
Ch'an Buddhism (Zen), 20, 84, 123, 145
Chandragupta Maurya, 168-69
Chandragupta II, 169
Chang, John M., 154
Chiang Kai-shek, 72, 102-3, 134

281